SÉRIE

PESSOAS E CONTEXTOS

PSICOLOGIA
CIÊNCIAS DA EDUCAÇÃO
SERVIÇO SOCIAL

IMPRENSA DA UNIVERSIDADE DE COIMBRA
COIMBRA UNIVERSITY PRESS

COORDENAÇÃO EDITORIAL

Imprensa da Universidade de Coimbra

Email: imprensa@uc.pt

URL: http://www.uc.pt/imprensa_uc

Vendas online: http://livrariadaimprensa.uc.pt

DESIGN

Carlos Costa

INFOGRAFIA

Margarida Albino

EXECUÇÃO GRÁFICA

KDP - Kindle Direct Publishing

ISBN

978-989-26-1769-5

ISBN DIGITAL

978-989-26-1770-1

DOI

https://doi.org/10.14195/978-989-26-1770-1

Fernanda Hellen Ribeiro Piske
Tania Stoltz
Alberto Rocha
Cristina Costa-Lobo

(Editors)

SOCIO-EMOTIONAL DEVELOPMENT AND CREATIVITY OF GIFTED STUDENTS

IMPRENSA DA UNIVERSIDADE DE COIMBRA
COIMBRA UNIVERSITY PRESS

TABLE OF CONTENTS

PREFACE

I smile when I think of Bradley, a student in a writing class I taught long ago. Personal computers were not yet common, and his handwriting was difficult to decipher. A teaching colleague said this handsome, affable student had problems focusing. I had already concluded that his mind was much brighter than the dismal academic marks in his school record.

The assignment was to write a tableau, with thick description and only minimal movement. To my surprise, Bradley wrote an impeccably metered parody of Poe's "The Raven" – based on the school lunchroom. It was fluid and reflected keen observation. I was in awe. It was beyond expectations at many levels. No student had ever written anything but straightforward paragraphs for that assignment in the past.

I had taken pride in offering open-ended assignments, giving only general parameters, and celebrating creativity, but I was also trying to nurture "correct" writing. The artistry of Bradley's paper clearly needed to be rewarded, and, for the first time, I completely ignored writing mechanics and posted it among a few others on a cork display board as "great work". Bradley, unknowingly and with verve, had jerked my reins, broadened my perspective, and reminded me how delicious creativity can be.

I brought that view to my next school. I fondly remember a "breakfast club" of gifted writers, mostly low academic achievers, who met with me weekly to share poetry, write short free verse in response to prompts, eat a pastry, and drink juice brought by a designated group member. I was directing the "gifted program", and the poetry group was 1 of 25 program options. The 25th option was small-group discussion about "just growing up", and nearly 100 participated in the groups each week. Almost all program options brought high and low achievers together, and I was inspired by the repartee, insights, and supportive relationships that developed. Regardless of achievement level, the students were among intellectual peers.

Future Problem Solving, a rigorous national program, was also an option. We usually had 6 teams, with 4 students each, who competed locally, and winners moved on to the state level and ultimately to national events. I learned how important it was to have a "closer" on each team – to watch the clock, since competitions were timed. I wanted an excellent, eager writer, since the end product was written. But I also hoped for creative minds, since outside-of-the-box thinking was valued. Some academic underachievers were the most creative.

These experiences instructed me. I witnessed joy, clever humor, passionate investment, and expressive language as the students learned together. Stereotyped perceptions of each other quickly disappeared, as did social hierarchies. The students allowed themselves to be emotionally vulnerable as they found common ground. I often felt "electricity" in group discussions about developmental concerns. Friendships developed, evident in casual groupings in a noon-hour philosophy class taught by a retired university professor during lunch, in exotic-language classes taught by local community members, and at weekly after-school lectures by community experts in fields outside of the school curriculum.

Too often "gifted programs" offer only "more and faster" curricula. I had intended for the complex program to go far beyond the many Advanced Placement classes available. Indeed, most students in the program were enrolled in them. However, students exulted in broad learning, shared insights, creative thinking, open-ended foci, and attention to their well-being in the rest of the special program. Almost all program options involved social interaction. Specific options purposefully helped students develop expressive language, and it was clear that their new skills and emotional openness also carried over to the other activities.

Every day I was busy organizing and facilitating the 25 options. However, the magic I observed as I "sat on the side" at the community lectures, problem-solving and poetry-writing sessions, and beyond-the-curriculum activities still inspires me.

High achievement does not necessarily mean "original ideas". For some, it might simply reflect a well practiced groove for learning what is known. Similarly, quantitative research methods in a measurement-oriented field like gifted education may miss the real ambiguity and uncertainty of "learning" and "knowing". The heightened sensitivity, intensity, and excitabilities that scholars and clinical professionals associate with giftedness argue for opportunities to follow passionate interests, generate insights, revel in positive repartee, self-reflect, respond emotionally, experience cross-disciplinary discussion, explore new territory, learn to tolerate ambiguity, and celebrate "not knowing anything for sure" – together with intellectual peers.

Academic underachievers are, like anyone else, developing, and perhaps they feel "stuck" in one or more areas of development. My own research has explored these phenomena – and has shown that accomplishing developmental tasks is related to movement forward. Underachievers need to be part of a community of intellectual peers at a crucial time of development – especially if they struggle with internal distress or difficult situations. I have long been fascinated with the notion that struggle is not only essential to advanced development, in Dabrowskian terms, but may also be rich soil for growing creativity. Underachievers may be able to contribute unexpected perspectives and insights to discussions, and the social and emotional development of both high and low achievers can be nurtured in the process.

Like Bradley. Like the poetry group. Like the Future Problem Solving teams. I have learned that gifted students like these are eager to invest in rigorous program options that broaden and deepen understanding and include ambiguity and uncertainty to wrestle with – that is, not just a "more and faster" curriculum. Given the current forces at work in a world increasingly interdependent, economically and socially stratified, and seemingly insecure, educators need to nurture creative thinkers and problem-solvers for whom collaborative interdisciplinary work is both encouraged and expected.

Jean Sunde Peterson
Ph.D., Professor Emerita, Purdue University, Indiana, U.S.A.

INTRODUCTION

The preface by Jean Sunde Peterson gives us the tone and the colors of the book. The author describes in a very dynamic way the emotions associated with her memories of enrichment programs for gifted students. These recollections open a set of hot topics about the education of students with high potential, such as inclusion and diversity, and present emotions and affectivity as the central theme of the book's foremost matter.

The course of the book deepens and develops the central theme of affectivity and creativity in high abilities. The journey through the eleven chapters provides us with an extensive and solid review of recent as well as classic literature, various qualitative research data that open the door to a broader understanding of innovative themes and some data that result from more quantitative and experimental research that allow us to support theoretical frames of reference. The chapters are chained together and motivate us to look further and in more detail. Reading the book helps us to systematize and restructure the ever-emerging knowledge about this passionate theme.

Susen Smith opens the first chapter with a challenging proposal in support of the social and emotional learning of students with dual exceptionality. If the advanced intellectual or creative abilities of gifted children and young people, as well as the asynchrony of their development and the dissonance with their peers, justify and reinforce per se the need to support the development of learning and socio-emotional skills, duality legitimizes even more all interventions at this level. The author emphasizes the relevance of Vygotskian and systemic approaches in the conceptualization of support based on the strengths of these students that enable them to go further and underlines the need to look at combined exceptionalities because they so often go unnoticed.

The importance of the socio-emotional development of the gifted is the theme of the second chapter by Fernanda Hellen Ribeiro Piske. The chapter begins by focusing on the concept of over-excitability, put forward by Dabrowski and defined as a prevalent and widespread perception of the environment that can lead to over-stimulation which in turn leads to an increase in the emotional reaction of the talented and gifted in their interaction with the world. The author then discusses the different forms of expression of emotional intensity and points out that a certain incongruity in development is intrinsic to the condition of being gifted. A set of very useful suggestions on various ways of dealing with the social and emotional issues of the gifted and talented is subsequently described. These strategies ultimately enable the gifted to have healthy interactions with their intellectual and artistic peers in order to feel comfortable with their talents and to develop deep friendships. The chapter highlights, in a tone of warning, that teachers and families can offer these children and young people support and encouragement, emphasizing that individual differences should be celebrated rather than altered to suit the classroom or societal standards. Gifted children and young people need to be encouraged to express their thoughts and feelings instead of keeping them hidden.

In the chapter that follows, Lola Prieto, Mercedes Ferrando, Marta Sainz, Rosario Bermejo and Carmen Ferrándiz give us an overview of the study of high ability (giftedness and talent) in Spain. They begin by explaining the history of the concern and intervention with gifted education dating back to the 1930s, and of the first scientific studies half a century later. Secondly they analyze the research carried out in recent years regarding identification procedures, cognitive, socio-emotional non-cognitive aspects of giftedness and present Murcia University as one of the leading research centers in Spain. They then explore in an interesting manner the different reasons 'why' and 'how' the Spanish identify students with such abilities and emphasize the importance of evaluating their creativity as well as their emotional intelligence. Programs and measures intended to deal with diversity used in the various autonomous regions in Spain are discussed as well as the difficulties that have been encountered. The chapter closes on a positive note mentioning the extensive increase in research on gifted and talented individuals and their education in the last decade and the way legislation has made progress. However, the authors point out concern about the lack of social awareness towards high-ability themes and hope that the efforts of researchers and educators may achieve greater social understanding and professional development in the field of high abilities.

In Chapter 4, Letícia Fleig Dal Forno and Sara Bahia explore the sum of educational specificities that emanate from the concepts of learning, inclusion, affectivity and giftedness. The authors explain that the recognition of giftedness requires a multidimensional understanding of the concept by those who evaluate and examine it. This analysis takes into consideration, besides academic performance, the sociocultural context and the opportunities that enable the expression of high abilities. They describe the data of their research that involved 245 childhood educators that incorporates the dimension of affectivity in the recognition and identification of the characteristics of giftedness.

In addition to development, learning rhythm, performance, learning style, memorization, outstanding performance, abilities and skills, educators also included in their conceptions divergent thinking, exceptionality in the production of ideas and their expression, attraction for challenge, ability of generating unexpected solutions and, not less relevant, affectivity. They recommend that the conceptualization of high abilities must incorporate non-intellectual dimensions. Both personal and environmental factors are significant in the expression of the potential of these children, even at a young age, such as 3, 4 or 5 years old.

Fernanda Bachini de Oliveira and Tania Stoltz explore the social and affective interaction of students with high skills in the fifth chapter. Based on an extensive literature review on the multidimensional character of giftedness, so often neglected by the educational system due to lack of knowledge or misrecognition on the part of teachers and school communities. The chapter presents us with data collected through three interviews and observation and systematic observations and concludes that the physical space of the school context allows social and affective interactions. The chapter also shows how activities are planned and proposed according to the space available. Classes are organized with the aim of promoting exchange of knowledge amongst students and this occurs both in intentional activities and games and also in the interchange arising from individual assignments. The authors lead us to a reflection on the relevance of factors that are not very well understood in theory and practice, thus opening up our own horizons.

In Chapter 6 Rocha and Matos show us how compassion, altruism, decentration, defense of others, empathy, solidarity and affective and moral sensibility are features of emotional overexcitability. Moreover, different standards and intensity of overexcitability play a decisive role in the development of human potential and should be valued in the conception and intervention of giftedness in all its richness. The authors explain how further research on the potential of empathy, affective sensibility and moral sensitivity is needed due to all the growing risks humanity faces, and the inherent necessity to make good use of intelligence along with moral development. Most of the research in this domain is unempirical and the results are largely considered to be inconsistent, thus reinforcing the need for more in-depth studies on empathetic compassion.

Susan J. Paik and Charlina Gozali, authors of Chapter 7, discuss the development of creative productivity in gifted students. They begin by defining "productive giftedness" as the ability to realize potential in the form of creative and productive results. They present the Productive Giftedness Model (PGM), a theoretical framework that outlines ten key factors of productive giftedness. Under Individual Aptitude, Instruction and Environment, PGM includes both alterable factors and contextual factors. This model helps us to better understand access of different opportunities, support and resources for students. They describe the literature on different climates of learning as well as the quality and the quantity of instruction as it relates to creativity. Creativity and productivity also require practice, discipline and commitment. The authors emphasize that the curriculum should be developed to enhance long-term development of students' talent and creativity. As talent cannot be cultivated alone, relationships with parents, teachers, mentors and peers are also important in sustaining creative productivity.

The motivational aspect of creativity as self-rewarding and autonomous is addressed by Eva Gyarmathy in the eighth chapter. The author makes a very relevant distinction between school giftedness identified and evaluated during school age and the creative and productive giftedness considered in adulthood. The first kind of gifted people are excellent at acquiring and storing knowledge whereas the latter, and in contrast, use knowledge to discover new things and prefer what can be discovered instead of what can be learned. The author emphasizes that good performance in formal education is not necessarily translated into talent and later notable creations and that motivational aspects determine to a good extent this continuity. Education must follow the process of acquiring natural knowledge, something that does not always happen. The last part of the chapter explains that creative functioning must be reinforced by a culture that treats diversity and different solutions as values, offers freedom and alternatives and considers congruence as natural.

In Chapter 9, Daiana Yamila Rigo, Romina Elisondo and María Laura de la Barrera present three current perspectives relevant to gifted education: commitment, creativity studies and neurosciences. They refer to dimensions interrelated with a wide variety of symbolic, physical and social resources and depend on the dynamic and reciprocal interaction of the individual with the educational, social and cultural context. The greater the interaction between people and formal, non-formal and informal educational environments, the greater the achievement of their genetic potential. Opportunities to participate in varied experiences bring more possibilities to creatively develop talents and abilities when interacting with the environment. The authors put forward arguments for understanding that social environment seen from the sociocultural perspective can maximize the potential of children and young people who are developing. However, they alert that a supportive environment that offers opportunities is not the only condition for developing a genetic potential. Commitment to interacting with the environment is essential for the development of creative thinking.

Chapter 10, by Otto Schmidt, presents a set of creative strategies for developing gifted students' creativity. It begins by stating that the creativity training of these students is one of the most important responsibilities of teachers and that it can improve the skills of all class students when planning and developing approaches to independent and self-directed learning. Teachers are responsible for inspiring these students to express their needs and ideas more openly so that everyone can understand and satisfy them. The author states that looking at creativity as "taking the ordinary and doing something unordinary" encourages people to think beyond the ordinary and think more deeply when involved in any task. The chapter also examines and proposes examples of existing creativity-promoting strategies that can be used in an innovative way and makes an interesting analysis of websites about creativity.

Fernanda Hellen Ribeiro Piske, Tânia Stoltz, Ettiène Guérios and Cristina Costa Lobo begin the last chapter with an analysis of the phenomenon of creative resistance based on Bourdieu's concept of "habitus", that is to say, the system of individual representations socially formed by structured arrangements and permanently configured by social functions and actions. For the authors, the school system is a reality composed of many rules that can constitute a barrier that blocks the abilities of the students who attend it. Knowing that development and expression of creativity depend not only on an individual's own efforts but also on the social context in which the person is immersed, it is important to reflect on the possibilities of developing creativity, avoiding resistance to this important attribute in the development of these students. Artistic practices can be an example of the re-signification of the teaching of students with high skills to the extent that the artistic object has in itself the means to instill emotions and culturally rich reactions to appropriation of the world. Thus it is the responsibility of the school to enable freedom of expression and encourage the development of the gifts, talents and potential of students in order to promote more creative and innovative teaching.

Written by authors from various parts of the world, this book is groundbreaking in that it touches on many of the hot topics of high abilities. Through the age range of the characteristics it analyzes, as young as three up to adulthood. Through the dimensions it covers, with particular emphasis on affectivity, but not neglecting the exploration of cognitive and artistic abilities. Through the multiplicity of models and theoretical approaches that surpass the more classic approaches on which we usually base our perspectives and practices. Through innovation in rethinking different conceptualizations like those of Steiner, Bordieu or Morin. Through proposals to implement strategies to promote talent not only in the classroom or in programs, but also in non-formal contexts such as the Web. Right up to the conceptual debates, surprising advances in definitions or unexpected clarifications of themes. All these perspectives contribute to orchestrate the central theme of the book: socio-emotional development and creativity of gifted students.

Lisbon, February 2020

Sara Bahia
FPULisboa

1

SCAFFOLDING THE SOCIAL AND EMOTIONAL LEARNING STRENGTHS AND CHALLENGES OF STUDENTS WITH TWICE-EXCEPTIONALITIES: DIFFERENCE AND DYNAMICITY

Susen Smith

GERRIC Senior Research Fellow

Honorary Senior Lecturer in Gifted & Special Education

School of Education, Faculty of the Arts and Social Sciences

University of New South Wales (UNSW), Sydney, Australia

ORCID: 0000-0002-4184-0706

E-mail: susen.smith@unsw.edu.au

Abstract: Gifted students can be as stable as their same-age typical peers in similar social and emotional circumstances. Nonetheless, gifted students may also experience difficulties because of their advanced intellectual or creative capabilities, asynchrony, dissonance with same-age peers' typical development, and the manifestation of psychosocial characteristics. These traits alone reinforce the need to support their Social and Emotional Competence (SEC) development with Social and Emotional Learning (SEL) in relevant educational programming and provisions. However, widespread misconceptions of giftedness and gifted education can inhibit provisions for diversely gifted students. Additionally, the disparity between the educational needs of gifted students and their educational context and provisions can contribute to their social and emotional difficulties. Nonetheless, some gifted populations are more at risk of additional psychosocial difficulties, such as students with twice-exceptionalities (2e). The combined exceptionalities of 2e may be imperceptible and not influential to the student's development, or the comorbidity or dynamics of their exceptionalities may result in incapacitating inhibition of development, learning, or achievement. The neurodiversity of 2e students suggests they may think quite differently, depending on their capabilities, conditions, or challenges. This chapter will focus on the neurodiverse conditions or differences of 2e students, that may be inhibiters or promoters of creativity or talent development, that is, having contrasting strengths or challenges, gifts or deficits. The Collaborative for Social, Academic, and Emotional Learning (CASEL) framework will be used to underscore 2e students' need for Social and Emotional Learning (SEL) within sensitive, inclusive, risk-free, and student-relevant learning ecologies. SEL includes scaffolding students' development of their social and emotional competences.

Keywords: Twice-exceptional, Social and Emotional Learning (SEL), Neurodiversity, Scaffolding dynamic strengths, CASEL.

Introduction

It is reiterated in the research that gifted students are as stable as their same-age peers and their social and emotional circumstances are similar to their typical peers (Hébert, 2011; Neihart, Pfeiffer, & Cross, 2015; Pfeiffer & Foley-Nicpon, 2018; Rogers, 2015). Nonetheless, gifted students may also experience difficulties because of their advanced intellectual or creative capabilities, asynchrony in their own development, dissonance with same-age peers' typical development, and the manifestation of psychosocial characteristics (Smith, 2017a). These alone reinforce the need to support their Social and Emotional Competence (SEC) development with Social and Emotional Learning (SEL). For a recent review of research on empirically validated psychological interventions for students with twice-exceptionalities see Foley-Nicpon and Candler (2018).

In the discourse widespread misconceptions of giftedness and gifted education that can inhibit provisions for diversely gifted students is reinforced (Smith, 2017a). In the research the disparity between the educational needs of gifted students and their educational context and provisions that contributes to their social and emotional difficulties is also reiterated (Smith, 2017a). Nonetheless, some gifted populations are more at risk of additional psychosocial difficulties, such as those students with twice-exceptionalities (Wormald, Rogers, & Vialle, 2015).

In this context, gifted exceptionalities are having the potential for achieving highly intellectually, creatively, physically, or in social/leadership domains (Gagné, 2010, 2016). Exceptional difficulties or disabilities or differences, however, can manifest at various levels of psychological/social-emotional, communication, neurodevelopmental/behavioural, physical/medical/sensory, or learning disabilities (Foley-Nicpon, Allmon, Sieck, & Stinson,

2011; Foley-Nicpon, Assouline, & Colangelo, 2013; Pfeiffer, 2015; Ronskey-Pavia, 2015). A student who displays more than one or two exceptionalities – inclusive of advanced learning capacity – has twice- or multiple-exceptionalities (Pfeiffer, 2015; Townend, Pendergast, & Garvis, 2014). For example, a student with high intellectual giftedness and a co-existing disability, such as Asperger's syndrome or a learning difficulty, has twice-exceptionalities (Wormald, Vialle, & Rogers, 2014). Students can also present with high cognitive capacity or other type of giftedness and two or more other exceptionalities, and these students have multiple-exceptionalities (Pfeiffer, 2015; Pfeiffer & Foley-Nicpon, 2018).

These co-existing exceptionalities may range from a mild to profound level in exceptionality or difficulty (Pfeiffer, 2015). The various exceptionalities that one student may have are not biologically, etiologically, nor phenotypically independent, but rather are interdependent, resulting in a melding that causes varying outcomes than for those individuals who may only experience one of the exceptionalities alone (Mayes, Harris, & Hines, 2016). Hence, the co-existence of giftedness and disability in one student causes three possible outcomes that add to the complexity of teaching students with 2e:

- the giftedness hides or masks the disability so the student achieves, but not to their expected advanced level and no support is provided for either the advanced ability nor the disability;
- the disability masks the giftedness so much that special services are provided to remediate the difficulties, but the giftedness is not identified nor supported; and,
- both conditions mask each other so much that the student performs at a typical level like their same-age peers, so neither exceptionality is recognized and no extra support is provided for either exceptionality (Baldwin, Baum, Pereles, & Hughes, 2015; Pfeiffer & Foley-Nicpon, 2018; Reis, Baum, & Burke, 2014).

Therefore, the combined exceptionalities may be imperceptible and not influential to the student's development, or the comorbidity or dynamics of exceptionalities may result in incapacitating inhibition of development, learning, or achievement (Pfeiffer, 2015). The terms *comorbidity* or *multi-morbidity* have derived from medical and psychiatric practice, where it is recognized that co-existing conditions exacerbate identification, behavioural outcomes, confuse the etiology of the 2e, and complicate possible treatment or support (Pfeiffer & Foley-Nicpon, 2018). However, comorbidity is historically based on the deficit model of disease with the medical model of care rather than strength-based provisions for exceptionality. In this chapter, comorbidity will be replaced with dynamicity – as *dynamicity* reinforces the influences of the dynamic overlap of the divergent exceptionalities in one person (Pfeiffer & Foley-Nicpon, 2018). For a detailed overview of the history associated with twice-exceptionalities the reader is referred to Baldwin, Baum et al. (2015), who detail the origins of terminology and recognition of 2e.

Neuropsychology, neuroscience, history, special education, and other fields have explored twice-exceptionalities linking high ability with high functioning autism and learning and behavioural disabilities. Additionally, the neurodiversity movement has arisen in recent years and supports the neurodiversity paradigm that suggests that all society is on a continuum of neurological development, and, as such, most of society thinks neorotypically, while there are pockets of neurominorities who are neurodivergent who think quite differently, depending on their capabilities, conditions, or challenges. This chapter will focus on neurodiverse conditions or differences, such as being highly able with co-existing autism and/or learning difficulties. Neurodivergent means having an extreme or different genetic predisposition that may be influenced by environmental interactions and is not a pathology or disease. Consequently, the neurological abnormality is identified rather than the ability/gifts or strengths resulting in the student attending special education support or presenting as typical (Buic-Belciu & Popovici, 2014). Neurodiverse differences can be viewed as inhibiters or promoters of creativity or talent development, that is, having contrasting strengths or challenges, gifts or deficits. Extremes in neurodiversity are those with neurodivergent conditions that are reflected in high functioning autism or Asperger's Syndrome or profound cognitive development for example.

The Collaborative for Social, Academic, and Emotional Learning (CASEL, 2015) framework reiterates five core social and emotional competencies, that are: *self-awareness* (i.e., understanding their emotions, strengths, and challenges); *self-management* (i.e., self-regulating their thinking, emotions, and behaviours); *relationships skills* (i.e., engaging in high-quality relationships); *social awareness* (i.e., empathetically understanding others); and *responsible decision-making* (i.e., making constructive choices) (CASEL, 2015; Collie, Martin, & Frydenberg, 2017; Smith, 2017a). Self-awareness, self-management, and responsible decision-making are intrapersonal (i.e., internal) competences, while social awareness and relationship skills are interpersonal (i.e., external) competences. Developing Social and Emotional Competence (SEC) includes understanding the relationships between intrapersonal and interpersonal agency factors that are crucial for 2e students' well-being as it influences achievement, social relationships, and health factors (Pfeiffer, 2015).

The academic achievement and positive intrapersonal and interpersonal well-being that results from the development of social and emotional competence is widely acknowledged (Collie, Martin, & Frydenberg, 2017; Foley-Nicpon, Allmon, Sieck, & Stinson, 2011; Gross, 2014; Rogers, 2015; Smith, 2017a). However, psychosocial difficulties may ensue if students' social and emotional competence is not developed through Social and Emotional Learning (SEL) within sensitive, inclusive, risk-free, and student-relevant learning ecologies (Collie, Martin, & Frydenberg, 2017; Rogers, 2015). SEL includes scaffolding students' development of their social and emotional competences (Smith, 2017a; Rogers, 2015). Durlak, Weissberg, Dymnicki, Taylor, and Schellinger's (2011) meta-analysis of over 200 studies showed how SEL can improve student capacity to manage depression and stress, increase student achievement, improve interrelationship skills and attitudinal factors.

> For gifted students to have their SEL needs met, they need a curriculum that accommodates their advanced abilities, alongside intentional SEL support. However, some gifted students have multiple special needs that may seem to contradict one another: they may be gifted and they may also have a learning difference such as attention deficit hyperactivity disorder or dyslexia. The giftedness of these twice exceptional (2e) students might be overlooked due to their learning weaknesses. (Galbraith, 2018, p. 146).

However, Smith (2017a) highlighted that most SEL programs are not designed for gifted students' unique needs, nor 2e students, but for students generally, so SEL provisions specifically for 2e's atypical needs are apposite.

Interrelated theoretical foundations

The interrelationship between positive psychology and social-constructivism within an ecological-systemic framework supported by gifted education research on scaffolding 2e well-being for talent development provides the theoretical foundation for SEL provisions. Positive psychology is the scientific study of the biological, personal, relational, educational, socio-cultural, and global aspects of how personal strengths and positive social systems foster emotional well-being.Hence, positive psychological attributes may result from either abilities or disabilities, so there is the need to promote provisions to support the development of intrapersonal and interpersonal well-being and accomplishments (Wang & Neihart, 2015).This is in contrast to the clinical treatment of pathologies by remediating or managing deficits of vulnerable populations like 2e students (Daniels & Freeman, 2018). The positive attributes include intrapersonal strengths, positive emotions and experiences, and meaningful interrelationships.

Social constructivism is defined as learning within an interpersonal context where more skilled others scaffold the student learner through their zone of proximal development (ZPD) – that is, teaching students just beyond their independent learning capacity to stretch their learning through scaffolding (Piske et al., 2016; Stoltz, Piske, de Freitas, D'Aroz, & Machado, 2015, Piske, 2018). Scaffolding is the support mechanisms or processes used to help students learn (Smith, 2017a, 2017b). For example, scaffolding strength development and achievement can enhance 2e students' self-efficacy (confidence or belief in one's capacity to achieve) and their self-concept (awareness of self based on personal experiences and beliefs) (Wang & Neihart, 2015).

In many studies on 2e the ecological systems view has been used to frame the research (e.g., Foley-Nicpon & Candler, 2018; Mayes & Moore, 2016).Bronfenbrenner's (1977) socio-ecological model based on the ecological-systems view provides an holistic foundation for recognizing the individual's development and interrelationships between varying entities within varying ecologies from their family to the broader cultural context (Bronfenbrenner & Ceci, 1994; Bronfenbrenner & Morris, 1998; Foley-Nicpon & Candler, 2018). The *Model of Dynamic Differentiation (MoDD)* (Smith, 2015, 2017b) was founded on Bronfenbrennor's (1977) developmentally based model and provides a foundation for planning the pedagogic approach to educational provisions. The MoDD (Smith, 2015, 2017b) transits from the 'developing' child generally to the 'student's academic, intrapersonal, and interpersonal development in differentiated educational contexts specifically. The MoDD highlights the dynamicity of human and contextual interrelationships between varying teaching and learning processes involving assessment of student strengths, enrichment based on interests, scaffolding individual needs according to learning readiness, and self-regulating learning within and across all the educational contexts from the student educating themselves, to the classroom, school, community, family, and global contexts (Smith, 2015, 2017b).

The conception of giftedness and talent most used in the Australian context is Gagné's *Differentiated Model of Giftedness and Talent (DMGT)*, a talent development model (Gagné, 2010, 2011, 2013, 2016). Gagné's DMGT (2010) separates 'domains of giftedness' and 'fields of talent' as two different entities on a continuum from transforming giftedness in one or more of many domains (e.g., intelligence, creativity) to talent emergence in any one or more fields of human endeavour (e.g., Science, Arts, Business, Academics). So, a 2e student may be gifted, but not yet talented, though still have the potential to develop their talent if supported. Gagné (2016) recognizes different domains of giftedness, of which being intellectually gifted and creatively gifted are two, while Neihart's and Betts' (1988; 2010) research adds to Gagné's DMGT by identifying different types and behaviours of giftedness within these domains, such as students with 2e, or at risk, or autonomous learners. For example, a student can be intellectually gifted and at risk of underachieving.

Gagné's DMGT (2010, 2016) also illustrates a developmental process the gifted child undergoes in order for their talent to be developed into excellent performance and outstanding achievement. In the DMGT, Gagné posits that gifted students' developmental processes are influenced by many interpersonal (e.g., social awareness, attitudes, teacher-student relationships, social engagement), intrapersonal (e.g., motivation, resilience, awareness of strengths) and environmental (e.g., teachers, classroom, resources, family) catalysts that either support or hinder talent evolvement. Therefore, in this context, and aligning with positive psychology, the ZPD of social constructivism, and scaffolding and self-regulation in the MoDD, the focus is on supporting 2e students' SEC development and growth of intrapersonal and interpersonal agency through SEL to promote well-being that may result in talent development (Smith, 2017a).

In the development of intrapersonal (i.e., self-awareness, self-management) and interpersonal (i.e., relationships skills) competencies, well-being should be nurtured to manifest outcomes, such as self-motivation, school enjoyment, achievement, and other resulting competences (Durlak et al., 2011, 2015; Martin, Cumming, O'Neill, & Strnadová, 2017). However, are problematic academic, intrapersonal, and interpersonal outcomes more likely to occur for students with 2e than for typical students or those with only one exceptionality?

Dichotomies of co-existing 2e strengths versus challenges

The duality of exceptionalities can result in the dynamicity of superior strengths and inhibiting challenges (Foley-Nicpon, 2015;

Hughes, 2017). The strengths may compensate for the challenges, so that the student appears as typical in their development, however psychosocial difficulties may still ensue (Baldwin, Baum, et al., 2015; Smith, 2017a; Townend et al., 2014). Alternatively, the challenges may hide or mask the underlying strengths, and inhibit potentially high achievement so underachievement ensues and talent is not developed (Bell, Taylor, McCallum, Coles, & Hays, 2015; Foley-Nicpon et al., 2011; Galbraith, 2018; Mayes et al., 2016; Reis et al., 2014).

While 2e students exhibit a number of strengths, these can be accompanied by difficulties and exacerbated by misconceptions about associated behaviours (Baum, Schader, & Hébert, 2014). For example, 2e students may learn quickly or attain large chunks of content knowledge very quickly, but become quite impatient and frustrated quickly when their peers do not understand as quickly and inhibit the 2e student's learning process.Likewise, 2e students can develop an extensive and advanced vocabulary, but their same-age peers may not comprehend their use of language or questions or directions. Additionally, 2e students can be very curious, but ask too many probing questions to the annoyance of others (Piske, Stoltz, & Machado, 2014). Students with 2e can also be very creative or innovative and problem-solve quickly, but be critical of others during their creative explorations (Piske et al., 2014). Also, 2e students can be socially well adjusted, but use their sophisticated sense of humor sarcastically (Smith, 2017a). Smith (2017a) further reiterated that due to the disproportionate differences between their exceptionalities, 2e students:

> may be more prone to having lower self-concept, which foregrounds cognitive processing difficulties and psychosocial problems (Townend et al., 2014). Psychosocial issues might cause frustration, demotivation, inappropriate

behaviours, fear of failure, poor interrelationships, negative school attitudes, or lack of belonging. (p. 150).

Twice-exceptional students, however, are not an homogenous group, hence, the chapter now focuses on different types of twice-exceptionalities. Three subgroups of twice-exceptionalities have the most prevalent empirical research or are most diagnosed, that is students with Giftedness and Learning Disabilities (GLD), Giftedness and Autism Spectrum Disorder (GASD), and Giftedness and Attention Deficit Hyperactivity Disorder (GADHD; Foley-Nicpon et al., 2013; Foley-Nicpon et al., 2011). In one recent study, the authors reinforced the outcome of the perception that 2e students' strengths and potential are not being nurtured in current educational contexts (Willard-Holt, Weber, Morrison, & Horgan, 2013). "One of the common barriers to developing educational interventions for twice-exceptional students relates to the lack of understanding about their specific skills and needs" (Foley-Nicpon & Candler, 2018, p. 550). Hence, in this chapter the SEC strengths and challenges, and SEL needs and provisions for students with GLD, GASD, and GADHD will be reiterated. The aforementioned theoretical framework, that is, experienced others scaffolding 2e students' SEL learning of SEC through their ZPD in supportive educational ecologies provides educators with the foundation for supporting 2e students' well-being.

Gifted students with Learning Disabilities (GLD)

Learning disabilities or difficulties are exhibited in many forms, such as dyslexia, dyscalculia, dyspraxia, and the like. Dyslexia is having difficulty with reading, writing, and other language expressions. Dyscalculia is difficulty learning mathematically (Williams, 2013), while Dyspraxia is difficulty with fine motor skill development. These learning difficulties impact intrapersonal and interpersonal agency factors, and may result in academic disengagement, disciplinary outcomes for adverse behavioural reactions, and poor social functioning (Martin et al., 2017). GLD combines giftedness and learning difficulties. LD seems to be the most prevalent or most diagnosed disability in twice-exceptionalities (Foley-Nicpon et al., 2011). In this chapter, the 'D' in LD will be replaced with the implication 'difference' rather than 'disability' to align with the neurodiversity developmental view.

Dichotomy of coexisting strengths versus challenges of students with GLD

The contradictions between the strengths and challenges of students with GLD are evinced in characteristics such as: having advanced vocabulary, but having difficulties with decoding and spelling (Wood & Estrada-Hernandez, 2009); being advanced reasoners with conceptual understandings that progress typically, though have memorization difficulties (Ottone-Cross et al., 2017); being able to use inductive learning strategies in problem-solving yet receptive and expressive communication are weak (Munro, 2002); having higher order thinking skills, divergent, and abstract thinking (VanTassel-Baska, 2016; Wood & Estrada-Hernandez, 2009), but have difficulties with long- and short-term memory; and having superior spatial skills, while being unable to express their thoughts in the written form (Ottone-Cross et al., 2017). These characteristic dichotomies have implications for identification, student engagement, achievement, social isolation, and talent development. For example, a GLD student may think creatively in visual images, but be unable to write about their innovative thoughts. In terms of interpersonal agency, students with GLD may be highly cognitively advanced enabling their awareness of their social difficulties, but lack the social skills to relate interpersonally, resulting in social isolation, that, in turn, impacts their intrapersonal agency factors, such as poor self-concept (Martin et al., 2017; Townend et al., 2014).

Gifted with a specific learning disability: Dyslexia

Daniels and Freeman (2018) suggest that dyslexia is a learning difference and not a disability, though they exhibit characteristics such as difficulties with "visual and auditory attention, processing, executive functioning, verbal fluency, math fluency, solving word problems, and such" (p. 258). Having high cognitive ability and being able to process verbal information easily (Berninger & Abbott, 2018) can mask their reading challenges. Conversely, GLD students may have advanced reading skills that could mask their specific processing difficulties (van Vierson, Kroesbergen, Slot, & de Bree, 2016).

GLD students with Dyslexia usually present with unique neurocognitive profiles (Crogman, Gilger, & Hoeft, 2018) and it has been suggested that it is this atypical neurological profile that enables their visual-spatial processing or innovative nonverbal problem solving (Diehl et al., 2014; Gilger, 2017; Gilger Allen, & Castillo, 2016). Indeed, Daniels and Freeman (2018) reinforced the neurological link between "certain cognitive weaknesses and certain cognitive strengths for students with dyslexia" (p. 258). While students with GLD with dyslexia do exhibit cognitive strengths and challenges, it is less clear if they do present as having strong compensatory skills in visual/spatial abilities (Gilger, 2017; Ottone-Cross et al., 2017). Crogman, Gilger, and Hoeft (2018) present a detailed review of 2e students with reading disabilities reiterating the dynamicity and complexity of 2e students' spatial visualization and that the research literature is so contradictory on the nonverbal and visual spatial processing characteristics needs of this population. Furthermore, Crogman et al. (2018), suggest a focus on individual developmental needs is preferable to labeling and more research is needed to verify GLD students' strengths.

Many anecdotal reports and reviews seem to support that GLD students with Dyslexia have visual/spatial strengths. However, to make this ascertain and apply provisions based on visual/ spatial learning processes only adds undue stress to an already stressed student (Gilger, 2017).

While neurological studies using brain imaging comparisons (Diehl et al., 2014; Olulade et al., 2012; Vandermosten, Hoeft, & Norton, 2016) show some differences in brain functioning between typical students' cognitive processing and GLD students' processing, more brain imaging research is needed on complex visual/ spatial reasoning to grasp what "these visual-spatial neurological differences mean and how they contribute to the dyslexic profile and potential" (Gilger, 2017, p. 111). Literature reviews (Crogman et al., 2018; Gilger, 2017; Gilger et al., 2016) question the research supporting the visual/spatial reasoning strengths of GLD students, so more rigorous empirical research to support such claims are needed before affirming such GLD characteristics, as it is:

> a social responsibility to determine to what extent the assertions of special talents in dyslexics can be supported, and then to identify how best to tailor clinical and educational interventions to help students make the best of the abilities they possess. (Gilger, 2017, p. 112).

SEC and SEL complexities of students with GLD and associated provisions

GLD intrapersonal agency factors likely include lower self-concept, poor self-esteem, and depression. GLD students may find the discrepancy between their exceptionalities difficult to cope with, contributing to contradictory thinking about their potential, which can decrease their self-concept and increase their anxiety (Townend et al., 2014). They may perceive themselves as being different to their peers, struggle with social-emotional problems, and have difficulty relating to their peers that often results in self-isolation. Focus on remediation alone is likely to emphasize challenges and difficulties, lowering self-esteem, reducing motivation, and increasing stressors or depression, while strength-based gifted education strategies and programs have been found to increase participants' self-concept (Baldwin, Baum et al., 2015; Baldwin, Omdal, & Pereles, 2015; Baum et al., 2014; Townend et al., 2014). Hence, provisions need to encompass strength-based SEL of these SEC alongside academic learning.

Crogman, Gilger, and Hoeft's (2018) review highlighted the:

> imbalance in the use of modern methodologies to study nonverbal skills in RD [reading disabilities] samples, with the majority of past research studies ... focusing on psychometric behavioral performance without consideration of neurology ... [as] similar behaviours do not necessarily mean the same neurological processes at work. (p. 249).

Bell et al.'s (2015) large-scale study reinforced the use of curriculum-based assessment to identify specific GLD student needs, especially those characteristics that mask each other. Hence, GLD students can achieve if identified accurately (Lovett & Sparks, 2013). This further reinforces the need for wide-ranging evaluations and accurate identification of both strengths and challenges of GLD students to prevent student disengagement and to foster accelerated pacing with advanced content in strength areas (Ottone-Cross et al., 2017; Rogers, 2015). When typical growth is evident then developmental instruction may be required, while their areas of strength may need scaffolding to develop further (Gilger et al., 2016). In turn, areas of challenge should be remediated with research-based interventions, such as using technologies to replace handwriting and to support grammar and syntax development, to decrease disengagement, and to increase achievement to enable giftedness to become unmasked (Gross, 2014; Ottone-Cross et al., 2017; Reis et al., 2014).

Teaching 2e students self-advocacy through role-playing and modeling is empowering and can increase their competencies, such as self-awareness and management skills (Galbraith, 2018).A social-constructivist interpersonal approach would utilize a mentor or grouping to support the development of SEC for GLD students. Interpersonal dynamics in small group contexts with like-minded peers allow students the opportunity to share their perspectives and experiences regarding how they are feeling or are treated, and also to focus on interests and strengths for group assignments (Galbraith, 2018).

> To support and promote creativity, innovation, and risk-taking, educators must create an environment where trying new things and making mistakes are okay – even desirable. Students who are fearful of mistakes and new things are at risk for undue stress, anxiety, and

underperforming. Educators can model healthy risk-taking [for 2e]. (Galbraith, 2018, p. 151).

In relation to interpersonal agency that may preclude or enhance positive peer relationships, open-ended tasks can provide opportunities for risk-taking during small group creative learning tasks (Galbraith, 2018). Teachers could model creative learning processes and teach creative thinking, and redirect student creativity, over-enthusiasm, or distracting responses into individual or small-group real world problem-solving tasks. Access to gifted education programs or other specialized provisions matched with their strengths and interests are also mooted in the literature to build innovative outcomes (Rogers, 2015; Smith, 2017b).

Gifted students with Asperger's or high functioning Autism (GASD)

Autism Spectrum Disorder (ASD) is a neurological developmental disability that is characterized by severe communication, social, behavioural, and/or emotional challenges that may manifest as social isolation, repetitive patterns of behaviours, obsessive routines, intense links with specific objects or interests, or extreme difficulties with oral communication, sensory difficulties, and/or depression. Those with high functioning autism or Asperger's can also have mild to profound intellectual or creative giftedness or talent (GASD) (Lerner & Girard, 2018).

Dichotomies of co-existing GASD students' strengths versus challenges

Students with GASD present with a complex amalgam of characteristics from ASD and whatever giftedness domain they identify with. Characteristic of ASD are social interaction and communication difficulties, obsessive interests, and repetitive behaviours, while single-mindedness, resilience, visual thinking, and problem solving are advantageous characteristics of students with GASD (Foley-Nicpon, 2015). However, the amalgamation of these characteristics presents differently to those with ASD alone or giftedness alone – e.g., GASD students may show some awareness of social differences, struggle with routines, and present with stereotypical behaviours – contributing to the unique cognitive dissidence and resulting non-social behaviours that GASD students present. Hence, GASD students' advanced cognitive capacity may change the phenotypic expression (Foley-Nicpon, 2015). For example, while they may have extremely deep content knowledge, especially in regard to their interest areas, they may lack the social awareness or interrelationship skills to work productively with peers in group contexts (Foley-Nicpon, 2015).

The dichotomy between GASD students' exceptional verbal expression and difficulties with processing information and short-term memory is evident in recent studies (Foley-Nicpon, Assouline, & Stinson, 2012). Foley-Nicpon et al.'s (2012) study found differences between students with GASD and those with autism, such that those students with GASD presented with significantly higher verbal comprehension than students with ASD alone, while students with ASD had significantly higher written expression than their GASD counterparts. As GASD students function with a lower processing speed their creativity may be inhibited by their more concrete, literal, and factual thinking processes. However, they do have the capacity to 'think outside the box' and provide unique and creative responses to questions and problems.

SEC and SEL complexities of students with GASD and associated provisions

While significant others "may observe symptoms of depression, inattention, hyperactivity, and difficulty in coping with change", students with GASD's lack of self-awareness may inhibit their understandings that they may be experiencing these aforementioned coexisting difficulties (Foley-Nicpon, 2015). In terms of intrapersonal and interpersonal skills, Doobay, Foley-Nicpon, Ali, and Assouline's (2014) study found that GASD students manifested more depression, inattention, and difficulty with social skill development than their peers with giftedness alone. High IQ is one protection against depression or may enable gifted students to deal with depression and build resiliency (Meuller, 2009). For example, advanced problem-solving skills can boost their coping capacity (Lo & Mantak, 2014).

A SEL strategy could tap into the students' interests and expertise by completing interest inventories, the results of which become the foundation for interest-based projects or assignments with choice (Galbraith, 2018). Educators can scaffold their transition between tasks and broaden their range of interests by relating their particular passion or obsession with other content knowledge or interdisciplinary issues.

As far as interpersonal skills, Lerner and Girard's (2018) empirical study found that GASD students' capacity for "novel, flexible social responses, rather than knowledge of concrete social rules, may be especially critical for development of real-world social communication skills" (p. 203-204). Hence, teachers or counselors could provide social constructivist social skills programs to enable the development of group-based skills, to build on their creative social skills, and increase their social competencies rather than their knowledge of social rules or etiquette (Gates, Kang, & Lerner, 2017). A number of recent programs highlighted by Lerner and Girard (2018) engage GASD students in collaborative grouping contexts that enable sharing unique social experiences and promote spontaneous innovations and creativity. Creativity development is enabled by providing spontaneous scenarios for improvised responses and encouraging opportunities for students with GASD to work with like-minded peers with like-interests for friendship-building and scaffolding learning in risk-free environments (Lerner & Girard, 2018). By creating the risk-free interpersonal environments using these strategies, successful SEL intrapersonal outcomes for students with GASD can reduce social anxiety, or enhance interrelationships, and self-esteem (Lerner & Girard, 2018).

Gifted students with Attention Deficit Hyperactivity Disorder (GADHD)

Students with GADHD present as having a neurobehavioural disorder that manifests in rapid speech, persistent non-social behaviours, extreme behavioural reactions, hyperactivity, impulsivity, distractibility, inattention, sensitivity to stimuli, and adverse competence beliefs that may impact development (Antshel, Hendricks, Faraone, & Gordon, 2011; Foley-Nicpon, 2015; Martin et al., 2017). This condition and these characteristics may co-exist with any type of giftedness or other conditions, which add different resulting behaviours for GADHD students.

Dichotomies of GADHD students' co-existing strengths versus challenges

Students with GADHD face many academic challenges. While lower working memory is often associated with students with ADHD, Fugate, Zentall, and Gentry (2013) found that GADHD students had greater creativity with increased capacity for problem solving than gifted students without ADHD. Additionally, GADHD students may also have difficulty with metacognitive skills, but have advanced divergent thinking skills supporting more innovative thinking (White & Shah, 2016). The advanced capacities of students with GADHD prompted Fugate and Gentry (2016) to re-title this population as Attention Divergent Hyperactive Gifted (ADHG), the divergence reinforcing their strengths and creativity, rather than possible difficulties or challenges. Hence, "identification and programming in creative domains may also be promising for twice-exceptional students, especially gifted students with ADHD" (Foley-Nicpon & Candler, 2018, p. 551).

SEC and SEL complexities of students with GADHD and associated provisions

While there is little research on the intrapersonal or interpersonal competencies associated with the well-being of students with ADHD (Martin et al., 2017), students with GADHD also contend with social-emotional difficulties. GADHD students may have executive functioning/learning problems, which means they have learning management difficulties, such as difficulty starting, organizing, and completing tasks, hence having difficulty maintaining effort and being motivated (Fugate & Gentry, 2016). Educators can teach intrinsic motivation to increase self-efficacy and learning enjoyment and decrease achievement anxiety. Psychosocial competencies, such as *effort* are pliable, hence, teachers can emphasize and praise individual effort and personal growth with feedback that matches goals. Setting short term goals increases student intrinsic motivation, so teach students to set personal goals to work towards mastery goals, where they learn new expertise that leads to improved SEC outcomes and talent development (Martin, 2013).

Difficulties with executive functioning can impact intrapersonal competencies, such as self-regulation skills development that can lead to difficulties working autonomously (Martin, 2012). Support for executive functioning development through guidance within their ZPD by a significant other is recommended. Teachers can teach self-regulation competences (i.e., identifying own strengths and challenges, setting small personal goals and increasing to larger ones, and self-assessing learning processes through daily journals) within well-structured interdisciplinary instruction. Scaffolding and modeling metacognition and providing systematic practice in authentic learning contexts using relevant, engaging, and challenging content can also assist self-regulation skill development (Sontag & Stoeger, 2015; Stoeger, Fleischmann, & Obergriesser, 2015).

Indeed, Martin (2012) and Martin et al. (2017) reiterate the link between ADHD difficulties with self-control that impact social interrelationships and well-being outcomes. Psychosocial difficulties may include inhibited school performance, poor social functioning, and mental health concerns (Antshel et al., 2007, 2011 in Foley-Nicpon, 2015). Specifically, GADHD studies have found differences in behavioural outcomes between gifted students with and without ADHD. Foley-Nicpon, Rickels, Assouline, and Richards (2012) found that GADHD students had adverse intrapersonal agency factors, such as lower levels of self-esteem, poor behavioural self-concept, and less happiness than gifted students without ADHD, while Antshel (2008), found that GADHD students:

> had higher levels of anxiety, exhibited more disruptive behavior, and experienced greater impairments in social, academic, and family functioning. [Additionally,] as students navigate the school system, they may internalize negative feelings of low self-esteem, self-doubt, and frustration as well as externalize aggressive and other problematic behaviors that make it challenging to maintain social relationships with peers and family. (Mayes & Moore, 2016, p. 168).

Many of these competencies can be enhanced through social skills programs or evidence-based counseling support (Foley-Nicpon & Assouline, 2015; Pfeiffer, 2015).

There are also similarities in social-emotional characteristics between giftedness and ADHD (Rinn & Reynolds, 2012), and educator misunderstandings of these characteristics may lead to misdiagnoses and inappropriate provisions (Webb et al., 2005). Conversely, Lovecky's (2018) review suggests that there is little evidence to support misdiagnoses of GADHD. Nonetheless, students may have ADHD and may not be gifted. Alternatively, students may be gifted, but not have ADHD. Additionally, there are students who have both giftedness and ADHD. Pfeiffer and Foley-Nicpon (2018) caution against misdiagnoses, under-treatment, and overtreatment – inclusive of under- or overmedication – of students with GADHD which may result in grave educational and social-emotional repercussions.

While medications can help self-regulation, inattentive or hyperactive behaviours have also been linked to inappropriate curriculum and pedagogy (Rogers, 2015). This reinforces the need to address the neuropsychological, social-emotional, and cognitive facets of both the giftedness and the neurodivergence (Pfeiffer, 2015). For example, Pfeiffer (2015) reports that, "contingency-based child behavioral procedures, behavioral parent training, and psychostimulant medication that adjusts neurotransmitter imbalance are considered the treatments of choice for a majority of children with ADHD" (p. 772). However, any evidence-based provisions for individual students with GADHD also needs to be based on comprehensive identification and ongoing monitoring that reflects the dynamicity and complexity of the overlap and similarity of characteristics evident in both exceptionality (Pfeiffer & Foley-Nicpon, 2018; Rinn, 2018; Ronskey-Pavia, 2015). This dynamicity and complexity suggest the need for greater flexibility in using strengths-based identification and provisions for students with GADHD for constructive social-emotional outcomes to ensue (Missett, Azanob, Callahan, & Landrum, 2016; Ronskey-Pavia, 2015). Many relevant curriculum and pedagogy for 2e students with ADHD are reported in the literature (Pfeiffer, 2015; Rogers, 2015; VanTassel-Baska, 2018). Additionally, outreach enrichment programs and whole schools for 2e students are gaining favour for supporting the academic and SEC of diversely gifted 2e students (Rankin, Smith, & Smith, 2017). Furthermore, Fugate and Gentry's (2016) small case study suggested that GADHD students learning intrapersonal competencies, such as self-regulation processes, could be assisted with learning interpersonal creative learning processes simultaneously.

Implications for practice

Usually students with twice-exceptionalities are confined by disability-focused provisions, and rarely gain entry to gifted education programs (Baum et al., 2014; Foley-Nicpon & Candler, 2018). Many researchers today reinforce the need for a strengths-based approach to provisions for students with twice-exceptionalities that address both the giftedness and the different disabilities (Assouline & Whiteman, 2011; Foley-Nicpon & Candler, 2018; Missett et al., 2016; Willard-Holt et al., 2013). Provisions should be relevant to 2e students' strengths to ensure their potential is not overshadowed by their difficulties or challenges, and also address the differences, so these do not mask their high potential (Baldwin, Baum et al., 2015).

A strength-based approach to provision for 2e students can increase cognitive and social-emotional development (Foley-Nicpon & Candler, 2018). Promoting a collaborative multidisciplinary team approach to planning provisions for 2e students in supportive school contexts is essential (Baldwin, Omdal, & Pereles, 2015; Coleman & Gallagher, 2015; Galbraith, 2018; Smith, 2017a; Wormald et al., 2015). Furthermore, Pfeiffer and Foley-Nicpon (2018) elaborate that in-school special education programs are the most cost effective interventions to support the psychosocial needs of 2e students. Varying strategies specific to students' 2e types, needs, and strengths are required to help transform giftedness into talent or excellence (Baldwin, Omdal, & Pereles, 2015; Gagné, 2011).

Both interpersonal and intrapersonal competences can be nurtured following the practical application of the developmental phase of Gagné's (2016) DMGT and the ecologically-based MoDD framework that reinforces scaffolding and self-regulating student SEL holistic needs across varying learning contexts

(Smith, 2017a, 2017b). Emotional well-being can be scaffolded further by open communication between teacher and student, modeling empathy towards others, explicitly teaching SEC, and providing coping strategies to deal with stressors (CASEL, 2015; Foley-Nicpon et al., 2011; Gross, 2014). These can be taught within small group contexts with like-minded peers that nurture interpersonal growth and address specific intrapersonal competencies.

Conclusion

It is evident from the research that students with twice-exceptionalities are a diverse group of students who have both diverse special abilities and divergent special needs according to their type or combination of exceptionalities. They are often misunderstood, misdiagnosed, or underachieving, and their intrapersonal and interpersonal agency remain largely unsupported. Ill-conceived deficits-based provisions can exacerbate their social-emotional development and difficulties. Replacing language, such as deficit, deficiency, and disability with difference and divergence and using a strength-based approach to provisions begins the journey to successful 2e students' SEC and SEL outcomes. The dynamicity of 2e students' overlapped exceptionalities needs special consideration for both the high ability and the complex challenges.Hence, their unique co-existing characteristics, which are different again to those with a single exceptionality or typical students, and their competences need scaffolding commensurate with both or all their exceptionalities. Based on social-constructivism and the ecological systems theory, specially planned SEL strategies and programs matched with 2e students' strengths and specific social and emotional competencies will go partway to addressing their unique social-emotional needs and promoting well-being and talent development in students with twice-exceptionalities.

References

Antshel, K. M. (2008). Attention-deficit hyperactivity disorder in the context of a high intellectual quotient/giftedness. *Developmental Disabilities Research Reviews,* 14(4), 293-299. doi:10.1002/ddrr.34

Antshel, K. M., Faraone, S. V., Stallone, K., Nave, A., Kaufmann, F. A., Doyle, A., & Biederman, J. (2007). Is attention deficit hyperactivity disorder a valid diagnosis in the presence of high IQ? Results from the MGH Longitudinal Family Studies of ADHD. *Journal of Child Psychology and Psychiatry,* 48(7), 687-694. doi: 10.1111/j.1469-7610.2007.01735.x

Antshel, K. M., Hendricks, K., Faraone, S., & Gordon, M. (2011). Disorder versus disability: The challenge of ADHD in the context of a high IQ. *The ADHD Report,* 19(2), 4-8. doi:10.1521/adhd.2011.19.2.4

Assouline, S. G., & Whiteman, C. S. (2011). Twice-exceptionality: Implications for school psychologists in the post-IDEA 2004 era. *Journal of Applied School Psychology,* 27(4), 380-402. doi: 10.1080/15377903.2011.616576

Baldwin, L., Baum, S., Pereles, D., & Hughes, C. (2015). Twice-exceptional learners: The journey toward a shared vision. *Gifted Child Today, 38*(4), 206-214. doi: 10.1177/1076

Baldwin, L., Omdal, S., & Pereles, D. (2015). Beyond stereotypes: Understanding, recognizing, and working with twice-exceptional learners. *Teaching Exceptional Children, 47*(4), 216-224. doi:10.1177/0040059915569361

Baum, S. M., Schader, R., M., & Hébert, T. P. (2014). Through a different lens: Reflecting on a strengths-based, talent-focused approach for twice-exceptional learners. *Gifted Child Quarterly, 58*(4), 311-327. doi: 10.1177/0016986214547632

Bell, S. M., Taylor, E. P., McCallum, R. S., Coles, J. T., & Hays, E. (2015). Comparing prospective twice-exceptional students with high-performing peers on high-stakes tests of achievement. *Journal for the Education of the Gifted, 38*(3), 294-317. doi: 10.1177/0162353215592500

Berninger, V. W., & Abbott, R. D. (2018). Differences between children with dyslexia who are and are not gifted in verbal reasoning. In S. B. Kaufman (Ed.), *Twice Exceptional:Supporting and educating bright and creative students with learning difficulties* (pp. 229-257). New York: Oxford University Press.

Betts, G. T., & Neihart, M. (1988). Profiles of the gifted and talented. *Gifted Child Quarterly, 32*(2), 248-251. Retrieved from https://www.davidsongifted.org/search-database/entry/a10114

Bronfennbrenner, U. (1977). Toward an experimental ecology of human development. *American Psychologist, 32*, 513-531. doi:10.1037/0003-066X.32.7.513

Bronfenbrenner, U., & Ceci, S. J. (1994). Nature-nurture reconceptualized in developmental perspective: A biological model. *Psychological Review, 101*(4), 568-586. doi: 10.1037/0033-295x.101.4.568

Bronfenbrenner, U., & Morris, P. A. (1998). The ecology of developmental processes. In R. M. Lerner (Ed.), *Handbook of child psychology*, 5(1), 993-1028. New York: Wiley.

Buic-Belciu, C., & Popovici, D-V. (2014). Being twice exceptional: Gifted students with learning disabilities. *Social and Behavioral Sciences, 127*, 519-523. doi:10.1016/j.sbspro.2014.03.302

Coleman, M. R., & Gallagher, S. (2015). Meeting the needs of students with 2e. It takes a team. *Gifted Child Today, 38*(4), 252-254. doi: 10.1177/1076217515597274

Collaborative for Academic, Social, and Emotional Learning [CASEL]. (2015). *The 2015 CASEL guide: Effective social and emotional learning programs – Middle and high school edition.* Chicago, IL: Author.

Collie, R. J., Martin, A. J., & Frydenberg, E. (2017). Social and emotional learning: A brief overview and issues relevant to Australia and the Asia-Pacific.

In E. Frydenberg, A. Martin, & E. Collie (Eds.), *Social and Emotional Learning in Australia and the Asia-Pacific:Perspectives, Programs and Approaches* (pp. 1-16). Singapore: Springer.

Crogman, M. T., Gilger, J. W., & Hoeft, F. (2018). Visuo-spatial skills in atypical readers: Myths, research, and potential. In S. B. Kaufman (Ed.), *Twice Exceptional:Supporting and educating bright and creative students with learning difficulties* (pp. 229-257). New York: Oxford University Press.

Daniels, S., & Freeman, M. (2018). Gifted dyslexics: MIND-Strengths, visual thinking, and creativity. In S. B. Kaufman (Ed.), *Twice Exceptional:Supporting and educating bright and creative students with learning difficulties* (pp. 258-269). New York: Oxford University Press.

Diehl. J. J., Frost, S. J., Sherman, G., Mencl, W. E., Kurian, A., Molfese, P., ... Pugh, K. R. (2014). Neural correlates of language and non-language visuospatial processing in adolescents with reading disability. *NeuroImage, 101*, 653-666. doi: 10.1016/j.neuroimage.2014.07.029

Doobay, A. F., Foley-Nicpon, M., Ali, S., & Assouline, S. G. (2014). Cognitive, adaptive and psychosocial differences between high ability youth with and without autism spectrum disorders. *Journal of Autism and Developmental Disorders, 44*(8), 2026-2040. doi: 10.1007/s10803-014-2082-1

Durlak, J. A., Weissberg, R. P., Dymnicki, A. B., Taylor, R., D., & Schellinger, K. B. (2011). The impact of enhancing students' social and emotional learning: A meta-analysis of school-based universal interventions. *Child Development, 82*(1), 405-432. Retrieved from https://www.casel.org/wp--content/uploads/2016/08/PDF-3-Durlak-Weissberg-Dymnicki-Taylor-_-Schellinger-2011-Meta-analysis.pdf

Durlak, J. A., Domitrovich, C. E., Weissberg, R. P., & Gullotta, T. P. (Eds.). (2015). *Handbook of social and emotional learning: Research and practice.* New York, NY: The Guilford Press.

Foley-Nicpon, M. (2015). The social and emotional development of twice-exceptional children. In M. Neihart, S. Pfeiffer & T. Cross (Eds.), *The social and emotional development of gifted children: What do we know?* (2nd ed., pp. 122-138). Waco, TX: Prufrock Press.

Foley-Nicpon, M., Allmon, A., Sieck, B., & Stinson, R. D. (2011). Empirical investigation of twice-exceptionality: Where have we been and where are we going? *Gifted Child Quarterly, 55*(1), 3-17.

Foley-Nicpon, M., & Assouline, S. G., (2015). Counseling considerations for the twice-exceptional client. *Journal of Counseling and Development, 93*, 202-211. doi: 10.1002/j.1556-6676.2015.00196.x

Foley-Nicpon, M., Assouline, S. G., & Colangelo, N. (2013). Twice-exceptional learners: Who needs to know what? *Gifted Child Quarterly, 57*(3), 169-180. doi: 10.1177/0016986213490021

Foley-Nicpon, M., Assouline, S. G., & Stinson, R. D. (2012). Cognitive and academic distinctions between gifted students with autism and Asperger Syndrome. *Gifted Child Quarterly, 56*(2), 77-89. doi: 10.1177/0016986211433199

Foley-Nicpon, M., & Candler, M. M. (2018). Psychological interventions for twice-exceptional youth. In S. I. Pfeiffer, E. Shaunessy-Dedrick & M. Foley-Nicpon (Eds.), *APA Handbook of Giftedness and Talent* (pp. 545-558). Washington DC:American Psychological Association.

Foley-Nicpon, M., Rickels, H., Assouline, S. G., & Richards, A. (2012). Self-esteem, self-concept examination among gifted students with ADHD. *Journal for the Education of the Gifted, 35*(3), 220-240. doi: 10.1177/0162353212451735

Fugate, C. M., & Gentry, M. (2016). Understanding adolescent gifted girls with ADHD: Motivated and achieving. *High Ability Studies, 27*(1), 83-109. doi: 10.1080/13598139.2015.1098522

Fugate, C. M., Zentall, S. S., Gentry, M. (2013). Creativity and working memory in gifted students with & without characteristics of Attention Deficit Hyperactive Disorder. *Gifted Child Quarterly, 57*(4), 234-246. https://doi.org/10.1177/0016986213500069

Gagné, F. (2010). Motivation within the DMGT 2.0 framework. *High Ability Studies, 21*(2), 81-99. doi: 10.1080/13598139.2010.525341

Gagné, F. (2011). Academic talent development and the equity issue in gifted education. *Talent Development & Excellence, 1*(3), 3-22.

Gagné, F. (2013). The DMGT: Changes within, beneath, and beyond. *Talent development and excellence, 5*(1), 5-19.

Gagné, F. (2016). From genes to talent: the DMGT/CMTD perspective. In F. H. R. Piske, T. Stoltz, J. Machado & S. Bahia (Eds.). *Altas habilidades/ Superdotação (AH/SD) e Criatividade: Identificação e Atendimento. [Giftedness and Creativity: Identification and Specialized Service].* (pp. 15-38). Curitiba: Juruá.

Galbraith, J. (2018). Twice exceptionality and social-emotional development: One label, many facets. In S. B. Kaufman (Ed.), *Twice Exceptional: Supporting and educating bright and creative students with learning difficulties* (pp. 145-153). New York: Oxford University Press.

Gates, J. A., Kang, E., & Lerner, M. D. (2017). Efficacy of group social skills interventions for youth with autism spectrum disorder: A systematic review and meta-analysis. *Clinical Psychology Review, 52,* 164-181. doi: 10.1016/j.cpr.2017.01.006

Gilger, J. W. (2017). Beyond a reading disability: Comments on the need to examine the full spectrum of abilities/disabilities of the atypical dyslexic brain. A special topics panel of The Dyslexia Foundation (TDF). *Annals of Dyslexia, 67*(2), 109-113. doi:10.1007/s11881-017-0142-x

Gilger, J. W., Allen, K., & Castillo, A. (2016). Reading disability and enhanced dynamic spatial reasoning: A review of the literature. *Brain and Cognition, 105,* 55-65.doi: 10.1016/j.bandc.2016.03.005

Gross, M. U. M. (2014). Issues in the social-emotional development of intellectually gifted children. In F. H. R. Piske, J. M. Machado, S. Bahia & T. Stoltz (Orgs.), *Altas Habilidades/Superdotação: Criatividade e emoção [High abilities/Giftedness: Creativity and emotion].* Curitiba: Juruá.

Hébert, T. P. (2011). *Understanding the social and emotional lives of gifted students.* Waco, Texas: Prufrock Press Inc.

Hughes, C. E. (2017). Focusing on strengths: Twice- exceptional students. In W. W. Murawski & K. L. Scott (Eds.) *What really works with exceptional learners.* Thousand Oaks, CA: Corwin.

Lerner, M. D., & Girard, R. M. (2018). Appreciating & promoting social creativity in youth with Asperger's syndrome. In S. B. Kaufman (Ed.), *Twice Exceptional: Supporting and educating bright and creative students with learning difficulties* (pp. 197-210). New York: Oxford University Press.

Lo, C. C., & Mantak, Y. (2014). Coping strategies and perceived sources of support among gifted students with specific learning disabilities: Three exploratory case studies in Hong Kong. *Gifted and Talented International, 29*(1-2), 125-136. https://doi.org/10.1080/15332276.2014.11678435

Lovecky, D. V. (2018). Misconceptions about giftedness and the diagnosis of ADHD and other mental health disorders. In S. B. Kaufman (Ed.), *Twice Exceptional:Supporting and educating bright and creative students with learning difficulties* (pp. 85-108). New York: Oxford University Press.

Lovett, B. J., Sparks, R. L. (2013). The identification and performance of gifted students with learning disability diagnoses: A quantitative synthesis. *Journal of Learning Disabilities, 46*(4), 304-316. doi: 10.1177/0022219411421810

Martin, A. J. (2012). Attention deficit hyperactivity disorder (ADHD), perceived competence, and self-worth: Evidence and implications for students and practitioners. In D. Hollar (Ed.), *Handbook of children with special health care needs* (pp. 47-72). New York, NY: Springer. doi:10.1007/978-1-4614-2335-5_3

Martin, A. J. (2013). Goal-setting and personal best goals. In J. Hattie & E. M. Anderman (Eds.), *International guide to student achievement* (pp. 356-358). New York, NY: Routledge.

Martin, A. J., Cumming, T., O'Neill, & Strnadová, I. (2017). Social and emotional competence and at-risk children's well-Being: The roles of personal and interpersonal agency for children with ADHD, emotional and behavioral disorder, learning disability, and developmental disability. In E. Frydenberg, A. Martin & E. Collie (Eds.), *Social and Emotional Learning in Australia and the Asia-Pacific: Perspectives, Programs and Approaches* (pp. 123-145). Singapore: Springer.

Mayes, R. D., Harris, P. C., & Hines, E. M. (2016). Meeting the academic and socio-emotional needs of twice exceptional African American students through group counseling. In J. L. Davis & J. L. Moore (Eds.), *Gifted Children of Color Around the World: Diverse Needs, Exemplary Practices, and Directions for the Future.* (pp. 53-69). Bingley, UK: Emerald Group Publishing Limited. doi:10.1108/S2051-231720160000003005

Mayes, R. D., & Moore, J. L. (2016). Adversity and pitfalls of twice-exceptional urban learners. *Journal of Advanced Academics, 27*(3), 167-189. doi: 10.1177/1932202X16649930

Meuller, C. E. (2009). Protective factors as barriers to depression in gifted and nongifted adolescents. G*ifted Child Quarterly, 53*(1), 3-14.doi: 10.1177/0016986208326552

Missett, T. C., Azanob, A. P., Callahan, C. M., & Landrum, K. (2016). The influence of teacher expectations about twice-exceptional students on the use of high quality gifted curriculum: A case study approach. *Exceptionality, 24*(1), 18-31.

Munro, J. (2002). The reading characteristics of gifted literacy disabled students. *Australian Journal of Learning Disabilities, 7*(2), 4-12.

Neihart, M., & Betts, G. (2010). *Revised profiles of the gifted and talented.* Retrieved from http://www.ingeniosus.net/wp-content/uploads/2010/11/PROFILES-BEST-REVISED-MATRIX-2010.pdf

Neihart, M., Pfeiffer, S., & Cross, T. (2015). *The social and emotional development of gifted children: What do we know?* (2nd ed.). Waco, TX: Prufrock Press.

Olulade O. A., Gilger J. W., Talavage T. M., Hynd G. W., McAteer C. I. (2012). Beyond phonological processing deficits in adult dyslexics: atypical fMRI activation patterns for spatial problem solving. *Developmental Neuropsychology, 37,* 617-635. doi 10.1080/87565641.2012.702826

Ottone-Cross, K. L., Dulong-Langley, S., Root, M. M., Gelbar, N., Bray, M. A., Luria, S. R., ... & Pan, X. (2017). Beyond the mask: Analysis of error patterns on the KTEA-3 for students with giftedness and learning disabilities. *Journal of Psychoeducational Assessment, 35*(1-2), 74-93. doi: 10.1177/0734282916669910

Pfeiffer, S. I., (2015). Gifted students with a coexisting disability: Thetwice exceptional. *Estud. Psicol., 32*(4), 717-727. doi:10.1590/0103-166X2015000400015

Pfeiffer, S. I., & Foley-Nicpon, M. (2018). Knowns and unknowns about students with disabilities who also happen to be intellectually gifted. In S. B. Kaufman (Ed.), *Twice exceptional: Supporting and educating bright and creative students with learning difficulties*, 109-126. New York: Oxford University Press.

Piske, F. H. R. (2018). *Altas habilidades/superdotação (AH/SD) e criatividade na escola: o olhar de Vygotsky e de Steiner* (Tese de Doutorado em Educação) Universidade Federal do Paraná, Curitiba, PR, Brazil.

Piske, F. H. R., Stoltz, T., & Machado, J. M. (2014). Creative education for gifted children. *Creative Education, 5*, 347-352. Retrieved from http://file.scirp.org/pdf/CE_2014042316202374.pdf

Piske, F. H. R., Stoltz, T., Machado, J. M., Vestena, C. L. B., de Oliveira, C. S., de Freitas, S. P., & Machado, C. L. (2016). Working with creativity of gifted students through Ludic teaching. *Creative Education, 7*, 1641-1647. doi:10.4236/ce.2016.711167

Rankin, S., Smith, S. R., & Smith, R. J. (2017). *2eMPower:Gifted students with learning disabilities attend STEM workshop at Imperial College London.* Funded by the National Heart & Lung Institute (NHLI). Retrieved from http://www3.imperial.ac.uk/newsandeventspggrp/imperialcollege/medicine/newssummary/news_4-10-2017-16-18-26

Reis, S. M., Baum, S. M., & Burke, E. (2014). An operational definition of twice-exceptional learners: Implications and applications. *Gifted Child Quarterly, 58*(3), 217-230.doi: 10.1177/0016986214534976

Rinn, A. N., (2018). Social and emotional considerations for gifted students. In S. I. Pfeiffer, E. Shaunessy-Dedrick & M. Foley-Nicpon (Eds.), *APA Handbook of Giftedness and Talent* (pp. 453-464). Washington, DC: American Psychological Association.

Rinn, A. N., & Reynolds, M. J. (2012). Overexcitabilities and ADHD in the gifted: An examination. *Roeper Review, 34*(1), 38-45.Retrieved from http://dx.doi.org/10.1080/02783193.2012.627551

Rogers, K. B. (2015). The academic, socialization, and psychological effects of acceleration: Research synthesis. In S. G. Assouline, N. Colangelo, J.

VanTassel-Baska & A. Lupkowski-Shoplik (Eds.), *A nation empowered: Evidence trumps the excuses that hold back America's brightest students* (Vol. 2, pp. 19-29). Iowa City: Belin-Blank Center for Gifted Education and Talent Development, University of Iowa.

Ronskey-Pavia, M. (2015). A model of twice-exceptionality: Explaining and defining the apparent paradoxical combination of disability and giftedness in childhood. *Journal for the Education of the Gifted, 38*(3), 318-340.doi: 10.1177/0162353215592499

Smith, S. R. (2015). A dynamic differentiation framework for talent enhancement: Findings from syntheses & teachers' perspectives. *Australasian Journal of Gifted Education, 24*(1), 59-72.doi:10.21505/ajge.2015.0008

Smith, S. R. (2017a). Responding to the unique social and emotional learning needs of gifted Australian students. In E. Frydenberg, A. Martin & E. Collie (Eds.), *Social and Emotional Learning in Australia and the Asia-Pacific:Perspectives, Programs and Approaches* (pp. 147-166). Singapore: Springer.

Smith, S. R. (2017b). Model of Dynamic Differentiation (MoDD): Innovation education for talent development. In T. S., Yamin, K. W., McCluskey, T. Lubart, D. Ambrose, K. C., McCluskey & S. Linke, (Eds.) Inno*vation Education* (pp. 41-66). Ulm, Germany: The International Centre for Innovation in Education (ICIE).

Sontag, C., & Stoeger, H. (2015). Can highly intelligent and high-achieving students benefit from a training of self-regulated learning in a regular classroom context? *Learning & Individual Differences, 41*, 43-53. https://doi.org/10.1016/j.lindif.2015.07.008

Stoeger, H., Fleischmann, S., & Obergriesser, S. (2015). Self-regulated learning (SRL) and the gifted learner in primary school: The theoretical basis of and empirical findings on a research program dedicated to ensuring that all students learn to regulate their own learning. *Asia Pacific Education Review, 16*, 257-267.

Stoltz, T., Piske, F. H. R., de Freitas, M. F. Q., D'Aroz, M. S., & Machado, J. M. (2015). Creativity in gifted education: Contributions from Vygotsky & Piaget. *Creative Education, 6*(1), 64-70. doi:10.4236/ce.2015.61005

Townend, G., Pendergast, D., & Garvis, S. (2014). Academic self-concept in twice-exceptional students: What the literature tells us. *TalentEd, 28*, 75-89. Retrieved from https://pdfs.semanticscholar.org/dbf0/b90bf264c2cd8b84e328f2a8c76 5f23bdf6d.pdf?_ga=2.236940417.1046177975.1580152109-1250395156. 158 0152109

Vandermosten, M., Hoeft, F., & Norton, E., S. (2016). Integrating MRI brain imaging studies of pre-reading children with current theories of developmental dyslexia: A review and quantitative meta-analysis. *Current Opinion in Behavioral Sciences, 10*, 155-161.https://doi.org/10.1016/j.cobeha.2016.06.007

VanTassel-Baska, J. (2016). Higher order thinking in gifted education. In J. Baer & A. Kauffman (Eds.), *Creativity and reason in cognitive development* (pp. 92-113). New York: Cambridge University Press.

VanTassel-Baska, J. (2018). Curriculum considerations for the gifted. In S. I. Pfeiffer, E. Shaunessy-Dedrick & M. Foley-Nicpon (Eds.), *APA Handbook of Giftedness and Talent*. Washington, DC: American Psychological Association.

van Vierson, S., Kroesbergen, E. H., Slot, E. M., & de Bree, E. H. (2016). High reading skills mask dyslexia in gifted children. *Journal of Learning Disabilities, 49*(2), 189-199.doi: 10.1177/0022219414538517

Wang, C. W., & Neihart, M. (2015). Academic self-concept and academic self-efficacy: Self-beliefs enable academic achievement of twice-exceptional students. *Roeper Review, 37*(2), 63-73. doi:10.1080/02783193.2015.1008660

Webb, J. T., Amend, E.R., Webb, N. E., Goerss, J., Beljan, P., & Olenchak, F. R. (2005). *Misdiagnosis and dual diagnoses of gifted children and adults: ADHD, Bipolar, OCD, Asperger's, Depression, and other disorders.* Scotsdale, AZ: Great Potential Press.

White, H. A., & Shah, P. (2016). Scope of semantic activation and innovative thinking in college students with ADHD. *Creativity Research Journal, 28*, 275-282.doi: 10.1080/10400419.2016.1195655

Willard-Holt, C., Weber, J., Morrison, K. L., & Horgan, J., (2013). Twice-exceptional learners' perspectives on effective learning strategies. *Gifted Child Quarterly, 57*(4), 247-262. doi:10.1177/0016986213501076

Williams, A. (2013). A teacher's perspective of dyscalculia: Who counts? An interdisciplinary overview. *Australian Journal of Learning Difficulties, 18*(1), 1-16. doi: 10.1080/19404158.2012.727840

Wood, S., & Estrada-Hernandez, N. (2009). Psychosocial characteristics of twice-exceptional individuals: Implications for rehabilitation practice. *Journal of Applied Rehabilitation Counseling, 40*(1), 11-17.doi: 10.1891/0047-2220.40.3.11

Wormald, C., Rogers, K., & Vialle, W. (2015). A case study of giftedness and specific learning disabilities: Bridging the two exceptionalities.*Roeper Review, 37*(3), 124-138.doi:10.1080/02783193.2015.1047547

Wormald, C., Vialle, W., & Rogers, K. (2014). Young and misunderstood in the education system: A case study of giftedness and specific learning disabilities. *Australasian Journal of Gifted Education, 23*(2), 16-28. Retrieved from https://ro.uow.edu.au/cgi/viewcontent.cgi?referer=https://www.google.com/&httpsredir=1&article=2697&context=sspapers

2.

THE IMPORTANCE OF SOCIO-EMOTIONAL DEVELOPMENT OF GIFTED STUDENTS

Fernanda Hellen Ribeiro Piske[1]

Doctor of Education from the Federal University of Paraná (UFPR), Brazil.

ORCID: 0000-0002-1516-6455.

E-mail: ferhellenrp@gmail.com

Abstract: *The aim of this chapter is to highlight the importance of the socio-emotional development of gifted students. The chapter begins by focusing on the concept of over-excitability, put forward by Dabrowski and defined as a prevalent and widespread perception of the environment that can lead to over-stimulation which in turn leads to an increase in the emotional reaction of the talented and gifted in their interaction with the world. The author then discusses the different forms of expression of emotional intensity and points out that a certain incongruity in development is intrinsic to the condition of being gifted. A*

[1] The author thanks the CAPES (Coordination for the Improvement of Higher Education Personnel) of Brazil for the Scholarships provided during her Master's course and sandwich Ph.D. course. Process number: 88881.134528 / 2016-01. ORCID: https://orcid.org/0000-0002-1516-6455. E-mail: ferhellenrp@gmail.com.

set of very useful suggestions on various ways of dealing with the social and emotional issues of the gifted and talented is subsequently described. These strategies ultimately enable the gifted to have healthy interactions with their intellectual and artistic peers in order to feel comfortable with their talents and to develop deep friendships. The chapter highlights, in a tone of warning, that teachers and families can offer these children and young people support and encouragement, emphasizing that individual differences should be celebrated rather than altered to suit the classroom or societal standards. Gifted children and young people need to be encouraged to express their thoughts and feelings instead of keeping them hidden.

Keywords: *Socio-emotional development; Dabrowski; Giftedness; Talent; Education; School.*

Introduction

The reality of gifted students at school brings constant concern, both because of lack of knowledge of their needs by many teachers and also because of lack of provision of adequate care. Facing this reality daily can cause anguish for these children, who often suffer from lack of understanding on the part of their classmates, their teachers and their families. This lack of understanding can cause social and emotional difficulties in gifted children. In this sense, this article aims to highlight the importance of the social-emotional development of the gifted. The article emphasizes that the role of emotion in the teaching of gifted people is fundamental for arousing their interest and desire to learn (Peterson, 2003, 2014; Piske, 2013, 2018).

In relation to research on the socio-emotional development of gifted individuals, Terman (1965) found a lower rate of difficulties in gifted children than in the populationin general. In contrast, Hollingworth (1942) found that people with extremely high intelligence test scores demonstrated greater difficulties than those with high or medium scores.

Like other characteristics related to giftedness, gifted children are more likely to have the same emotional experiences as their inexperienced peers, but experience these emotions differently as a result of their giftedness (Dabrowski, 1972).

In his theory of the emotional development of gifted children, Dabrowski (1972) described this difference, which he referred to as superexcitability. He defined superexcitability as a widespread and expanded perception of the environment, which can lead to overstimulation. He established that the talents and cognitive abilities of gifted children increase their emotional reaction when interacting with the world.

The discrepancies in the literature may contribute so that the answer is nota dichotomy, i.e. yes or no, but rather a spectrum. Neihart (1999) points out that giftedness affects the social and emotional adjustment of gifted children, adolescents and adults. However, whether the impact is positive or negative depends on the type of giftedness, educational setting and personal characteristics of each child. In his studies, it has also been postulated that there are more differences within the group, that is, gifted children, than in the group with differences, that is, between gifted and non-gifted children.

Dealing with the emotions of the gifted may not be so simple. There are scholars (Renzulli, 2005; Piechowski, 2014; Pfeiffer, 2016) who affirm the importance of gifted people interacting with their peers in homogeneous groups. In contrast, Piske (2018) argues for the importance of these children having contact with heterogeneous groups because the difference between them can be an enriching aspect in several ways. It can be said that there is a need to consider different types of work, in homogeneous and heterogeneous groups, for the social-emotional and cognitive development of the gifted.

Hollingworth (1942) was one of the pioneers in researching the social and emotional development of the gifted, and found, in her research, some relevant changes in the behavior of these exceptionally intelligent children when they could interact with their peers in intelligence. Such changes are revealing because this fact is demonstrated when some of these children who felt socially withdrawn and seemingly unmotivated to carry out their tasks, over time began to participate more in school activities when they were in contact with other children with similar interests and mental age. For the author, homogeneous groups are more significant because children may feel better when they encounter others similar to them. This author highlights that the results of her studies point out the importance of giving the gifted contact with their peers in order for them to feel more satisfied and motivated at school.

Most of the time, the reactions, feelings and emotions that the gifted present are limited to their age group, and may also be influenced by the feelings of other children in their group; for this reason, their parents, teachers and psychologists must be attentive to their social and emotional needs.

Regarding these needs, Lewis Madison Terman (1965) identified that subjects with an IQ above 170 expressed problems of social adjustment, and during school follow-up, their teachers perceived them as subjects with little expressiveness in their interactions with their classmates, besides being considered solitary because of lack of attitude in relation to making friendships.

Terman's (1965) research had a large sample of 1528 gifted subjects, who had been identified through IQ tests since childhood, and had follow-up over a long periodof time. Terman (1965) found that, unlike exceptionally intelligent subjects, subjects with an

IQ of 150 on average were able to interact adequately without presenting significant social problems, and were considered to be psychologically stable and not vulnerable to conflicts and isolation.

Miraca Gross (2002), when carrying out research in Australia, found that many students who had exceptional intelligence had many limitations, frustrations and problems related to self-esteem, because they had difficulty relating to other subjects in their school environment; in addition, they had no chance to participate in acceleration programs to advance their activities. Gross (2002) points out that there is a large difference in behavior and needs between gifted students and those with exceptional intelligence; this difference can be perceived in several spheres of development, including, also, the emotional and moral aspect; their expectations are relatively distinct in relation to school work, task performance, involvement with subjects in their group, interaction with other students in the classroom, and the way they evaluate their way of living together; they present values, reactions and attitudes proper to their personality.

Terman (1965) Gross (2004, 2014, 2016) found that students with exceptional intelligence, usually with IQ above 160, may face situations that lead them to difficulties in relating, social problems that cause their isolation in the context in which they live, difficulties that compromise their affective aspect.

Jean Charles Terrassier (1979), a French psychologist and specialist in the area of highly developed abilities/giftedness, indicates the dyssynchrony syndrome to characterize the misfit of the different forms of gifted development. This asynchrony can be ofan internal origin: affective-intellectual that refers to the mismatch between affective and cognitive development and, in this case, the level of intellectual development is above the social and emotional level; the intellectual-psychomotor refers to the mismatch between intellectual and psychomotor development;

it can be exemplified as writing and reading during the learning process, the mental rhythm may be faster than the physical act, feelings such as anxiety and concern in performing this process may be reasons for this lack of synchrony; language and reasoning may also present a mismatch in development; for example, the gifted subject may find it very easy to calculate, but have difficulty explaining how they processed this reasoning.

According to Piske (2013), asynchronism can also be of an external origin: the social-school, in which the subject has above average abilities, when compared to other subjects; however, they have difficulties in their social life, often for presenting more advanced ideas than their colleagues; in this sense, they may feel misunderstood and excluded by their group; this exclusion may mean social or emotional maladjustment; asynchronism in the family relationship refers to the mismatch between the cognitive and affective development that the gifted subject can present in the family environment, causing disagreement and confusion.

Gifted adolescents can display interests which are not very common to their age group, causing their families to be surprised and expect attitudes that are not always compatible with the mentality of their children, since, for the most part, parents do not understand that their children can react with childish attitudes, even though they have a high capacity for reasoning (Terrassier, 1979).

In his research, Terrassier (1981) points to the Pygmalion Effect, also known as the Rosenthal effect, which can occur in the school context, even with gifted students. This effect is defined in psychology as a result caused by expectations and perception of reality, which depend on how subjects relate to what is experienced in their social environment. This effect was found in a study that indicated how students were affected by their teachers' expectations. It was found that, in certain situations, some teachers perceived the potential and good characteristics of their students and stimulated them; consequently, these students could achieve better school performance.

An inverse effect was found when teachers, instead of stimulating and perceiving the good side of their students, did not care about their performance and did not motivate them; in this case, these students did not obtain good results during the learning process, because they were influenced in a negative way.

According to Terrassier (1981), the teacher needs to have a real perception of their students' potential, especially when it comes to gifted students, because if they do not perceive that these subjects have superior capacity, instead of stimulating their potential, the teacher will be inhibiting their school performance through attitudes and limited work, hindering even more the teaching process offered to meet their demands.

Each gifted child may develop differently, that is, many, but not all aspects of the development of these children occur at a fast pace. It is important to understand that although the cognitive abilities of a gifted child are developing rapidly, their bodies and, most likely, their emotions are also developing into a more age-appropriate continuum. This out of sync or asynchronous development occurs when a child's intellectual development proceeds on a trajectory that is outside the norm, while physical, social and/or emotional development does not occur.

Silverman (2013) noted that developmental asynchrony often intensifies as the child's intelligence increases, resulting in an even greater divergence between mental and chronological age. Silverman (2013) points out that lack of synchrony in cognitive and affective development can mean the origin of social problems, conflicts and tensions. When lack of adjustment between developmental spheres increases, it is likely that the gifted person will have even more difficulty coping with social and emotional issues that occur in their environment. According to Silverman

(1993), although there are many studies on the mismatch between the different dimensions of development, this question has not yet been clarified in depth; it is supported only by clinical observations of gifted subjects, based on the analysis of their phenomenological experience; there should be, indeed, a deeper understanding of asynchronous development (Silverman, 1993).

Developmental mismatches can sometimes be related to the condition of being gifted, when high intellectual capacity and intense anxiety combine and consequently lead to the subject having different internal experiences. Good student performance depends on the condition of how they live and are treated at school and at home. School and family structures should be modified in order to give support and motivation to the gifted.

Silverman (1993) explains that giftedness is an asynchronous form of development in which "advanced cognitive abilities and great intensity combine to create inner experiences and consciousness that are qualitatively different from the norm" (Silverman, 1993, p. 3).

As for the moral sensibility of the gifted, Silverman (1993) indicates that this is a fundamental aspect for the well-being of every society. There are also studies that were found in the Gifted Development Center, which Silverman coordinates, which highlight some important characteristics of the pro-social morality of the gifted; among them: sensitivity to the suffering of others, empathy, compassion for the other members of their peer group, protection of the needy and a sense of justice. It has also been found that the exaggerated sensitivity of the gifted makes them more sensitive to external factors, such as air pollution, sounds, some types of food and some textures.

In these studies, we also find information that these subjects present introversion and a high degree of perfectionism, which is another great problem that the gifted can face if they cannot deal with their limitations.

Piske (2013) explains that gifted children may want to do things close to perfection. Dealing with perfectionism is not simple. This aspect can be defined as a desire to do things in an accurate, error-freeway, and to the highest possible standard. Some common features associated with perfectionism include attention to detail, an innate drive to achieve the highest standards, total commitment to the task, fear of never being good enough, and frustration when these goals cannot be achieved. Like introversion, perfectionism is not an inherently negative personality trait. On the contrary, there are many benefits in striving for excellence.

In relation to the perfectionism that the gifted can present, Patrícia Schuler (2000) explains that it is related to a set of behaviors and ideas that encompass great expectations regarding performance itself. Perfectionism may oscillate to a degree that ranges from what is considered healthy to neurotic.

According to Schuler (2000), there are gifted individuals who are considered healthy perfectionists, since the perfection they seek leads them to personal fulfillment in a positive way. These subjects are usually committed to their activities, study over a long period of time, devote many hours to their school work; their expectations match what they are capable of and do not cause frustrations, they accept their limitations and recognize that they have difficulties in some areas of knowledge.

On the other hand, there are gifted people who are never satisfied with their performance; their performance is never considered enough to make them feel good. They face great fear of failure, they are extremely sensitive to criticism from other subjects in their circles, become excessively self-critical, do not admit error, for error can mean a humiliation that must be constantly avoided. These subjects become neurotic because they try to accomplish the same task several times and waste a lot of time in those attempts that are essential for them. They cannot understand their limitations (Schuler, 2000).

For Alencar (1986), many are the characteristics that can differentiate the gifted student from other young people in their group. This student may also present a differentiated psychological profile, requiring more attention and understanding on the part of the people in his or her life.

Alencar (1986) believes that one of the main aspects that must be fundamental in the classroom is gifted students' self-concept. Positive self-concept can mean the development and use of the creative potential of students, and also good social-emotional development. If the degree of confidence increases, consequently production at school comes to life. The way gifted students perceive themselves can be a stimulus for new discoveries and great achievements.

There are decisive measures that the teacher, as a mediator of the teaching and learning process, can take in relation to their students' self-concept; some of these measures include: making changes in students' self-concept, even if they are negative; helping students create a sense of personal value through actions that make them feel good: this can be through a friendly greeting or a reference to a quality that the students present (Alencar, 1986, 2014).

Some social-emotional characteristics that the gifted student can present in the school context are pointed out in some national and international studies (Alencar, 2007; Piechowski, 1991; Lovecky, 1993); among these characteristics, it is possible to emphasize: perseverance and persistence related to great concentration in activities of interest; passion for learning; idealism and a sense of justice; emotional sensitivity; sharp perception of themselves, which leads them to perceive their own characteristics, their high capacity and their educational needs; perfectionism related to the requirement to produce increasingly better activities that are of interest to them; sensitivity to the expectations of people with whom they live and who admire their creative potential; in which case they may be concerned about criticism and comments that may arise in relation to their production and activities.

Piske (2013) points out that despite the array of behavioral characteristics that differ from those of other subjects in their social group and despite emotional difficulties that the gifted may present in Brazil, emotional development is discussed in a superficial and very limited way. Unlike the United States, which is considered the largest investor in gifted education, Brazil does not have sufficient care programs to meet the high demand of gifted students, nor specific programs that help these individuals to overcome their affective difficulties.

Emotional Intensity of Gifted Students

The area of giftedness covers emotional and intellectual dimensions. The intellectual aspect with its unlimited complexity is related to the emotional depth of the gifted, just as their thinking is more complex and has more depth if compared to that of other students. Their emotions are also more complex and more intense and are experienced in different ways in the school context. Complexity is perceived through the wide range of emotions that gifted children can experience at any moment, and emotional intensity is evident from their involvement in various situations.

Since gifted children show greater maturity than others in some domains, they may be at greater risk of specific types of socio-emotional difficulties if their needs are not met.

These aspects may include increased awareness, anxiety, perfectionism, stress, difficulties with peer relationships, and concerns about identity and adjustment. Their teachers and families need to be attuned to the specific needs of their children and help shape a solid framework for socio-emotional health.

Specialists in the area of Giftedness (Silverman, 2013; Piechowski, 2014, Peterson, 2003, 2014; Gross, 2014, 2016; Piske & Stoltz, 2012, 2020) point out that people who live with gifted children need to be aware that:

- Not all gifted children are the same, including their own socio-emotional profile; there is no single, definitive recipe for maintaining a child's emotional balance;
- A gifted child in one area of knowledge does not mean being gifted in every way;
- Giftedness may lead to masking and misunderstanding of problems of various origins and causes that the child may present;
- Gifted children's families need to maintain balance and define the best way to deal with their special needs, always with the guidance of trained professionals, to reduce the stress / anxiety in the lives of these children.

In relation to the emotional intensity of the gifted, it is not a question of feeling more sensitive than other people, but a different way of experiencing the world by absorbing feelings, putting themselves in the shoes of others, it is a pervasive, comprehensive, complex way of being because it expresses a way of being tremendously alive.

Many experts (Gross, 2014, 2016; Peterson, 2003, 2014; Piechowski, 2014; Renzulli, 2005, Bahia, 2016; Piske & Stoltz, 2020) point out that the emotional intensity of the gifted can be expressed in several ways, such as:

- emotional bonds and connections with others, empathy and concern for others, sensitivity in relationships, attachment to animals, difficulty adapting to new environments, loneliness, conflicts with others in relation to the depth of relationships;
- intensity of feelings – positive feelings, negative feelings, positive and negative feelings together, extremes of emotion, complex emotions that seemingly move from one feeling to another in a short period of time, identification with other people's feelings;
- strong emotional memory – emotionally intense children can remember the feelings that accompanied an incident and often re-live and re-feel them much later;
- through the body – the body mirrors the emotions and feelings that are often expressed as bodily symptoms, such as tense stomach, tight heart, flushing, headache, nausea;
- inhibition and shyness;
- fears and anxieties, feelings of guilt, feelings of being out of control;
- worries about death, feeling depressed;
- critical self-evaluation and self-judgment, feelings of inadequacy and inferiority.

Through emotional intensity, in emotional bonds, interpersonal interactions, when feeling fears and anxieties at different times, it is always worth emphasizing the importance of psychologists, teachers and families being mediators of the reassurance of the feelings of the gifted who need to feel safe and welcomed in any situation and context.

How to deal with social and emotional issues of the gifted

According to Piske (2018) programs geared to the needs of the gifted can provide gifted children with much-needed interactions with peers of intellectual, artistic or musical inclinations of various ages with whom they share common interests and skills among other areas of knowledge. This allows gifted children to feel comfortable with their talents and develop intimate and deep friendships that may not be possible with their peers of the same age. At the same time, staying with children of the same age allows gifted children to enhance social skills in general, such as problem solving and the development of realistic expectations of others.

Emotional bonds and friendship can be decisive for the good development of gifted children. Peer relationships help them learn how to solve problems, regulate their emotions, seek help and support, and trust and be trustworthy. As they grow up, children's concepts of friendship grow and develop based on their experiences and interactions with family members, other adults, and colleagues. From this point of view, Gross (2006) postulated five stages of friendship development.

The first stage is when a friend is seen as someone to playwith and share toys. In the second stage, friendships are no longer defined just by playing, on the contrary, a sharing of interests and conversations related to those interests becomes important. In the third stage, in addition to shared interests, a friend is now perceived as someone who offers support, help and encouragement, although the child still does not recognize the importance of providing support in return. As for the fourth stage, the child now recognizes the aspects of giving and receiving support and encouragement. And finally, the fifth stage characterizes friendship as a long-term and emotionally profound connection, full of mutual interests, respect, support and trust.

Gross (2006) helps us understand not only how children develop friendships, but also how talents can affect development of friendship through these stages. Both in bonds and in friendships, the support of teachers and families of gifted children can be reflected in their behavior. Teachers and families of these children can offer support and encouragement to all of them, noting that individual differences should be celebrated rather than altered to suit the classroom or society's rules. In addition, these children need to be encouraged to express their thoughts and feelings about their school experiences, rather than keeping them hidden for some reason. Understanding these children, therefore, becomes the basis upon which all decisions on their education rests. In this sense, it is essential that teachers and families work together and carefully consider the options for the individual needs of these children academically, socially and emotionally for them to develop in a healthy way.

References

Alencar, E. M. L. S. de. (1986). *Psicologia e educação de superdotado.* São Paulo: EPU.

Alencar, E. M. L. S. de. (2007). Características sócio-emocionais do superdotado: questões atuais. *Psicologia em estudo* [online], 12 (2), 371-378, mai/ago. Retrieved from <http://www.scielo.br/pdf/pe/v12n2/v12n2a18.pdf>. Acesso em: 09/04/2010.

Alencar, E. M. L. S. de. (2014). Ajustamento Emocional e Social do Superdotado: Fatores Correlatos. In F. H. R. Piske, J. M. Machado, S. Bahia, & T. Stoltz. (orgs.), *Altas habilidades/Superdotação (AH/SD): Criatividade e emoção. [Giftedness: Creativity and Emotion].* (pp. 149-162). Curitiba: Juruá.

Bahia, S. (2016). Criatividade na avaliação e intervenção na sobredotação. In F. H. R. Piske, T. Stoltz, J. M. Machado, & S. Bahia. (orgs.), *Altas habilidades/ Superdotação (AH/SD) e Criatividade: Identificação e Atendimento. [Giftedness and Creativity: Identification and Specialized service].* (pp. 145-164). Curitiba: Juruá.

Dabrowski, K. (1972). *Psychoneuroses is not an illness.* London, England: Little Brown & Co.

Gross, M.U.M. (2002). Social and emotional issues for exceptionally intellectually gifted students. In: *Neihart, M.; Reis, S.M.; Robinson, N. M.; Moon, M.M.* (Eds.). *The social and emotional development of gifted children: what do we know?* Waco: Prufrock, 19-20.

Gross, M. U. M. (2004). *Exceptionally gifted children* (2nd ed.). London: RoutledgeFalmer.

Gross, M. (2006). Tips for parents: Gifted children's friendships. *Davidson Institute for Talent Development.* Retrieved from www.giftedserives.com. au._

Gross, M. U. M. (2014). Issues in the Social-Emotional Development of Intellectually Gifted Children. In F. H. R. Piske, J. M. Machado, S. Bahia & T. Stoltz (Orgs.). *Altas habilidades/Superdotação (AH/SD): Criatividade e emoção. [Giftedness: Creativity and Emotion].* Curitiba: Juruá, 85-96.

Gross, M. U. M. (2016). Developing programs for gifted and talented students. In F. H. R. Piske, T.Stoltz, J. M. Machado & S. Bahia (Orgs.). *Altas habilidades/ Superdotação (AH/SD) e Criatividade: Identificação e Atendimento. [Giftedness and Creativity: Identification and Specialized Service]* (pp. 61-75). Curitiba: Juruá.

Hollingworth, L. (1942). *Children above 180 IQ: Origin and development.* New York: World Books.

Lovecky, D. V. (1993). The quest for meaning: Counseling issues with gifted children and adolescents. Em L.K. Silverman (Ed.), *Counseling the gifted and talented* (pp. 29-50). Denver. CO: Love.

Neihart, M. (1999). The impact of giftedness on psychological well-being: What does the empirical literature say. *Roeper Review,* 22 (1), 10-17.

Peterson, J. S. (2003). Underachievers: Students who don't perform. In: J. F. Smutny (Ed.), *Underserved gifted populations* (307-332). Creskill: Hampton.

Peterson, J. S. (2014). Paying Attention to the Whole Gifted Child: Why, When, and How to Focus on Social and Emotional Development. In F. H. R.Piske, J. M. Machado, S. Bahia & T. Stoltz (Orgs.). *Altas habilidades/Superdotação (AH/SD): Criatividade e emoção [Giftedness: Creativity and Emotion]* (pp. 45-66). Curitiba: Juruá.

Pfeiffer, S. (2016). Leading Edge Perspectives on Gifted Assessment. In F. H. R. Piske, T. Stoltz, J. M. Machado, & S. Bahia (Eds.) *Altas habilidades/ Superdotação (AH/SD) e Criatividade: Identificação e Atendimento [Giftedness and Creativity: Identification and Specialized Service].* (pp. 95-122). Curitiba: Juruá.

Piechowski, M. M. (1991) Emotional development and emotional giftedness. Em: N. Colangelo & G.A. Davis (Eds.), *Handbook of gifted education* (pp. 285-306). Needham Heights, MA: Allyn and Bacon.

Piechowski, M. M. (2014). Identity. In F. H. R. Piske, J. M. Machado, S. Bahia & T. Stoltz (Orgs.). *Altas habilidades/Superdotação (AH/SD): Criatividade e emoção. [Giftedness: Creativity and Emotion]* (pp. 97-114). Curitiba, Juruá.

Piske, F. H. R. (2013*). O desenvolvimento socioemocional de alunos com altas habilidades/ superdotação (AH/SD) no contexto escolar: Contribuições a partir de Vygotsky. [The socio-emotional development of gifted students in the school context: Contributions from Vygotsky].* (Thesis). Universidade Federal do Paraná. Curitiba, PR, Brazil.

Piske, F. H. R. (2018). *Altas habilidades/superdotação (AH/SD) e criatividade na escola: o olhar de Vygotsky e de Steiner. [Giftedness and creativity at school: Vygotsky and Steiner view's]* (Dissertation P.h.D in Education) Universidade Federal do Paraná. Curitiba, PR, Brazil.

Piske, F. H. R. & Stoltz, T. (2012). O Desenvolvimento Afetivo de Alunos Superdotados: Uma Contribuição a partir de Piaget. *Schème: Revista Eletrônica de Psicologia e Epistemologia Genéticas*, 4, 149-166.

Piske, F. H. R. & Stoltz, T. (2020). *Altas Habilidades/Superdotação (AH/SD) e Criatividade: Contribuições do Sociointeracionismo de Vygotsky e da Pedagogia Waldorf de Rudolf Steiner.* Curitiba, Juruá.

Renzulli, J. S. (2005). The Three-Ring Conception of Giftedness: A developmental Model for Creative Productivity. In R. Sternberg, & J. Davidson (Eds.), *Conception of Giftedness.* Cambridge: University of Cambridge. doi:10.1017/CBO9780511610455.015

Schuler, P. A. (2000). Perfectionism and the gifted adolescents. *Journal of Secondary Gifted Education, 9,* 183-196.

Silverman, L. K. (1993). Counseling needs and programs for the gifted. In K. A. Heller, F. J. Mönks& A. H. Passow (Eds.), *International handbook of research and development of giftedness and talent* (pp. 631-647). Oxford: Pergamon.

Silverman, L. K. (2013). Asynchronous development: Theoretical bases and current applications. In C. S. Neville, M. M. Piechowski, & S. S. Tolan (Eds.), *Off the charts: Asynchrony and the gifted child* (pp. 18-47). Unionville, NY: Royal Fireworks Press.

Terman, L. M. (1965). The discovery and encouragement of exceptional talent. In W. B. Barbe (Ed.), *Psychology and education of the gifted: Selected readings* (pp. 8-28). New York: Appleton-Century-Crofts.

Terrassier, J. C. (1979). Gifted children and psychopathology. The syndrome of dyssinchrony. In J. J. Gallagher (Ed.), *Gifted children: Reaching their potential* (pp. 434-440). Jerusalem: Kollek& Son.

Terrassier, J. C. (1981). The negative pygmalion effect. In A. H. Kramer (Ed.), *Gifted children: Challenging their potential: New perspectives and alternatives* (pp. 82-84). New York: Trillium.

3.

75

GIFTED & TALENTED IN SPAIN:
CREATIVITY AND EMOTIONAL INTELLIGENCE

Lola Prieto

Professor of Educational Psychology (Emeritus)

University of Murcia (Spain)

ORCID: 0000-0003-3149-3197

Mercedes Ferrando

Full Professor

University of Murcia (Spain)

ORCID : 0000-0001-9198-1390

Marta Sainz

Professor at the Department of Evolutionary Psychology and Education,

University of Murcia (Spain)

ORCID: 0000-0002-5573-9748

Rosario Bermejo

Full Professor

University of Murcia (Spain)

ORCID: 0000-0002-2430-9200

Carmen Ferrándiz

Full Professor

University of Murcia (Spain)

ORCID: 0000-0002-4066-4595

Abstract: *The aim of this work is to analyze the importance of Creativity and Emotional Intelligence (EI) in students with 'high ability' (giftedness and talent) in Spain. First, it explains the history and early contributions regarding high abilities in Spain. Second, it analyses research carried out in recent years, considering it from three points of view: a) regarding identification procedures; b) in relation to cognitive configuration of students with high abilities; c) in relation to these students' socio-emotional and non-cognitive aspects. The third part of this research focus on understanding the socio-emotional profile of students with extraordinary abilities. The results may be summarized as follows: 1) differences between G & T and non-G & T students are found repeatedly for the Adaptability dimension. Thus, G & T students perceived themselves as having more flexibility and skills to adjust to new situations as well as better ability to identify and overcome problems and implement effective solutions. That could be explained by the nature of giftedness, as it implies creative thinking and flexibility, tolerance to ambiguity, open-mindedness, desire to take risks and better capacity to propose new ideas; 2) when studying differences between gifted versus talented students, differences have been confirmed for stress management, intrapersonal and total Emotional Intelligence favouring gifted students; 3) other studies found that gifted and talented students are characterized by vital satisfaction and high self-esteem; they often feel they are not being understood and that they are envied for their special aptitudes, which leads them to feel ashamed about their giftedness and to hide it.*

Keywords: Gifted and Talented, Cognitive Configuration, Creativity, Emotional Intelligence.

Introduction

The aim of this work is to analyze the study of 'high ability' (giftedness and talent) in Spain. First, it explains the history and first contributions of high abilities in this country.

Second, it analyses the research carried out in recent years, considering it from three points of view: a) regarding identification procedures; b) in relation to its cognitive configuration; c) according to its socio-emotional configuration and non-cognitive aspects. Third, it explains the different reasons 'why' and 'how' to identify students who have such abilities; in addition, it analyses the identification procedure and the tests used. We must emphasize the importance of evaluating creativity as well as the emotional intelligence of the gifted and talented (G&T).

Fourth, it includes comments made on programs and/or measures intended to deal with diversity which are used in the various autonomous regions in Spain; additionally, it analyses the existing difficulties in producing appropriate programs to cater for the diversity present in high ability people (G&T). Fifth, it states its conclusions.

Finally, there is a list of bibliographical references used in this study.

What are the most important contributions to gifted education that have been made in Spain

The aim is to explain Spanish Gifted and Talented (G&T) policy and how it is being developed in Spain.

Background Studies on High Abilities (giftedness and talent).

Between 1930 and 1934 there was concern about the education of the highly gifted. This pedagogical attitude toward the highly gifted consisted of considering them as having very specific personality problems and showing very high levels of performance. Between 1931 and 1939 the "Madrid Workers School Selection Institute" (*Instituto de Selección Escolar de Madrid*) was founded, under the direction of Laura Luque. Its objective was to study the Spanish gifted and talented and their personality traits (Linares, 1931).

In 1939 the "Valencia Municipal Orientation and Management School" (*Escuela de Orientación y Aprovechamiento del Excmo. Ayuntamiento de Valencia, EEOA*) was founded, the aim of which was to select highly gifted children, as well as those with intellectual disabilities. Gifted students were observed by their teachers and their intelligence was assessed by means of psycho-technical instruments; they received a differentiated type of education, adapted to their special needs; there were differentiatedprograms and stimulation (Garmendía de Otaola, 1950, 1954). Around that time a combination of individualized political principles appeared, which brought together the Spanish experience on institutionalization of intellectually gifted and disabled students. The studies on gifted studentswere enthusiastically pursued during the 50s, but decreased as a result of the school protection programs during the 60s.

The Beginnings of Scientific Studies on High Abilities

The first scientific-experimental research in Spain was carried out by García Yagüe (1986) drawing attention to this type of student and their education. 17.028 children between 6 and 9 years old from 16 Spanish provinces were studied. This pioneer Spanish project was very complex as regards its application, and it received some criticism on the grounds that it lacked theoretical basis.

Some of its results were: a) high percentage of children selected as gifted (*'bien dotados'*), according to the author, over 6% of the sample; b) the gifted were not able to make the most of their special abilities during the initial stage of their schooling due to the scarce stimulation they received; c) in spite of achieving good results, these students showed serious shortcomings in their learning processes. For that reason, a recommendation was made to design a differentiated education program to stimulate and promote the development of their abilities.

In 1981, the 'International Gifted and Talented Seminar' was held in Madrid. It was very successful and had several international specialists among its participants. It was then that systematic and generalized research on giftedness and talentedness started in Spain. Gifted children's parents associations began to appear, which aimed at paying special attention to the educational needs of those children and disseminating information on research carried out in that area.

Studies conducted by Spanish Universities.

In 1980 the "Gifted and Talented Boys and Girls Research Team" (*Equipo de Investigación sobre Niños y Niñas Superdotados, EINNS*) was founded, within the Education Psychology Department of Barcelona Autonomous University, lead by Genovard. From 1982 to 1991, the team increased its activities in the field of talent and giftedness: a) it organized the First National Symposium on

Psychopedagogy of Diversity. One of its aims was to analyze the degree of knowledge and attention given to gifted and talented individuals in Spain (Genovard, 1982); b) it provided training for the professional development of the team members; c) it raised awareness on the matter in different spheres: social, political and academic; d) it organized courses and seminars; e) it encouraged attendance and participation in international forums; f) it promoted the creation of basic instruments to conduct the team's work and publication there of (Genovard & Castelló, 1990).Today, Genovard and his team continue working on the subject of teachers of high-ability students, as they are an important source of information for detecting these students. With regard to the profile of these teachers, they mention: a) there is not an ideal teacher for these students; b) they must take into account the students' intellectual, motivational, cultural diversity and other resources, in their approach to the teaching-learning process; c) tutoring must be defined in terms of students' potentialities and motivation; d) they must pay attention to students' individual differences, and learning must be in a one-to-one context, bearing in mind personal characteristics, styles and resources; and e) they must encourage creativity (Genovard, Gotzens, Badía, & Dezcallar, 2010).

At Madrid Complutense University, during the 1988/89 academic year Elena García-Alcañiz developed a macro-research study following Genovard's lines, on the identification, performance, creativity features, meta-memory andleadership processes of high-ability students (García-Alcañiz, 1995). Later on, Pérez and her team focused their attention on the features and profiles of those students, such as detecting linguistic talents (Pérez, López-Cobeñas & González, 2008) and gender differences, and also proposed various programs to respond to the educational demands ofthese children.

High Abilities at Murcia University.

Study of high abilities formally started at this university in 1992 with a research project entitled 'Identification, assessment and education of high-ability students', under the leadership of Prieto. That was when the "High Abilities Research Group" was formed at Murcia University, also under the direction of Prieto. The aims of the group pivot around three points:

a) Identification of students with high abilities (gifted and talented)

In the identification process two tests were used to measure intelligence: a) a traditional 'g' factor test; and a cognitive assessment STAT test (Sternberg Triarchic Abilities Test, 1993). The sample was taken from 2055 students (aged between 11 and 13), from 22 schools from Murcia (Spain). Then they took a sub-sample of 1255 students assessed with those two intelligence tests. And from that, another sub-sample of 208 students was taken, who were grouped according to the following criteria: a) IQ higher than 120 for both tests; b) higher than 120 by 'g' factor; c) higher than 120 by STAT; and d) IQ lower than 120 for both tests. The data showed that: a) STAT is a valid and reliable test for identifying students in terms of their intellectual abilities; b) both tests measure intelligence abilities, but STAT has specific elements which differ from the traditional means of assessing those abilities; the processes needed to solve the STAT tasks are not the same as the ones required to do other tests, such as Cattell 'g' factor; and c) STAT has been designed to assess intelligence within the school context, in such a way that students are required to undertake certain selective processes in order to handle the information contained in each element of this test

(Sternberg, Castejón, Prieto, Hautamaki, & Grigorenko, 2001; Sternberg, Prieto & Castejón, 2000).

b) Studies on specific features (insight and creativity).

Their aim was to make an in-depth observation of the way gifted students handle 'insight' processes (codification, combination and selective comparison). To that end, 'insight' activities were used (Davidson & Sternberg, 1986). The results showed the importance of 'insight' as a key variable for studying high-ability students cognitive complexity. They did better than their peers in the following processes: a) they had greater capacity in distinguishing relevant from irrelevant information (selective codification); b) they had greater aptitude and cognitive complexity in combining independent pieces of information in a unified structure (selective combination); c) they showed greater ability in relating new information to that obtained in the past (selective comparison); d) their higher performance was apparentin their processing of information and their efficiency in finishing their tasks; and e) it was confirmed that gifted students were more able than those with average intelligence when dealing with 'insight' problems, whether mathematical or verbal; in conclusion, they performed better when facing this type of problem (Prieto, Castejón, & Bermejo, 1998).

c) Teacher Training

The aim of the project was to elaborate a teaching program for gifted student teachers in Primary Education, to give an educational response to those students considered to have special needs under the LOGSE (1990) legislation, which was in force at that time. One of its conclusions was that teachers of high-ability students must facilitate learning; and although they do not need to have the same abilities, they must adjust to individual differences; they must be able to manage curricular competencies (contents knowledge, abilities and attitudes); besides, they must have training and information on high abilities.

At present we are re-defining the concept of 'High Ability' with a view to continue exploring the configuration of a study model, identification and support to individual diversity at nursery school and in primary and secondary education. We are assessing and studying abilities in connection with the profiles of students showing those abilities (gifted, mathematical, verbal and scientific talents) with a view to offering parents, teachers, learners and education professionals advice and teaching in those areas related to giftedness and talent in the school context.

What have been the most important research findings that have emerged during recent years?

The proliferation of associations and legislative provisions in the several autonomous communities have led to a growing interest in high abilities, both in the research area as well as in the area of teaching-learning practice. We have witnessed a surge in scientific publications dealing with this matter. In the last six years five studies on high abilities have been published: "New Horizons in the Study of High Ability: Gifted and Talented" (Prieto & Ferrando, 2016), "Critical Issues on Gifted Education and Talent Development" (Tourón, 2015), "Emotional Intelligence and High Ability" (Prieto & Hernández-Torrano, 2011) and "High Abilities: Giftedness and Talent' (Prieto, 2010). The work of researchers should be added to this list, such as Tourón and his team (UNIR: Rioja International University; Prieto and her team (Murcia University); Pérez (Complutense University, Madrid);

Borges (Laguna University, Canary Islands); Sastre-Riba (La Rioja University); and Pomar (Santiago de Compostela University). The topics dealt with by them have been grouped into the following categories.

About Identification Procedures

Psychometric intelligence tests are being used in a non-conventional way, analyzing the scores to find the differential profiles within high ability. Tourón & Tourón (2006) adapted the 'School and College Ability Test' to our context. The test is used at John Hopkins University. Furthermore, given the 'ceiling effect' present in some tests, they proposed an "out of level" rating, which facilitates distinction and differentiation within a given high-ability group; to that end, the scales for the test were calculated for different age groups and abilities.

There has been some interest in looking for alternative measurement tests, besides the IQ and the 'divergent thinking' tests. The 'High Abilities Research Group' from Murcia University has adapted the 'Aurora Battery', which features a new model to identify gifted and talented individuals, and is based on Sternberg's 'successful intelligence' theory (Kornilov, Tan, Elliott, Sternberg, & Grigorenko, 2012). This procedure allows understanding of cognitive resources management of students with high abilities in synthetic, practical and analytical intelligence. Emphasis is on the use of new resources to generate new ideas, create imaginative stories, solve problems in unusual ways, discover new connections, as well as on the application of knowledge to solve both school and everyday life problems, aspects rarely considered by traditional intelligence and standardized intelligence tests (Prieto, Ferrándiz, Ferrando, & Bermejo, 2015).

Montero, Navarro, Aguilar & Ramiro (2006) studied the usefulness of Piaget's approach and the psychometric approach (Raven's progressive matrices test) for assessing high abilities. After analyzing the various forms for identifying gifted and talented children, they found statistically significant correlations between Piaget's tests and those rating psychometric intelligence. In fact, there were significant relations between mental attention and Piaget's studies, considering the importance of the 'Intersection of Figures Test' as an instrument to identify the gifted and talented. The authors mainly highlight the use of 'mental attention and work memory' tests for the detection of high ability.

Regarding the 'screening' procedure, Barraca & Artola (2004) devised a screening scale: 'High capability/aptitude Individuals Detection Scale' (EDAC), based on Renzulli's scale. It contains four sub-scales that assess: cognitive abilities, divergent thinking, motivational characteristics and personality and leadership. Their work confirms adequate psycho-metric properties in terms of internal consistency and construct validity. The authors also highlight the usefulness of the scale for building programs which allow for the individual differences of gifted persons and different types of talent.

The study conducted by Tourón, Repáraz & Peralta (2006) found that the teachers were not able to identify students with high abilities. There was disagreement between identification by nomination and by standard procedures (IQ). Teachers tend to nominate excessively, obtaining 83% false positive cases. Given these results, the authors strongly recommended implementing active policies for the identification of gifted and talented students. The study by Castro, Campo, Álvarez, López & Álvarez (2011) showed how subjective kindergarten teachers were when they had to fill-in the Renzulli observation scales.

Salazar, Bermejo, Ferrando & Ferrándiz (2015) used the Teachers' nomination scale for students, parents and teachers. It is based on Renzulli's theory and the main objective is to assess the three main characteristics of giftedness: above average ability, Task commitment and Creativity. They concluded that students and parents were more generous than teachers when assessing high abilities. They found statistically significant effects depending on the children's ages: the older ones obtained higher ratings. There was also a significant effect according to teacher filling in of the scale. Briefly, this Checklist instrument helps teachers to identify characteristics of high ability students in a very significant way, because it can be very effective in identifying of the abilities of gifted students. An advantage of this system is that, once a teacher recognizes the ability, they usually become interested in designing adequate forms of measuring the diversity of the extremely gifted (educational provisions). Identification provision and educational provision have been always seen to be very close to each other: good provision allows ability to surface, while good identification leads to adequate provision (Prieto, Parra, Ferrándiz & Sánchez, 2004).

Screening tests based on multiple intelligences (MI) were also used (Llor et al., 2012), in particular the Screening Scale for the Evaluation of Multiple Intelligences – Teacher, Parents and Students Form (SSEMI). The aim is to assess seven areas in which students can show MI strengths or weakness. It is a 28-item rating scale in which teachers, parents and students express their agreement about student characteristics and behaviors on a 4-point scale ranging from 1 (never) to 4 (always), in terms of Gardner's MI (1983). The seven areas in which students can show strengths or weakness assessed by teachers are: linguistic (ability to effectively manipulate language to express oneself when writing and speaking), logical-mathematical (ability to detect patterns, reason deductively, and think logically), naturalist (ability to identify and classify patterns in nature), spatial (ability to manipulate and create mental images to solve problems), musical (ability to recognize and compose musical pitches, tones, and rhythms), bodily-kinesthetic (ability to use one's mental abilities to coordinate one's own bodily movements), and social intelligences – intrapersonal and interpersonal intelligences from the original scale were combined – (ability to understand and discern the feelings and intentions of oneself and others). These authors found important differences in the perception of linguistic, logical-mathematical and naturalist intelligences (according to the parents, teachers and student's reports) in favour of high ability students. Agreement between those judging (parents, teachers and students) was also studied. The results showed significant differences in the perception of students' MI (between the three groups of informants) in the areas of linguistic, mathematical and naturalist intelligence favoring high ability students. No significant differences were found in less academic areas like musical, kinesthetic and social intelligence. With regard to gender, there were significant differences favoring girls in social and musical intelligences, and favoring boys in mathematical intelligence.

What are the characteristics leading teachers to nominate gifted students in Spain? To answer this question, several demographic characteristics (i.e. gender, grade) and psychological characteristics (i.e. multiple intelligences, emotional intelligence, intellectual aptitude, and divergent thinking) of 563 secondary students nominated as gifted by their teachers were analyzed. Results showed a general gifted profile of the nominated students defined by higher scores in their naturalist and social intelligences, stress management, and verbal, mechanical, and spatial reasoning. Additional analysis indicated that students' gender and grade also influenced teachers' nominations of gifted students. Based on the associations between the demographic and psychological characteristics included in this study, nominated students could be classified into five specific gifted profiles, namely, moderately gifted students, social emotionally gifted students, artistically gifted students, intellectually gifted students, and generally gifted students (Hernández-Torrano, Prieto, Ferrándiz, Bermejo & Sainz, 2013).

Overall, the data presented here provide evidence that MI theory is a valuable construct for studying and identifying high ability students. Our studies offer two components that allow us to analyze the broad spectrum of high skill beyond the information provided by conventional intelligence and aptitude tests. These components can be used to identify strengths and talents in the academic areas, as well as high ability students who excel in less academic areas such as sports, dance, music, or the social area. Furthermore, the possibility of collecting information from the perspective of different informants (i.e. students, parents, and teachers) greatly enhances the identification process. Thus, this procedure covers the information provided by the teacher about the school context, by the parents about the family context, and by the student about his/her personal context. Additionally, the application and interpretation of the MI scales is very easy, facilitating the identification process. The academic and non-academic components converge in the three MI scales, which yields very practical effects when analyzing the student's cognitive profile and comparing the information provided by distinct informants. Future studies should be directed toward improving the internal consistency of the scales, especially the scale for assessing students' MI. Finally, the approach presented here allows taking detailed profiles regarding different intelligences to be taken into account, which can help all individuals reach their maximum development potential, both in the academic and non-academic contexts (Hernández-Torrano, Ferrándiz, Ferrando, Prieto & Fernández, 2014; Salazar, Bermejo, Ferrando & Ferrándiz, 2015).

About the Cognitive Configuration of High Abilities

The research conducted by Sastre-Riba (2013) focused on understanding cognitive functioning and the difference between exceptionally able individuals, according to Castelló and Batlle (1998), who categorize them into gifted and talented, whereby the latter can be single or complex. Gifted individuals have extraordinary, convergent intelligence (logical-deductive) and divergent intelligence (creativity). Single talent persons are those with an extraordinary intellectual configuration in only one specific aptitude (verbal, mathematical, spatial, creative or logical); while complex talent persons have an extraordinary intellectual combination of different specific aptitudes; for example, artistic, figurative talent, involving an extraordinary combination of perception management and very good spatial aptitude, or high creativity level and an adequate level of logical reasoning; another example is academic talent, requiring an extraordinary combination of verbal and logical resources, and very good memory management. The study carried out by Sastre-Riba shows that higher cognitive complexity correlates with better management of intellectual resources, better meta-cognitive strategies and better executive functions; as well as greater use of information and more complexity in its organization.

In fact, the authors claim that there are differences between subjects with high intellectual aptitude and those with average intellectual aptitude as regards the organization of information received; differences in the way gifted and talented people solve problems, as the latter show more organizational complexity of received information; moreover, the number of ideas they produce is also significantly greater. These results confirm the differential cognitive functioning appearing in high intellectual capability. In addition, in the case of complex talent, work memory is also higher, and becomes apparent in better executive functioning, greater flexibility and inhibition. Additionally, the profiles of individuals with complex talents show better management of meta-cognitive abilities (Sastre-Riba, 2013; Sastre-Riba & Viana-Saenz, 2016).

In her doctoral thesis, González-García (2015) analyzed the correlation between various identification criteria (BadyG[2], 'g' factor, academic performance and creativeness) and found a low degree of correspondence between them. The results demonstrated that although students with a high intellectual ability do not form a homogeneous group, there are heterogeneous cognitive profiles, which can be categorized as follows: high intellectual aptitude, high academic performance, high creativeness and a combination of high-level aptitude and low performance.

The research carried out by Ferrando, Ferrándiz, Llor & Sainz (2016) aimed to study the different giftedness and talent patterns which can result from the combination of analytical, creative and practical abilities, according to Sternberg's 'successful intelligence' theory. He suggests seven possible profiles: three pure ones, as well as the combination of creative-analytical, creative-practical, analytical-practical talents, and the combination of analytical-creative-practical talents. Six out of the seven profiles proposed

---

[2] BADyG: Battery of Differential and General Aptitudes.

by Sternberg were found in their research. The only missing one was the purely analytically gifted and talented profile.

Socio-emotional configuration

Part of this research is dedicated to better understanding of the socio-emotional profile of students with extraordinary abilities. Worthy of mention here is the work of the Murcia University "High Abilities Research Group", which used the Emotional Quotient Inventory – Young Version (EQ-i:YV; Bar-On & Parker, 2000). The results found by the Group's research may be summarized as follows: 1) differences between gifted and non-gifted are found repeatedly for the Adaptability dimension. G&T students self-perceived themselves as having more flexibility and skills to adjust to new situations as well as better ability to identify and overcome problems and implement effective solutions (Ferrándiz, Hernández-Torrano, Bermejo, Ferrando, & Sainz, 2012; Ferrando et al., 2010; Prieto & Ferrando, 2008). That could be explained by the nature of giftedness, as it implies creative thinking and flexibility, tolerance to ambiguity, open-mindedness, desire to take risks and better capacity to propose new ideas (Sternberg & Lubart, 1993).

2) When studying differences between gifted versus talented students, differences have been confirmed for stress management, intrapersonal and total Emotional Intelligence in favour of the gifted (Ferrando, et al., 2010; Prieto, & Ferrando, 2008). We need to bear in mind that in the Spanish context talented is defined by specificity, whereas giftedness shows a broader domain in different areas. Thus a talented child can have good verbal intelligence, for instance, but a gifted child has the intellectual resources to perform above average in any area of knowledge.

This generality may be explaining a better performance of the gifted in emotional intelligence. Due to the identification procedure followed, we did not identify "emotionally talented students" who would perform better than gifted students in the Emotional Intelligence dimension (Ferrando, 2006; Prieto & Ferrando, 2008).

Peñas (2006) found that gifted and talented students are characterized by vital satisfaction and high self-esteem; they often feel they are not being understood and that they are envied for their special aptitudes, which leads them to feel ashamed about their giftedness and to hide it. The author claimed she found a lack of adjustment between the gifted student's stereotype and their own image.

The study done by Del Caño, Palazuelo, Marugán, & Velasco (2011) analyzed the relationship between high aptitudes, socialization and optimism, as well as the teachers' ability to identify them. The results showed that: a) the most intelligent students are considered by their peers as leaders, having good social relationships and ready to help others; b) students with a high intellectual aptitude obtained significantly higher ratings for optimism and attitude; c) students considered to be more intelligent by their teachers achieved higher ratings than those of their peers in the cognitive aptitude tests, and were also regarded by their peers as leaders and assertive; and d) according to their peers, students chosen as being optimistic by their teachers show a helping, collaborative and supportive attitude towards others, as well as ability to solve conflicts. In general, students with a high intellectual aptitude are perceived as showing greater maturity and empathy.

Why and how to identify pupils who are gifted?

There are several reasons justifying the need to identify students with high abilities and to have suitable instruments available to detect them.

Why is it necessary to study gifted and talented students?

1. Because it is necessary to understand the cognitive, social and emotional complexity of these students.
2. Because it is necessary to understand the way intellectual resources are articulated in the different 'high-ability' types.
3. To get to know the different intelligence patterns (analytical, synthetic and practical), the gaps, as well as strong points in the management of different abilities or talents. This would allow us to offer action guidelines and personalized advice according to talent type. The specific capability patterns vary to a large extent (Ferrando, Ferrándiz, Llor & Sainz, 2016; Sternberg, 2000).
4. To comply with the 'equal-opportunities' principle, which determines that each person should be educated according to their own educational needs; as well as to promote excellence. Our education system approaches talents as a potential, emerging factor, which can be developed through education, but only when the appropriate conditions are given.
5. To adjust the curriculum to the individual's needs and competences (knowledge, abilities and attitudes), i.e. to offer differential education.
6. To elaborate programs which are suitable to high abilities, which allow students to make progress at school according to their learning pace and competence.

7. Because there is a need for counselors to undertake screening in order to gather additional information regarding the student's school, family, and social context. The aim is to assess the interaction that G&T students develop with their peers, teachers, and their social context, in order to work together to improve the development of G&T students.

8. Because information regarding teachers' and parents' expectations for the child should betaken into account, as both teachers and parents face many issues and challenges. Once the child, parents, and teachers are aware of the special needs of the child, it becomes easier to manage, counsel and give guidance to the child, school or family.

9. Lastly, the child and family may need counseling in order to channel giftedness in appropriate ways, as G&T children learn first from their parents. Parents who spend time with their gifted child are more able to tune in to their child's interests and respond by offering appropriate educational enrichment opportunities. Home stimulation and support of interests is vital to the development of these talents and this will help the child to flourish. Moreover, it is important for parents of any children with special needs to meet with teachers early in the school year. When parents and teachers work together, appropriate programs can be developed and problems can be dealt with early. It is helpful for parents to offer to assist their child's teacher by making or locating supplementary materials, helping in the classroom or library, offering expertise to small groups of students, or finding others who can provide other enrichment experiences.

Identification process: how to identify gifted and talented children?

Both state and private schools need to develop a gifted student identification process that suits their own school context but which can also be adopted as a school-wide approach. Many tools are available to assist identification and a combination of techniques is necessary, including teachers' informed observations and professional judgment.

According to our law, the key to the identification process is psychological assessment and educational provisions for these children (ordinary, extraordinary and exceptional educational provisions).

Psychological assessment

This is a complex process in which counselors must take the following steps into account:

Screening Phase

The Screening Phase consists of some first-step assessment procedures aimed at selecting students who may have special needs. To do so, students' strengths and needs are assessed. The screening assessment is important because data will be obtained not only as to whether the child is gifted or talented, but in what ways he/she is gifted so that their academic, social, emotional and psychological needs can be met (Hernández-Torrano, Ferrándiz, Ferrando, Prieto & Fernández, 2014). We wish to point out that in our school district (Murcia, Spain), we measure a diversity of abilities, talents and strengths.

Second Phase: Identification

Intelligence Aptitude Test: For primary schools we use the Battery of Differential and General Aptitudes (BADyG). The aim is to assess the following abilities: analogical relations, numerical verbal problems, logical matrixes, numerical calculus, complex verbal orders, rotated figures, immediate memory, alterations in writing, discrimination of differences, sentence completion, verbal analogies, numerical series, number problem-solving, shapes-fitting, memorizing oral texts and visual orthographic memory (Yuste, 1998a, b).

This test allows us to find the IQ related to pupils' general intelligence, as well as partial scores regarding verbal factors, numerical factors, spatial factors and logical factors.

For secondary schools we use the Differential Aptitude Test – Level 1 (DAT-5; Bennett, Seashore & Wesman, 2000). The aim is to assess the following abilities: verbal (ability to find relationships between words), numerical (ability to understand numerical relationships and handle numerical concepts), abstract (ability to discover an implicit rule that relates a series of non-verbal designs), mechanical (ability to understand basic mechanical principles), and spatial reasoning (ability to imagine and rotate an object in three dimensions).

Creativity assessment

The Torrance Test of Creative Thinking: Creative Thinking Test (TTCT Torrance Tests of Creative Thinking, Torrance, 1974). The object of this test is to assess the four fundamental dimensions of creativity: fluency (number of meaningful responses given), flexibility (number of changes of response category), originality (number of statistically infrequent responses), and elaboration (number of items to embellish the ideas). It contains a verbal and a figural part. Previous studies have shown that the third subtest explains a higher percentage of variance. Our results show that it is a very good instrument for identifying G&T students (Almeida, Prieto, Ferrando, Oliveira & Ferrándiz, 2008; Ferrando, Ferrándiz, Bermejo, Sánchez, Parra & Prieto, 2007; Hernández-Torrano, Prieto, Ferrándiz, Bermejo & Sainz 2013; Oliveira, Almeida, Ferrándiz, Ferrando, Sainz & Prieto, 2009).

Assessment of non-cognitive aspects

The aim is to assess the components of emotional intelligence of G&T.

Student's, parents' and teachers' perception of Emotional

Intelligence

To assess the competencies of emotional intelligence, the 'Bar-On and Parker Questionnaire' (Emotional Quotient Inventory: Young Version: EQ-i: YV and EQ-i:YV-O, 2000) was used. It contains 38 items which appear in a Likert-type scale consisting of four points, which assesses five factors of emotional intelligence: capacity to understand their own emotions (intra-personal intelligence); capacity to understand and appreciate others' emotions (inter-personal intelligence); flexibility and efficiency to solve conflicts (adaptability); ability to direct and control their own emotions (stress management); and the ability to take a positive attitude towards life (state of mind). In addition, it offers a total rating for emotional intelligence, which is the result of the combination of the factors mentioned before. Its psychometric features are adequate (Ferrándiz, et. al., 2012; Sainz, Ferrándiz, Fernández & Ferrando, 2014).

Educational provisions: enrichment workshops

According to educational policy in Spain, we have different programs and opportunities for gifted and talented children.

Enrichment Workshops

Under our policy for the education of gifted students, their primary school teacher has high responsibility during the fourth year. Teachers must ensure that these students are provided with opportunities to develop their abilities and to meet their potential for outstanding achievement. Enrichment activities may include introducing students to other fields or activities, such as art, music, journal writing, clubs or field trips, assigning additional work at the same level of difficulty, or assigning various school responsibilities tothe advanced student, such as being a classroom aide.

In addition to the teachers' efforts within the class and school, in Murcia specific three-hour workshops for the G&T have been carried out every two weeks. The aim is to offer enrichment activities according to the students' interests, motivation and needs.

The principal goal of our enrichment and extension program is to foster the development of high-level abilities, creativity and critical thinking. To summarize, the educational provisions or the enrichment activities are oriented to: enabling all pupils to achieve success at school; providing specific assistance and targeting programs to students who are gifted; ensuring effective provision for individual students who are gifted (state schools need to consider a range of options for their curriculum and their school organization); emphasizing higher-order skills such as problem-solving, critical thinking, evaluation and analysis;

the use of more complex language and demanding resources; and emphasis on the development and use of pupils' research abilities. Also, it is important for teachers to improve teaching strategies that foster creativity in gifted in order to incite their curiosity and their desire to learn (Piske, Stoltz, & Machado, 2014; Piske, et al., 2016).

Differentiated Programs for gifted and talented students

Among the after-school programs aimed at the enrichment and care for diversity in high-ability students, we can mention some initiatives carried out by some autonomous communities, such as:

The 'Canarias Government Education, Culture and Sports Counseling Board'*(Consejería de Educación, Cultura y Deportes del Gobierno de Canarias)*, through its 'General Department of Educational Management and Innovation', aware of the needs of high-ability students and receptive to the interests of the families and the whole school community, has brought about an initiative to promote actions tending to adequately respond to the possibilities, interests and learning pace of this group of students. This initiative comprises a series of programs aimed at stimulating divergent thinking in primary school learners. These have been carried out since 2001, and there have been different versions. Some of the activities in these programs, known as 'PREPEDI', have been published (Rodríguez, Ramos, Artiles & Jiménez, 2004).

For students in 'Compulsory Secondary Education' (ESO) and *'Bachillerato'* (high school level) there is an 'After-school Premium Enrichment and Mentors Program', which, by means of tutoring provided by university teacher-mentors or secondary education teachers, helps them develop interest areas which cannot be addressed during in-school activities. This program also offers online courses and workshops offering contents which are loosely related to the school curriculum.

Another after-school program is that known as 'Star'. Its objectives are: to achieve personal development and prevent disintegration and lack of synchronicity at school; to prevent behaviors and motivational problems deriving from the application of the curricular subjects; to strengthen cognitive development; to foster the use of learning strategies and develop relational abilities among peers. This program includes the following components: 1) cognitive training through enrichment activities; 2) personal-social counseling; 3) promotion of self-examination and creative thinking processes. There are also workshops given by well-known experts in the fields of arts, creativity and robotics (Pérez, López, del Valle & Ricote, 2008).

The 'University of La Rioja research group', conducted by Sastre-Riba (2013), has prepared an 'After-school Enrichment' program. It is structured around the following objectives: 1) to modify contents (ideas, concepts, facts and information), processes and teaching-learning contexts (psychological atmosphere and places); 2) to optimize cognitive and personal development, aiming at and sustaining the accomplishment of high potentialities; 3) to promote the use of intellectual processes and cognitive management; 4) to promote interaction abilities among peers; to prevent dysfunctional behavior and/or learning; 5) to avoid motivational difficulties. The conclusions of the program assessment show that a high percentage of participants and parents are happy with the after-class activities and can see improvements in the students' cognitive and emotional management; students state that they are achieving the program goals relating to their personal development and cognitive resources management.

Parents say that the program develops and stimulates their children's abilities and capabilities. The author claims that the feedback given by the parents and the students involved shows that participation in the program is satisfactory and leads to awareness of the preferences indicated by such improvement.

The Santiago de Compostela University, in collaboration with the 'High Abilities Association' (ASAC), carries out after-class extracurricular enrichment programs aiming at: offering integrated education to individuals with high aptitude/abilities, as well as adequate training for parents and teachers, with a view to achieving their correct interaction with persons who have high abilities. This program has been modified and adjusted in relation to the permanent follow-up assessment results carried out through all the social groups involved. It entails various activities for children and parents. Children's work groups are organized according to their ages and the types of workshops available, although flexibility allows them to change groups if the situation calls for that (Fernández, Pomar & Rodríguez, 2005).

The Andalucia Council has different means available for approaching and supporting diversity of the gifted and talented. A number of those documents containing identification procedures and educational responses can be found on the web (Calero, García & Gómez-Gómez, 2007).

Worthy of note is the so-called 'MENTORAC-UMA' program, the aim of which is to offer activities orientated towards students' integrated development. It is important to mention the multicultural nature of the students attending the program.

The 'High Abilities (aptitudes) Integrated Programmed' (*PIPAC, Programa Integral para Altas Capacidades*, Rodríguez,

Rodríguez, Díaz, Borges & Veladez, 2015), is orientated to support the integral development of gifted individuals, both at cognitive and socio-affective and family levels. It includes learning strategies, study habits and self-managed learning; in addition the program offersadvice to parents of gifted and talented children.

The results show the efficiency and effectiveness of the program, as the participants state that they are happy both with the program and their monitors, in addition to changes in the children and their parents' expected attitudes being apparent.

ESTALMAT (Mathematical talent stimulus) started in Madrid in 1998, thanks to Professor Guzmán's decisive efforts (2002). This initiative has been incorporated in other large cities (in Cataluña, Andalucía, Canarias, León, Valladolid, Segovia, Valencia, Cantabria and Castilla La Mancha). The project stems from an initiative of the 'Royal Academy of Science', which aims at detecting 25 youths every year, aged between 12 and 13, who have Mathematical talent. Its objectives are: to detect students having special aptitudes/abilities and talent for Mathematics; to develop and promote knowledge and positive attitudes towards the Mathematical sciences; to develop their abilities to the highest degree according to their psychological development (from the beginning of formal thought to abstract thinking); to enhance their Mathematics background with interesting, motivating topics which are not included in the curriculum; to increase and consolidate their inquisitive attitude, raising questions, formulating hypotheses and processes, and specific Mathematical knowledge; to facilitate autonomous work and give a humanistic view of Mathematics; to teach the importance of Mathematics in the development of scientific thinking; as well as to explore the use of new technology.

Online education for students with high intellectual abilities in the area of Mathematics (Tourón, Marcos & Tourón, 2009), the so-called *"Destination Math"* (property of Houghton Mifflin Harcourt Learning Technology), has been translated into Spanish. Each of its units always has a fetching start, intended to capture the student's attention. Emphasis is placed both on concepts as well as on practice. Learning takes place in contexts that are meaningful for the student, and they are helped by the use of models. It employs cartoons and dynamic graphs in a meaningful way, giving them teaching guidance both within the lessons and the questions they contain. It also offers students the tools for exploratory learning and a large variety of interaction modes, besides promoting links with other disciplines. It was applied with 215 learners (9 to 10 years old) whose verbal or mathematical abilities were 10% higher than that of their peers in the same age group. The program lasted for twelve weeks. The assessment the children made of their learning experience was highly positive; 82% of them said that they would repeat the experience and 94% of them stated that they would recommend the program to a friend. The assessment of the students' learning process indicated significant gains between pre-test and post-test, with ratings between 5 and 20 points. For the final assessment the students were required to generally summarize three aspects of the program: a) their opinion of it in terms of its contents, level of challenge it presented them with, type of activities, challenges presented by the tutor, etc.; b) their own opinion about the tutorials they had been given; and c), having the whole experience in mind, how they would rate it, considering the program, tutorials, peers, challenge and difficulty levels. It was also taken into account whether the student would be happy to repeat the experience with another online program and if they would recommend it to a friend. The results obtained for all these aspects show the usefulness of the program and the satisfaction felt by students, tutors and parents.

The 'Extracurricular Enrichment Workshops for high-Ability Students' were created in the Murcia Autonomous Community. These were started in 2006 under the auspices of the High-Abilities Research Group (Murcia University). The aim of the activities and materials of these workshops was to offer those students certain learning experiences which allowed them to work in an entertaining and creative fashion. The program objectives were: to achieve the integral development of the students' personal aptitudes; to offer enriched learning environments and to encourage an autonomous learning attitude; to develop divergent thinking; to strengthen social abilities to improve relationships with others in a qualitative way and to promote personal growth; as well as to collaborate and offer advice to the educational centers and families involved (Rojo et al., 2010). One of the main weaknesses found in relation to these workshops, however, was the failure to assess their effects, which occurred due to administrative limitations.

The Scientist's Workshop

At present we are working with a group of students with various high-ability profiles using a program aimed at developing their competences in the area of science. It is based on a program or 'Cognitive Model for Science Teaching' (Esparza, Ruiz-Melero, Bermejo, Ferrando, & Sainz, 2016), which follows a range of perspectives of science teaching which have proved to be useful and innovative in the process of science teaching-learning (Feist, 2013; Simonton, 2011).

Esparza et al., (2016) build their model on three basic aspects, which take place in the laboratory.

1. Teaching and development of contents proper to sciences: a) declarative (to know what is happening in connection with a given specific content: facts, definitions and descriptions); b) procedural (to know how to act in terms of the production and the application of rules, steps to follow, etc.); c) schematic (to know why a specific fact occurs, laying down principles, conceptual schemes and relations between concepts); and d) strategic (to know when, where and how to apply knowledge, strategies, heuristic methods, etc.).

2. Promotion of abilities proper to scientific-creative thinking: observation, hypotheses generation, hypotheses assessment and evidence verification; and learning strategies: questioning, discovery and Socratic learning methods. Matters related to chemistry, physics and biology have been used as a source of interest.

3. Competence development and skills to use learning strategies. The model includes different skills levels, and as such offers varied difficulty levels in order to achieve students' learning goals.

Thus, being aware of the variety of activities and problems which may ensue from the area of sciences, it is worth mentioning that this instrument should be understood as an innovative, dynamic and flexible model. Its structure takes into account the synergy between different reasoning types and the abilities of scientific-creative thinking, throughplanned practice which is performed along various stages.

This program was carried out with the participation of 30 students (between 12 and 13 years of age). They had previously been identified as gifted and talented, according to Castelló & Battle's model (1998). The data from the qualitative assessment showed that the teachers informed that all the students had managed to solve the problems assigned in a satisfactory way, in some cases even surpassing expectations in terms of contents knowledge, abilities and strategies. They point out that during the sessions the students showed remarkable initiative and autonomy, triggering debates and questions which led to a more in-depth treatment of matters of interest.

The students think that the experience has been useful and, in practice, this is reflected in the accomplishment of creative and meta-cognitive abilities, in the content knowledge and even in the surprise factor. The usefulness and efficacy of the model used should be noted. Besides, the satisfactory experiences have led to the enrichment of knowledge, abilities and strategies typical of scientific-creative thinking, which is necessary in the area of science. In conclusion, the organization and implementation of the model has made it possible to develop students' critical thinking, as reflected in the various stages of the activities carried out, when they were required to assess, judge and justify the validity of the tasks from their beginning through to their solution. Moreover, in the various stages students have achieved a certain degree of competence in the management of the abilities and strategies proper to the scientific-creative thinking. Thus, students have shown competence and ability to offer solutions which are not only innovative and original but also useful and suitable for problems appearing within a social context. The improvements made in the methodological strategies to encourage analogical, associative, critical and creative thinking have decisively contributed to the understanding of more abstract topics in the area of sciences (e.g., atmospheric pressure). Given that talented individuals are a very important human asset, especially prepared for taking part in the production and advancement of scientific-technological knowledge, it should be highlighted that the main purpose of this work at all times has been that of stimulating the potentialities of scientific talent within the educational system (Gluckman, 2011). Likewise, it can be stated that the present study follows and adjusts to the European Framework Program for Research and Innovation' Horizon 2020' (*Horizonte,* 2020), the objective of which is to promote science by and for society, making university studies and scientific education more attractive for young people, and encouraging gender equality in research and innovation.

Additionally, it poses an innovative alternative to meeting the needs of diversity and heterogeneity in students with a scientific talent, training future scientists in order to be ready to respond to the requirements and demands of the 21st Century; promoting scientific research; stimulating the curricular innovation process in the area of science through specifically orientated practices; introducing and relating acquired content knowledge to the natural context and the development of technology; and encouraging thinking and debate on topics referring to scientific knowledge.

To sum up, it can be claimed that although efforts in this direction have been made in our country, the lack of available resources has been the main reason why they have been isolated and we do have data explaining the achievement of objectives and the effects obtained. Moreover, we have observed in this research that at times there is no correlation between the identification model and the educational response; very rarely have the social-emotional factors or personality traits been includedin studies on this matter, which introduce great variability among the participants, and which should be under control. The amount of empirical studies on the efficacy of the programs on psycho-pedagogical intervention on High Aptitudes/Abilities is poor. However, the assessment of such programs is a necessary means to grasp their efficacy and the effects of their implementation on the personal development of the students taking part in them, as well as their intellectual management within and outside them.

Why should Talent be Cultivated through extracurricular experiences?

According to different authors there are several reasons for stimulating talent development (Eliot et al., 2013; Tourón, 2010; Tourón, Santiago & Díez, 2014).

Because it is necessary to comply with and guarantee the 'equal-opportunities' principle.

Because if talent is not cultivated it is lost.

Because attention to such students demands a type of education aimed at the diversity of aptitudes, interests, expectations and needs of all of them, as well as at the changes society and students experience.

Because students need programs and resources which are at the same level and adequately follow the development of their abilities.

Because the very heterogeneity of talented students demands a personalized and differential education.

Because it is not possible to have a school program which can meet all the needs of all talented learners.

Because it is necessary to develop and apply school programs which allow for the students' individual differences through curricular flexibility.

Because learning may take place anywhere, not only at school.

Because generally educational planning includes only those courses that are within the school system.

Because students with academic talent need to interact with their peers as regards special talents, referred to as 'intellectual partners'.

Because cultivating and promoting talent is a requirement of the 'equal opportunities' principle, which entails giving everybody the type of education they need, making all educational systems really egalitarian.

Because it is necessary to do away with the myths and social prejudice which hinder the acceptance and development of talent and excellence.

Because the talents of the most able individuals, if used to serve society, will enable us all to build a better future for everybody.

Conclusions

Firstly, in recent years there has been an important increase in research on gifted and talented individuals and their education. Even legislation has made progress, although there is still a lack of philosophy and social awareness toward high-ability matters. Therefore, such a cultural vacuum regarding high abilities/ aptitudes determines their not being included in academic plans; thus, the school system does not have guidelines for screening, identification and paying special attention to these students' specific needs (differentiated programs for gifted and talented students).

Secondly, there are no available differential curricula for gifted and talented students. They are expected to comply with and exceed the normal educational standards according to their level or course.

Thirdly, there has been a significant involvement of parents and some education professionals concerned with high ability, especially with regard to identification and orchestrating of educational actions; however, that is not enough, and the aims should be, on the one hand, to achieve greater social understanding and professional development in the field of high ability; on the other hand, to get access to more resources, support, funding and time availability from the educational authorities and schools.

References

Almeida, L., Prieto, M. D., Ferrando, M., Oliveira, E., & Ferrándiz, C. (2008). Torrance Test of Creative Thinking: the question of its construct validity. *Thinking Skills and Creativity, 3,* 53-58.

Bar-On, R., & Parker, J. D. A. (2000). *The Bar-On Emotional Quotient Inventory: Youth Version (EQ-i:YV).* Toronto, Canada: Multi-Health Systems.

Barraca, J. y Artola, T. (2004). La identificación de alumnos con altas capacidades a través de la EDAC. *EduPsykhé: Revista de psicología y psicopedagogía, 3*(1), 3-18.

Bennett, G. Seashore, G. &Wesman, A. (2000). *DAT-5, Test de Aptitudes Diferenciales.* Madrid: TEA Ediciones.

Calero, M. D., García, M. B., & Gómez-Gómez, M. T., (2007). *El alumnado con sobredotación intellectual. Conceptualización, evaluación y respuesta educativa.* Sevilla: Junta de Andalucía.

Castelló, A. & Batlle, C. (1998). Aspectos teóricos e instrumentales en la identificación del alumno superdotado y talentoso. Propuesta de un protocolo. *FAISCA. Revista de Altas Capacidades, 6,* 26-66.

Castro, P., Campo, M. A., Álvarez, M., López, C., & Álvarez, E. (2011). Cuestionario para detectar niños de altas capacidades. El problema de las diferentes interpretaciones. *Revista de Investigación en Educación 1*(9), 73-83.

Davidson, J. E. & Sternberg, R. J. (1986). What is insight? *Educational Horizons, 64,* 177-179.

Del Caño, M., Palazuelo, M., Marugán, M.& Velasco, S. (2011). Socialización, alta capacidad intelectual y optimismo disposicional. International Journal of Developmental and Educational Psychology: INFAD. *Revista de Psicología, 1*(1), 613-620.

Eliot, Ch. et al. (2013) *Teaching Students Who Are Gifted And Talented: A Handbook for Teachers.* Newfoundland and Labrador Department of Education.

Esparza, J., Ruiz-Melero, M. J.; Bermejo, M.R., Ferrando, M. & Sainz, M. (2016). Diseño de un programa para favorecer habilidades y estrategias del pensamiento científico-creativo. In F. H.R. Piske; T. Stoltz; J.M. Machado (org.). *Altas Habilidades/Superdotaçao (AH/SD) e Creatividades. Identificação e Atendimiento* (pp. 39-60), Brasil: Jurua Editora.

Feist, G.J. (2013). The Scientific Personality. In G.J., Feist, & M.E. Gorman (Eds.), *Handbook of the Psychology of Science* (pp. 95-121). New York: Springer Publishing Company.

Fernández, O., Pomar, C., & Rodríguez, L., (2005). La identificación en superdotación: un estudio de la comunidad autónoma de Galicia. *FAISCA. Revista de Altas Capacidades, 10*(12), 5-26.

Ferrándiz, C., Hernández-Torrano, D., Bermejo, R., Ferrando, M., & Sainz, M. (2012). Social and Emotional Intelligence in Childhood and Adolescence: Spanish Validation of a Measurement Instrument.*Revista de Psicodidáctica, 17*(2), 309-340.

Ferrando, M. (2006).*Creatividad e Inteligencia Emocional: Un Estudio Empírico en* Alumnos con Altas Habilidades (Tesis Doctoral) Universidad de Murcia.

Ferrando, M., Ferrándiz, C. Almeida, L., Prieto, L. Sáinz, M, Fernández, M.C., … & Soto, G. (2010). Emotional intelligence in gifted and talented students: review of the research conducted. In E. Perzycka (Ed). *Towards a Better School (International perspectives)* (pp: 141-156). Boise (Indiana, USA): Educational Research Council.

Ferrando, M., Ferrándiz, C., Bermejo, M. R., Sánchez, C. Parra, J., & Prieto, M. D. (2007). Estructura Interna y Baremación del Test de Pensamiento Creativo de Torrance. *Psicothema, 3* (19), 489-496.

Ferrando, M., Ferrándiz, C., Llor, L., &Sainz, M. (2016). Successful intelligence and giftedness: an empirical study. *Annals of Psychology, 32* (3), 672--682.

García-Alcañiz, E. (1995). Test de inteligencia y medición de la superdotación. Aspectos teóricos y metodológicos. *Revista de Psicología Generaly Aplicada, 48* (4), 539-551.

García Yagüe, J. (1986). *El niño bien dotado y sus problemas. Perspectivas de una investigación española en el primer ciclo de E.G.B.* Madrid: CEPE.

Gardner, H. (1983). Frames of mind. New York, Basic Books. Garmen día de Otaola, A. (1950). Clasificación de los talentos dentro del paradigma psicológico. *Revista de Psicología Generaly Aplicada, 2*, 29-38.

Garmendía de Otaola, A. (1954). Democraciay selección. *Revista Española de Pedagogía, 12* (45), 5-24.

Genovard, C. (1982). Hacia un esquema previo para el estudio del superdotado. *Cuadernos de Psicología, 6* (1), 115-144.

Genovard, C., & Castelló, A. (1990). *El límite superior. Aspectos psicopedagógicos de la excepcionalidad intelectual.* Madrid: Pirámide.

Genovard, C., Gotzens, C., Badía, M., & Dezcallar, T. (2010). Los profesores de alumnos con altas habilidades. In M.D. Prieto (Coord.) Monográfico sobre alumnos con altas habilidades. *Revista Electrónica Interuniversitaria de Formación del Profesorado, 13* (1), 21-31.

Gluckman, P. (2011). *Looking ahead: Science education for the twenty-first century. A report from the Prime Minister's Chief Science Advisor.* Auckland, New Zealand: Office of the Prime Minister's Science Advisory Committee.

González-García, M. (2015). *Perfiles cognitivos asociados a alumnos con altas habilidades intelectuales.* (Tesis Doctoral) Universidad de Alicante.

Guzmán, M. (2002). *Un programa para detector y estimular el talento matemático precoz en la Comunidad de Madrid En La Gaceta de la RSME,* 5.1, 131--140.

Hernández-Torrano, D., Ferrándiz, C., Ferrando, M., Prieto, L., & Fernández, M. C. (2014). The theory of multiple intelligences in the identification of high ability students. *Annals of Psychology, 30* (1), 192-200.

Hernández-Torrano, D., Prieto, M. D., Ferrándiz, C., Bermejo, R., &Sáinz, M. (2013). Characteristics leading teachers to nominate secondary students as gifted in Spain. *Gifted Child Quarterly, 57* (3), 181-196.

Kornilov, S. A., Tan, M., Elliott, J. G., Sternberg, R. J., & Grigorenko, E. L. (2012). Gifted identification with Aurora: Widening the spotlight. *Journal of Psychoeducational Assessment, 30* (1), 117-133.

Linares, A. (1931). Diagnóstico de los niños anormales y superdotados. *Revista Pedagogía, 50*, 412-417.

Llor, L., Ferrando, M., Ferrándiz, C., Hernández, D., Sáinz, M., Prieto, M. D., & Fernández, M. C. (2012). Inteligencias múltiples y alta habilidad. *Aula abierta, 40* (1), 27-38.

LOGSE. Ley Orgánica 1/1990, de 3 de octubre, de Ordenación General del Sistema Educativo.

Montero, J., Navarro, J. I., Aguilar, M., & Ramiro, P. (2006). Comparación de los enfoques psicométrico y operatorio. *Revista Mexicana de Psicología, 23* (2), 185-191.

Oliveira, E. P., Almeida, L., Ferrándiz, C., Ferrando, M., Sáinz, M., & Prieto, M. D. (2009). Tests de Pensamiento Creativo de Torrance (TTCT): Elementos para la validez del constructo en adolescentes portugueses. *Psicothema, 21* (4), 562-567.

Peñas, M. (2006). *Características socioemocionales de las personas adolescentes superdotadas. Ajuste psicológico y negación de la superdotación en el concepto de sí mismas.* (Tesis doctoral). Secretaria General Técnica de Educación, Madrid.

Pérez, L., López-Cobeñas, E. T., & González, C. (2008). La detección del talento lingüístico. *FAISCA: Revista de Altas Capacidades, 13* (15), 124-159.

Pérez, L., López, E., del Valle, L. & Ricote, E. (2008). Más allá del currículo: Programas de Enriquecimiento Extraescolar. La experiencia del Programa Estrella. *FAISCA: Revista de Altas Capacidades,* 15, 4-29.

Piske, F. H. R., Stoltz, T., & Machado, J. (2014). Creative Education for Gifted Children. *Creative Education, Online Submission, 5*, 347-352.

Piske, F. H. R., Stoltz, T., Vestena, C. L. B., de Freitas, S. P., de Fátima Bastos Valentim, B., de Oliveira, C. S. A., & Machado, C. L. (2016). Barriers to Creativity, Identification and Inclusion of Gifted Student. *Creative Education, Online Submission, 7*, 1899-1905.

Prieto, M.D. (Coord.) (2010). Monográfico: Alta habilidad: Superdotación y Talento. *Revista Electrónica Interuniversitaria de Formación del Profesorado, 32* (13, 1), 1-174.

Prieto, M. D., Castejón, J. L. & Bermejo, M. R. (1998). Identification and analysis of differential characteristics among able pupils. *Educating Able Children, 3*, 28-31.

Prieto, M.D., Ferrándiz, C., Ferrando, M., & Bermejo, M. R. (2015). Aurora Battery: A new assessment of successful intelligence. *Revista de Educación, 368*, 132-157.

Prieto, M. D. & Ferrando, M. (2008). Prejudices about Emotional Intelligence in Gifted and Talented Children. In T. Balchin, B. Hymer & D. Matthews (Eds.). *The Routledge International Companion to Gifted Education* (pp. 149-154). New York: Routledge-Farmer.

Prieto, M. D. & Ferrando, M. (Coord) (2016) Monographic theme: High Ability (G&T). *Annals of Psychologhy, 32* (3), 617-701.

Prieto, M. D., & Hernández, D. (Coord) (2011). Monográfico: Inteligencia Emocional y Alta Habilidad. *Revista Electrónica Interuniversitaria de Formación del Profesorado, 38* (14, 3), 1-163.

Prieto, M.D., Parra, J., Ferrándiz, C. & Sánchez, C. (2004). *The role of the teacher within the identification of gifted students.* Paper presented at the European Conference on Educational Research, University of Crete.

Rodríguez, C., Ramos, S., Artiles, C., & Jiménez, J.E. (2004). *Developing creativity in Spanish gifted children.* Poster presentado a la 9th ECHA Conference, 11-14 Septiembre, Pamplona.

Rodríguez, E., Rodríguez, M., Díaz, M., Borges, A. & Veladez, M.D. (2015). *Programa integral para altas capacidades "Descubriéndonos": Una guía práctica de aplicación*. México: Manual Moderno.

Rojo, Á., Garrido, C., Soto, G., Sáinz, M., Fernández, M.C. & Hernández, D. (2010). Talleres de enriquecimiento extracurricular para alumnos de altas habilidades. *Revista Electrónica Interuniversitaria de Formación del Profesorado, 13* (1), 137-146.

Sainz, M., Ferrándiz, C., Fernández, C., & Ferrando, M. (2014). Propiedades psicométricas del Inventario de Cociente Emocional EQ-i: YV en alumnos superdotados y talentosos. *Revista de Investigación Educativa, 32* (1), 41-55.

Salazar, M., Bermejo, M.R., Ferrando, M.&Ferrandiz, C. (2015). Altas habilidades: valoración de padres, profesores y alumnos en la identificación de la superdotación y el talento. In J. I. A. Roque, P. M. Martínez, A. E. Frutos (Eds.) *Investigación en Educación Primaria desde y para el aula* (pp 309-321). Murcia: Editum.

Sastre-Riba, S. (2013). High intellectualability: Extracurricular enrichment and cognitive management. *Journal Educational Gifted, 36*, 119-132.

Sastre-Riba, S., & Viana-Sáenz, L. (2016). Funciones ejecutivas y alta capacidad intelectual. *Revista de Neurología, 62* (Supl 1), 65-71.

Simonton, D. K. (2011). Creativity and discovery as blind variation: Campbell's (1960) BVSR model after the half-century mark. *Review of General Psychology, 15*, 158-174.

Sternberg, R. J. (2000). Patterns of giftedness: A triarchic analysis. *Roeper Review, 22* (4), 231-235.

Sternberg, R. J., Castejón, J. L., Prieto, M. D., Hautamäki, J. & Grigorenko, E. L. (2001). Confirmatory factor analysis of the Sternberg Triarchic Abilities Test in three international samples: An empirical test of the triarchic theory of intelligence. *European Journal of Psychological Assessment, 17* (1), 1-16.

Sternberg, R. &Lubart, T. (1993). Investing in creativity.*PsychologicalInquiry, 4*(3), 229-232.

Sternberg, R. J., Prieto, M. D., & Castejón, J. L. (2000). Análisis factorial confirmatorio del Sternberg Triarchic Abilities Test (nivel-H) en una muestra española: resultados preliminares. *Psicothema, 12* (4), 642-647.

Torrance, E. P. (1974). *The Torrance Tests of Creative Thinking – Norms – Technical Manual Research Edition – Verbal Tests, Forms A and B – Figural Tests, Forms A and B*. Princeton NJ: Personnel Press.

Tourón, J. (2010). El desarrollo del talento y la promoción de la excelencia: exigencias de un sistema educativo mejor. *IV Congreso Iberoamericano de Pedagogía*. Toluca: Mexico, 7-10 Septiembre.

Tourón, J. (Ed.) (2015). Critical Issues On Gifted Education and Talent Development. *Revista de Educación, 368,* 1-211.

Tourón, J., Marcos, G. &Tourón, M. (2009). La educación online con alumnos de alta capacidad intelectual. Evaluación de una intervención en el ámbito de las Matemáticas. *Revista Interuniversitaria de Formación del Profesorado, 24,* 21-31.

Tourón, J., Repáraz, C. & Peralta, F. (2006). Las nominaciones de los profesores en la identificación de alumnos de alta capacidad intelectual. *Sobredotação, 7,* 7-25.

Tourón, J., Santiago, R., & Diez, A. (2014). *The Flipped Classroom: Cómo convertir la escuela en un espacio de aprendizaje*. México DF: Grupo Océano.

Tourón, J., & Tourón, M. (2016). Identification of Verbal and Mathematical Talent: The Relevance of 'Out of Level' Measurement. *Annals of Psychology, 32* (3), 638-651.

Yuste, C. (1998a). *Batería de Aptitudes Diferenciales y Generales (BADyG-E1)*. Madrid: CEPE.

Yuste, C. (1998b). *Batería de Aptitudes Diferenciales y Generales (BADyG-E2)*. Madrid: CEPE.

4.

LEARNING AND INCLUSION: AFFECTIVENESS AND GIFTEDNESS, A SUMMATION OF EDUCATIONAL SPECIFICITIES

Letícia Fleig Dal Forno

Professor at the Master's program in knowledge management in organizations at Unicesumar, Brazil.

ORCID: 0000-0002-3102-8757

Sara Bahia

Professor of Developmental and Educational Psychology at the Faculty of Psychology of the University of Lisbon.

ORCID: 0000-0002-0206-7925

Abstract: *This chapter presents a discussion and an analysis of the need for teachers to be attentive not only to the process of identifying giftedness, but to perceive the relevance of their attitude towards the student's learning process. The perspective of the two theorists stands out in the attempt that while Wallon analyzed and studied child development, Dewey addressed clashes about methodology and the meaning of the teaching-learning process in the teacher-student relationship. According to the descriptions of some researchers on the topic* *of overcrowding, it is recognized that the clash and discussions in relation to: methodology; understanding of the teaching and learning process; verification of the affective and intellectual development of the gifted, reflect on an understanding that these students have specificities in their educational path. Through the analysis of the perception of child educators in Brazil and Portugal regarding the characteristics that indicate giftedness in children, it has become possible to verify the importance of affection on the part of the education professional when working with this target audience. What has been lacking in actions aimed at inclusion of gifted students is to understand the integral development of these individuals, and to recognize that affection is a variable recognized since the beginning of the studies of educational psychology as a means of promoting motivation in and of learning.*

Keywords: Teacher; Inclusion; Affectiveness; Giftedness.

Last century, in the 1990s, Sprinthall & Sprinthall described how the teaching agenda, from a general perspective, was structured on four points of intersection between education and psychology, relating by means of process analysis a contribution made by pedagogy and psychology with variables that influence learners in their construction of knowledge.

For these authors, firstly schoolchildren need to be recognized as they are, in order to perceive that they are all unique and individual, although close as far as the systematization of teaching is concerned. This makes it necessary for the teacher to recognize all individual differences as well as similarities in groups, as well as to combine these two analyses (individual and group) (Sprinthall & Sprinthall, 1993).

Secondly, teachers' attitudes and conceptions about learning as well as teachers' feelings about their role are emphasized as factors that influence the organization of the classroom and the need for them to be taken into consideration in the teaching agenda.

The third theme presents teaching strategies in the process of meaning that teachers fail to do their own way and begin to recognize that it is necessary to identify their competencies before then acting based on teaching strategies, seeking to relate their perceptions of learning with pedagogical actions (Sprinthall & Sprinthall, 1993).

In fourth place, the subject of teaching content is described. Teachers must recognize and know the subject, because in this way they can also share with students the content and its sequence, so that the learning process occurs within a perspective of exchanges (Sprinthall & Sprinthall, 1993).

In this context it is possible to identify that the authors' proposal was to emphasize that teaching and the factors that influence learning are two axes that must converge. And this convergence should be for the teacher-school relationship, so that both are recognized in the context of the classroom, with an organization of roles, tasks and purposes. This refers to John Dewey's (1859-1952) study and conception that teaching and learning "interact, and that the learner is as much part of the learning context as the teacher" (Sprinthall & Sprinthall, 1993, p.19).

Feldman (2015) argues that this identification of the duality between teaching and learning, i.e. this understanding that teaching strategies influence the learning process in the classroom, denotes the cognitive theory of learning in that it involves the consideration of external and internal factors that promote school engagement and interest in learning.

When considering that learning happens through the influence of external and internal factors, it is possible to recognize that social interactions play a significant role in the student's development process, and that affectivity is a relevant means of connection therein. According to Henry Wallon (1879-1962), affectivity has a relevant role in child development, whereby there is oscillation between affectivity and intelligence.

Two theoretical frameworks are thus stressed. Wallon analyzed and studied child development. Dewey addressed the methodology and meaning of the teaching-learning process in the teacher-student relationship. According to the descriptions of some researchers on the subject of giftedness, it is recognized that the debate and the discussion regarding methodology, understanding of the teaching and learning process as well as evaluation of the affective and intellectual development of the gifted, have repercussions on an understanding that such students have specificities along their educational path (Bahia & Trindade, 2012; Fleith & Alencar, 2007; Piske & Stoltz, 2012; Valentim, Vestena & Neusmann, 2014; Virgolim, 2007).

The specific case of giftedness

The definition of giftedness is based on the idea that an individual expresses in his or her development and learning an above-average potential, differing in rhythm and performance, emphasizing their abilities and capabilities through domains and areas of interest, which single out giftedness and the style of challenges and motivations that promote creative production (Bahia, 2006; Corte, 2013; Cross & Coleman, 2014; Gagné, 2014; Gallagher, 2008; Heller, Mönks, Sternberg, & Subotnik, 2002; Pérez & Freitas, 2011; Renzulli, 2010).

Recognition of giftedness requires a multidimensional understanding of this concept by those who evaluate and analyze it, taking into account, in addition to academic performance, the sociocultural context, and the contributions that allow the expression of skills, competencies, and domains (Sternberg, Jarvin, & Grigorenko, 2011).

The theories that describe giftedness have in common the notion that environmental and personal factors are significant in expressing potential, and refer to how much one needs to feel stimulated and recognized for the expressiveness of giftedness in their performance. This means that school, professional educationand the process of identification and evaluation of giftedness are truly significant for the learner (Almeida & Capellini, 2005; Bahia, 2006; Kaufman & Sternberg, 2008).

This is because the recognition of giftedness in an educational context enables the student to feel at ease with his or her abilities and performance (Almeida & Capellini, 2005; Bahia, 2006; Kaufman & Sternberg, 2008). Given the importance of the assessment of giftedness, the following section presents ways of carrying out evaluation in a school context, taking into account the learner's perspective at different levels of education.

In this sense, giftedness can be identified through characteristics such as: engagement, learning rhythm, performance, learning style, memorization, performance, abilities (Dal Forno, Veiga & Bahia, 2015). Divergent thinking, fluidity, exceptionality in the production of ideas and expression of ideas, creative movement, creative thinking and kin esthetic behavior can also characterize the gifted learner, in addition to cognitive test results, necessary to consider what is natural for the child or young person (Torrance, 1965).

Giftedness is a characteristic of the learner's performance, represented by the particularities of the individual as regards the cognitive, affective and moral level, and that goes beyond the learner's interests, choices and attitudes (Bahia, 2011).

According to Pfeiffer & Blei (2008), teachers perceive giftedness through more specific characteristics such as creativity, fast and easy learning, learning initiative, curiosity, broad knowledge, academic talent and motivation, and there is a tendency to treat differently learners who have academic potential higher than theirpeers.

Therefore, the criteria adopted by a teacher, based on a certain theory about giftedness, define the characteristics that will be considered in the behavior and performance of the gifted learner. Thus, characterization of giftedness will be dependent on what the learner expresses and what the teacher intends to observe regarding cognition, affectivity and morality, highlighting the learning rhythm and performance of the learner (Almeida, Fleith, & Oliveira, 2013; Bahia, 2011; Delpretto & Zardo, 2010; Kaufman & Sternberg, 2008; Pfeiffer & Blei, 2008).

In this approach it is possible to recognize that the perceptions regarding giftedness hardly involve recognition of questions about the affectivity and learning of a gifted learner, but rather the specificity that this individual should have a differentiated educational performance. According to Freitas & Pérez (2012) one can observe certain characteristics as indicators of giftedness. These are: precocity and taste for reading, varied and different interests from their peers, asynchronism (affective, intellectual, language, child-school, or family relationship), preference for working or studying alone, developed sense of humor, perfectionism, higher observation skills, leadership, and a preference for games that require strategies.

When affectivity is approached as a variable that is seldom analyzed by education professionals in the context of the pedagogical approach of educational interventions, and in the process of identification of giftedness, the conception appears that giftedness is seen as mostly related to cognition, academic content and little linked to the social and the global development of the learner (Dal Forno, Veiga & Bahia, 2015). Therefore, identification of giftedness is linked to the fact that the quality and the "scope of the effect of the educational process are largely circumscribed by what is emphasized in the system of measurement and evaluation" (Lück & Carneiro, 1983, p. 13).

Thus, as Bahia & Trindade (2012) describe, it is necessary to recognize the meaning of the affective and emotional dimensions of the learner and not only the meaning of the cognitive and rational dimensions. In relation to the latter, it is as if the consideration of the learner's performance or engagement, or his or her motivation and performance were associated with cognitive potential, disregarding or giving little consideration to the significance of the social, emotional and relationships established in the classroom.

Tapia (1997; 2005) described how motivation of the learner is a dependent variable and related to the classroom climate, the relationship established between teacher and student, the relationship established between peers and the way learners relate to their own learning profile, pace and style. This challenges us to review identification of giftedness over the academic course of the student which disregardstheir feelings and perceptions as an apprentice and a developing individual.

Some studies on the myths of giftedness and some research with gifted people have revealed that some individuals are not recognized as gifted because their performance or their learning style are incongruent with what is expected from the school and the learning system. In spite of the recognition of studies that de-characterize giftedness linked only to high intellectual quotient or to high academic performance, it is noted that some education professionals still associate giftedness with academic factors and contents linked to logic-mathematics and language.

A study with kindergarten teachers regarding their perception of giftedness and characteristics that are recognized as being those of a gifted learner concluded that these professionals tend to value characteristics linked to academic factors and, in the case of the teachers of 3 to 5-year-old children, they consider items related to logical thinking, knowledge domain, attraction for challenge and ability to generate unexpected solutions (Dal Forno, Veiga & Bahia, 2015). The Characterization of Giftedness Scale (*Escala de Caracterização da Sobredotação – ECS*) was developed and fully studied to this end.

Table 1 shows the distribution of Brazilian and Portuguese kindergartenteachers in relation to ECS variable disagreement (D) and agreement (C) according to the nationality of the educator. It should be emphasized that the perception of the kindergarten teachers is reflected in the understanding of characteristics linked to the dimension of high cognitive abilities.

TABLE 1 – Distribution of ECS variable disagreement (D) and agreement (A) according to the nationality of the educator

Dimension	Item		Brazil	Portugal	Total (N=245)
	Vivacity	D	12.1%	22.9%	17%
		A	87.9%	77.1%	83%
	Sense of humor	D	27.6%	37.3%	32%
		A	72.4%	62.7%	68%
	Ease of expression	D	25.8%	12.6%	19.8%
		A	74.2%	87.4%	80.2%
	Flexibility with ideas	D	19.4%	13.6%	16.8%
		A	80.6%	86.4%	83.2%
	Taste for innovation	D	6.7%	13.6%	9.8%
		A	93.3%	86.4%	90.2%
	Sensitivity	D	12.7%	14.8%	13.6%
		A	87.3%	85.2%	86.4%
	Sense of justice	D	23.1%	19.3%	21.4%
		A	76.9%	80.7%	78.6%
	Honesty	D	18.0%	21.6%	19.7%
		A	82.0%	78.4%	80.3%
	Self-confidence	D	11.3%	31.2%	20.2%
		A	88.7%	68.8%	79.8%
Adaptability	Creativity	D	4.5%	14.5%	9.1%
		A	95.5%	85.5%	90.9%
	Taste foradventure	D	17.2%	31.8%	23.8%
		A	82.8%	68.2%	76.2%
	Solidarity	D	24.8%	29.4%	26.9%
		A	75.2%	70.6%	73.1%
	Ease in establishing relationships	D	34.3%	52.7%	42.6%
		A	65.7%	47.3%	57.4%
	Self criticism	D	17.5%	24.5%	20.7%
		A	82.5%	75.5%	79.3%
	Leadership	D	20.1%	30.3%	24.7%
		A	79.9%	69.7%	75.3%
	Ability to cooperate	D	28.4%	33.0%	30.5%
		A	71.6%	67.0%	69.5%
	Organizational skills	D	18.9%	28.4%	23.2%
		A	81.1%	71.6%	76.8%
	Ability to adapt (ideas, people)	D	26.1%	41.8%	33.2%
		A	73.9%	58.2%	66.8%
	Self-consciousness	D	18.7%	17.4%	18.1%
		A	81.3%	82.6%	81.9%

Category	Characteristic				
High Cognitive Abilities	High performance	D	6.0%	11.7%	8.6%
		A	94.0%	88.3%	91.4%
	Autonomy	D	10.4%	25.5%	17.2%
		A	89.6%	74.5%	82.8%
	Perfectionism	D	19.4%	21.6%	20.4%
		A	80.6%	78.4%	79.6%
	Precocity in development	D	12.9%	6.4%	9.9%
		A	87.1%	93.6%	90.1%
	Learning ease	D	7.5%	3.6%	5.7%
		A	92.5%	96.4%	94.3%
	Good memory	D	9.0%	2.7%	6.1%
		A	91.0%	97.3%	93.9%
	Abstraction Ability	D	7.5%	17.1%	11.9%
		A	92.5%	82.9%	88.1%
	Domain of knowledge	D	5.3%	1.8%	3.7%
		A	94.7%	98.2%	96.3%
	Logical thinking	D	3.0%	2.7%	2.9%
		A	97.0%	97.3%	97.1%
	Self demanding	D	8.3%	7.3%	7.9%
		A	91.7%	92.7%	92.1%
	Attraction for complexity	D	8.2%	4.6%	6.6%
		A	91.8%	95.4%	93.4%
	Demanding towards others (parents, educators, colleagues)	D	8.2%	8.2%	8.2%
		A	91.8%	91.8%	91.8%
	High academic ability	D	11.3%	16.4%	13.6%
		A	88.7%	83.6%	86.4%
	Attraction for challenges	D	2.3%	6.3%	4.1%
		A	97.7%	93.7%	95.9%
	Need for privacy	D	16.5%	9.1%	13.2%
		A	83.5%	90.9%	86.8%
	Restlessness	D	11.3%	11.9%	11.6%
		A	88.7%	88.1%	88.4%
Learning management	Critical questioning with others	D	7.5%	4.5%	6.1%
		A	92.5%	95.5%	93.9%
	Wittiness	D	5.3%	10.8%	7.9%
		A	94.7%	89.2%	92.1%
	Analytical ability	D	15.3%	6.5%	11.3%
		A	84.7%	93.5%	88.7%
	Ability to generate differentiated solutions	D	3.8%	6.5%	5.0%
		A	96.2%	93.5%	95.0%
	Persistence	D	7.5%	17.8%	12.0%
		A	92.5%	82.2%	88.0%
	Observational skills	D	5.2%	8.3%	6.6%
		A	94.8%	91.7%	93.4%

Nonconformity	Disinterest in routine activities	D	21.6%	8.1%	15.5%
		A	78.4%	91.9%	84.5%
	Indiscipline	D	41.8%	30.9%	36.9%
		A	58.2%	69.1%	63.1%
	Developmental dyssynchrony	D	26.8%	12.4%	20.3%
		A	73.2%	87.6%	79.7%

The recognition of giftedness through these characteristics shows that the majority (≥90%) of the 245 educators who participated in this study recognize giftedness and characterize it as a variable in the learning process, but little linked to issues that refer to characteristics such as self-confidence or sense of humor (Dal Forno, Veiga& Bahia, 2015). This information can be seen in the items highlighted in this chapter, and which reflect that approximately 237 (97.1%) of kindergarten teachers consider logical thinking as the main characteristic of giftedness, followed by knowledge domain (96.3%) and attraction to challenge (95.9%).

Table 2 shows the distribution of Brazilian and Portuguese schoolchildren in relation to ECS variable disagreement (D) as a function of the educator's perception. It can be seen that some education professionals still disregard some characteristics related to giftedness. The following table lists items with a percentage higher than 20%, i.e. representing a margin of 50 kindergarten educators.

TABLE 2 – Distribution of ECS variable disagreement (D) according to the educator's perception

Dimension	Item		Brazil	Portugal	Total (N=245)
	Sense of justice	D	23.1%	19.3%	21.4%
	Solidarity	D	24.8%	29.4%	26.9%
	Ease in establishing relationships	D	34.3%	52.7%	42.6%
	Self criticism	D	17.5%	24.5%	20.7%
Adaptability	Leadership	D	20.1%	30.3%	24.7%
	Ability to cooperate	D	28.4%	33.0%	30.5%
	Organizational skills	D	18.9%	28.4%	23.2%
	Ability to adapt (ideas, people)	D	26.1%	41.8%	33.2%
High Cognitive Abilities	Perfectionism	D	19.4%	21.6%	20.4%
	Indiscipline	D	41.8%	30.9%	36.9%
Nonconformity	Developmental dyssynchrony	D	26.8%	12.4%	20.3%

Table 2 depicts that ease in establishing relationships is disregarded by approximately 104 kindergarten teachers as being related to giftedness. Items such as adaptability and ability to cooperate are also discordant. This allows us to recognize that the perception of kindergarten teachersdoes not include in its characterization of the gifted learner items pertaining tobehavior regarding social relations and attitudes. This understanding is based on the finding that for approximately 91 kindergarten teachers there is disagreement as to indiscipline as a characteristic of giftedness, but also that most of the items on the scale that are judged to be in disagreement with characterization of giftedness belong to the Adaptability dimension.

The Adaptability dimension refers to the items of characterization of giftedness from the perspective that the gifted show ease in establishing relationships in the classroom context and in relation to their interests and styles. This dimension accounts for that part of the scale with most items with percentage disagreement. On the other hand, the High Cognitive Abilities dimension refers to the items related to performance precocity that the gifted learner should present in the teaching-learning process, and this dimension stands out as having highest percentage agreement with characterization of giftedness.

It is possible to recognize that early childhood teachers participating in the 2015 study by Dal Forno, Veiga and Bahia, as well as education professionals who took part in studies conducted by Al-Hadabi (2010), Almeida et al. (2001), Hany (1993), and Nogueira (2003) consider giftedness based on schoolchildren's development and academic learning, and distanced themselves from behavioural factors. Educational professionals tend to consider and attribute giftedness to intellectual factors, to academic development of schoolchildren, and diverge from factors that could relate to the accelerated behavior and social development of schoolchildren.

Seeking to single out gifted schoolchildren based on their characteristics as described in the literature can lead to their identification and suggests that the recognition and evaluation of a possible diagnosis of giftedness by means of the most common features and characteristics described are exactly those that can more easily be verified. This has repercussions on the discussion presented in Dewey's theory that education professionals need to understand that there is a practice that must be added to educational conceptualizations, not just a technicality of the evaluation and teaching process (Mattar, 2010).

The removal of emotional, social and affective factors can occur due to the use of concepts that describe a gifted learner as an individual who has emotional problems and lack of social inclusion (Bahia &Trindade, 2012). Therefore, assessments and evaluations made by educational professionals are based on descriptive elements, without an analysis of the context of the learner, the classroom and the specific process regarding development and learning, such as pace and style of learning. It should be emphasized that all these descriptors should collaborate with the inclusion process, with the pedagogical approach and interventions, as support for inclusive education and a pedagogical practice oriented towards equal rights, opportunities and pedagogical strategies involving the promotion of autonomy and access to citizenship for all (Brazil, 2008; Fleith et al., 2010; Miranda & Almeida, 2012).

In this perspective, one of the reflections that arises concerns the extent to which teachers and educators promote pedagogical interventions and considerthemselves asmere facilitators of learning, and not as mediators who can and should intervene beyond academic issues in social, relationship and learning about citizenship and individuality. This strategy approachesintelligence as a process, and not as a product, as if the gifted learner already possesses all the conditions for more autonomous development, considering onlyresults, seen as excellent academic performance.

The process of inclusion of the gifted infers that the education professional needs to identify the specificities of the learner, analyze strategies that collaborate towards the overall development of the learner, rather than strictly focusing on the constraints of the literature and failing to consider the individual who lives in the classroom.

Proposal for inclusion of affectivity in conceptions about giftedness

When giftedness is recognized as the presence of differentiated and specific factors and it is recognized that the gifted person can be identified as a learner with special educational needs (Brazil, 2015), the action of school inclusion has repercussions on what education proposes to achieve. This implication influences the way in which the teacher seeks to organize interventions, and how the learner's content, methodology and specificities converge.

The inclusion of the gifted impacts on understanding what their specificities are, how their differences are identified and inquiring as to how pedagogical interventions can promote development and learning. That is to say, perception of the learner's development and learning is gained through a sum of the details of their achievements in performing school tasks which allow the teacher to observe and analyze learning styles, level of development and rhythm of the interlocution between the processes that take place in the construction of the individual (Azevedo&Mettrau, 2010; Barreto&Mettrau, 2011).

Affectivity is seldom referred to in the literature on inclusion and giftedness. The concept of inclusion is perceived as an action to adapt methodology and educational proposals to the needs of the learner, thus promoting classes that are congruent with the learner, the classroom, and the role of the school (Brazil, 2015). The concept of giftedness is related to cognitive issues, and even when approaches are made as to possibilities of high abilities in the psychomotor or social area, a characterization based on performance and results is presented.

Valentim, Vestena and Neumann (2014) have described how it is relevant for educational professionals to identify, based on childhood education, how children construct their knowledge, how they relate to peers, and how they create and promote their affective bonds. In the case of giftedness, there is a common recognition that the child is advanced in terms of intellectual development and emotional immaturity (Pérez &Freitas, 2011). However, little is discussed about the importance of this variable in children's development and learning, when their learning and skills are above average.

As described by Wallonian theory, affectivity and affective development are important for schoolchildren, "as a means of obtaining a balanced and necessary construction for their personal and social adjustment" (Lück & Carneiro, 1983, p.13). This lack of verification and attention to affectivity within the process of schoolchildren's development and learning may well be reflected in the indifference or difficulties that gifted schoolchildren present in their performances.

Some authors indicate that isolation, need for individual work, concern for personal issues, immaturity and questioning behavior are characteristic of gifted individuals. Not recognizing them as a part of the gifted may suggest that there are no problems and that teachers should not intervene when the learner demands that these characteristics be respected and accepted.

In Dewey's conception, school is a space that should encourage learners to understand their social role and educational roles. The inclusion process ends up, therefore, surpassing methodological and pedagogical issues, and demands of the educational professional a mediating role for the global development of the learners, without disregarding all the spheres in which it occurs.

What stands out is that the process of including gifted learner demands attention to personal variables and not excessive focuson the pace and style of learning in order to identify above average potential and abilities. It is necessary to understand that when accompanied during the school process, a pupil with giftedness presents different outcomes, according to personal variables. Or as described by Tapia (1997, 2005), the gifted at school go through different moments in the development and learning process in accordance with the type of feedback, pedagogical proposal of the education professional and the climate between peers.

It is not congruent to believe that a gifted student does not need teacher mediation, or that he or she does not have to be accompanied in the course of knowledge development, because he or she already possesses conditions of cognitive autonomy, for example. We still have in the classroom a learner who has the need to be recognized, perceived, understood and engaged by the education professional. A gifted learner who has abilities, aptitudes and specificities, who needs to be viewed beyond academic questions, and who has a specific affective need, since he or she sometimes has characteristics of isolation, difficulty in relation to peers, or shyness, as stated in literature. The teacher should not understand this characterization as something irreversible, constant, and common to the gifted individual.

When some kindergarten teachers fail to recognize the ability to work with peers, the ability to organize and the ability to establish relationships as characteristics of a gifted learner, it can be seen that what has stood out from this type of school education is that it has or should have homogeneous development, but that this does not occur. Bahia and Trindade (2012) argue that the emotional development of gifted learners is a result of their adaptability in relation to their spaces, to what is required of them, and to how they recognize themselves in different universes, which again reinforces the relevance of the role of the classroom and educational strategies of an educational professional as a means of influencing. Recognition of this reverberates the idea that the response of the school environment is not only its own product.

Adapted from this discussion is an approach developed by Lück and Carneiro (1983), which describes that one of the problems of promoting affective development in school refers to the "lack of positive attitudes and adequate understanding of teachers and technicians in education, with respect to the need to promote affective development"with the purpose of recognizing and encouraging the complete development of the school. It is important to highlight the importance of creating "situations, conditions, mechanisms and resources necessary to promote affective development" (Lück&Carneiro, 1983, p. 14).

What is perceived is that in the process of inclusion of giftedness, a variable that needs to be identified and elaborated in educational strategies is affectivity. In the sense of the affective development of the school, with the intention of providing the learner not only with moments and processes that refer to cognition, but retaking the perspective of Dewey's theory as to the promotion of the school and social role of each school or in the perspective of Wallon's theory regarding the intercalations of intelligence and affectivity in students' learning. It can be identified that "becoming aware of oneself is fundamental to those who choose to be educators, since educating has the principle to change something and change is based on self-development" (Valentim et al., 2014, p. 722).

To learn is to develop, or to develop is to learn.The appropriate order of these variables is consistent with learning theories. However, what has been lacking in actions aimed at inclusion of gifted students is understanding of the integral development of this individual, and recognition that affectivity is a variable that has been recognized since the beginning of the studies of the psychology of education as a means of promoting motivation in learning and motivation of learning.

References

Al-Hadabi, A. (2010). Yemeni Basic Education Teacher's Perception of Gifted Students' Characteristics and the Methods used for Identifying these Characteristics. *Procedia Social and Behavioral Sciences,* 7(C), 480--487.

Almeida, L., Fleith, D., & Oliveira, E. (2013). *Sobredotação: Respostas Educativas.* Braga: ADIPSIEDUC.

Almeida, M., & Capellini, V. (2005). Alunos Talentosos: Possíveis Superdotados não Notados. *Revista Educação, 1* (55), 45-64

Almeida, L., Silva, E., Oliveira, E., Palhares, C., Melo, A., & Rodrigues, A. (2001). Conhecimento e Perceções dos Professores na Área da Sobredotação. *Sobredotação, 2* (2), 139-153.

Azevedo, S., &Mettrau, M. (2010). Altas Habilidades/Superdotação: Mitos e Dilemas Docentes na Indicação para o Atendimento. *Psicologia, Ciência e Profissão, 30*(1), 32-45.

Bahia, S. (2006). Estimular Talentos na Sala de Aula: Os Múltiplos Prismas da Questão. In A. Candeias, *Múltiplos Olhares Sobre Como Intervir* (pp. 160--174). Évora: Universidade de Évora.

Bahia, S. (2011). A vida emocional e afetiva dos alunos sobredotados. *Revista Diversidades, 34,* 7-10.

Bahia, S., & Trindade, J.P. (2012) Emoções na Sobredotação: da teoria à prática. *Revista AMAzônica,* X(1), 165-185.

Barreto, C., & Mettrau, M. (2011). Altas Habilidades: Uma Questão Escolar. *Revista Brasileira de Educação Especial, (17)3,* 413-426.

Brazil, MEC. (2008, january*). Política Nacional de Educação Especial Na perspectiva da Educação Inclusiva.* Ministério da Educação/ SEESP. Retrieved from http://portal.mec.gov.br/arquivos/pdf/politicaeducespecial. pdf.

Brazil, MEC. (06 de Julho de 2015) *Lei Federal de Inclusão.* Ministério da Educação/ MEC. Retrieved from www.planalto.gov.br/ccivil_03/_ato2015-2018/2015/lei/l13146.htm

Corte, E. (2013). Giftedness considered from the perspective of research on learning and instruction. *High Ability Studies, 34(1)*, 3-19.

Cross, T., & Coleman, L. (2014). School-Based Conception of Giftedness. *Journal for the Education of the Gifted, 37(1)*, 94-103.

Dal Forno, L., Veiga, F., & Bahia, S. (2015) *Indicios de Sobredotação e Criatividade na Criança: Perceções de educadores do pré-escolar no Brasil e em Portugal.* (Tese de Doutorado) Instituto de Educação: Universidade de Lisboa.

Delpretto, B., & Zardo, S. (2010). Alunos com Altas Habilidades/Superdotação no Contexto da Educação Inclusiva. In B. Delpretto, *A Educação Especial na Perspectiva da Inclusão Escolar: Altas Habilidades/Superdotação* (pp. 19-24). Brasília: Ministério da Educação/SEESP.

Feldman, R.S. (2015) *Introdução à Psicologia.* Artmed: Porto Alegre.

Fleith, D. S., & *Alencar*, E. M. L. S. (2007) *Desenvolvimento de talentos e altas habilidades: orientação a pais e professores.* Artmed: Porto Alegre.

Fleith, D., Almeida, L., Alencar, E., & Miranda, L. (2010). Educação do Aluno Sobredotado no Brasil e em Portugal: uma análise comparativa. *Revista Lusófona de Educação, 16*, 75-88.

Freitas, S., & Pérez, S. (2012). *Altas Habilidades/ Superdotação: atendimento especializado.*Marília: ABPEE.

Gagné, F. (2014). The DMGT: Changes within, beneath, and beyond. In F. Piske, J. Machado, S. Bahia, & T. Stoltz, *Altas Habilidades/Superdotação (AH/SD): Criatividade e Emoção* (pp. 19-42). Curitiba: Juruá Psicologia ABDR.

Gallagher, J. (2008). Psychology, Psychologists, and Gifted Students. In S. Pfeiffer, *Handbook of giftedness in Children: psychoeducational theory, research, and best practices* (pp. 1-11). New York: Springer Verlag.

Hany, E. (1993). How Teachers Identify Gifted Students: Feature Processing or Concept Based Classification. *European Journal of High Ability, 4(2)*, 196-211.

Heller, K., Mönks, F., Sternberg, R., &Subotnik, R. (2002). *International Handbook of Giftedness and Talent* (2nd ed.). London: Pergamon.

Kaufman, S., & Sternberg, R. (2008).Conceptions Of Giftedness. In S. Pfeiffer, *Handbook of Giftedness in Children: psychoeducational theory, research, and best practices* (pp. 71-91). New York: Springer Verlag.

Lück, H., & Carneiro, D.G. (1983).*Desenvolvimento afetivo na escola: Promoção, medida e avaliação*. Vozes: Rio de Janeiro.

Mattar, S. (2010) *Sobre arte e educação: Entre a oficina artesanal e a sala de aula*. Papirus: Campinas.

MEC. (2008, january). *Política Nacional de Educação Especial Na perspectiva da Educação Inclusiva*. Ministério da Educação/ SEESP. Retrieved from http://portal.mec.gov.br/arquivos/pdf/politicaeducespecial.pdf.

Miranda, L., & Almeida, L.S. (2012) Sinalização de alunos sobredotados e talentosos: Perfil de desempenho em provas psicológicas e percepção dos professores. *Revista AMAzônica, 3*, 146-164.

Nogueira, S. (2003). A sobredotação vista por docentes do pré-escolar e do 1º ciclo do ensino básico. *Sobredotação, 4(1)*, 95-107.

Pérez, S., & Freitas, S. (2011). Encaminhamentos Pedagógicos com Alunos com Altas Habilidades/ Superdotação na Educação Básica: Cenário Brasileiro. *Educar em Revista, 41*, 109-124.

Pfeiffer, S., & Blei, S. (2008). Gifted Identification Beyond the IQ Test. In S. Pfeiffer, *Handbook of Giftedness in Children: psychoeducational theory, research, and best practices* (pp. 177-198). New York: Springer Verlag.

Piske, F., & Stoltz, T. (2012) O desenvolvimento afetivo de alunos superdotados: Uma contribuição a partir de Piaget. *Revista de Psicologia e Epistemologia Genética, 4*(1), 149-166.

Renzulli, J. (2010). El Rol del Profesor en el Desarrollo del Talento.*Revista Electrónica Interuniversitaria de Formacion del Profesorado REIFOP, 13*(1), 33-40.

Sprinthall, N., & Sprinthall, R. (1993). *Psicologia Educacional: Uma abordagem Desenvolvimentista*.Portugal: McGraw–Hill.

Sternberg, R., Jarvin, L., & Grigorenko, E. (2011). *Explorations in Giftedness*. New York: Cambridge University Press.

Tapia, J.A. (1997)*Motivar para el aprendizaje: Teorías y Estrategias*. Edebelé: Spain.

Tapia, J.A. (2005) Motivación para elaprendizaje: La perspectiva de los alumnos. In *Ministerio deEducación y Ciencia. La orientación escolar en centros educativos*. Madrid: MEC, 209-242.

Torrance, E. (1965). *Cómo es el NiñoSobredotado y Cómo Enseñarle*. Buenos Aires: Paidós.

Valentim, B.F.B., Vestena, C.L., & Neumann, P. (2014) Educadores e estudantes: um olhar para a afetividade nas Altas Habilidades/Superdotação. *Revista Educação Especial*, 27(50), 713-724.

Virgolim, A. (2007). Altas Habilidades e Desenvolvimento Intelectual. In D. Fleith, & E. Alencar, *Desenvolvimento de Talentos e Altas Habilidades* (pp. 25-40). Porto Alegre: Artes Médicas.

5.

SOCIAL AND AFFECTIVE INTERACTION OF GIFTED STUDENTS

Fernanda Bachini de Oliveira

Graduated in Pedagogy from the Federal University of Paraná, Brazil.

ORCID: 0000-0003-2400-1190

Tania Stoltz

Full Professor at the Federal University of Parana, Brazil.

ORCID: 0000-0002-9132-0514.

Abstract: *This chapter explores the social and affective interaction of students with high skills. Based on an extensive literature review on the multidimensional character of giftedness, so often neglected by the educational system due to lack of knowledge or misrecognition on the part of teachers and school communities. The chapter presents us with data collected through three interviews and observation and systematic observations and concludes that the physical space of the school context allows social and affective interactions. The chapter also shows how activities are planned and proposed according to the space available. Classes are organized with the aim of promoting exchange of knowledge amongst students and this occurs both in*

intentional activities and games and also in the interchange arising from individual assignments. The authors lead us to a reflection on the relevance of factors that are not very well understood in theory and practice, thus opening up our own horizons.
Keywords: *Social; Affective; Interaction; Gifted.*

Introduction

Giftedness is, according to Joseph Renzulli (2004), the interrelation of three factors: above-average ability, creativity and involvement with the task. Notwithstanding, when most people talk about this issue they relate it to brilliant subjects who create extraordinary and unique things, learning by themselves, without the need for help. According to Winner (1998), this reveals myths that hinder both the identification and the guarantee of provision of adequate attention to these subjects.

High ability subjects are present in classrooms and demonstrate the most diverse abilities, not just in academic areas, but also in productive and creative areas, and this may be just one or several areas. This is a fact that many authors refer to as the multidimensional character of giftedness.

Nevertheless, in our education system, these students are often neglected, not by legislation, but rather in practice, owing to lack of knowledge or misconceived knowledge on the part of teachers and school communities, as well as lack of specialized and inclusive schooling for these students. Initiatives in this area are still at the embryonic stage and need to be scaled up.

The definition of giftedness is also neither clear nor precise. Notwithstanding, it is our understanding that this is a result of this field being raveled in myths, lack of knowledge and lack of understanding of its multidimensional character and the need for specialized service provision. As such, the aim of this paper is to understand how social and affective development of high ability/gifted students occurs in the multifunctional resources classroom of a municipality in the metropolitan area of Curitiba. Not all cities provide differentiated schooling for these students, and schooling is also precarious both with regard to differentiated activities in regular classrooms and curricular adaptations, and also with regard to curricular enrichment initiatives for these students during free school periods.

The need therefore exists to observe the perspective of the multifunctional resources classroom teacher who is in contact with various students, with different characteristics and abilities, grouped together in the most diverse forms, as well as being in contact with their families and regular education teachers, specifically in order to understand how social and affective interaction occurs in this space. Social and affective interaction is often relegated to second place by the education system, with much emphasis on maximizing academic potentials to the detriment of harmonious and integral student development.

Literature review

The field of Giftedness is quite new with regard to Brazilian academic production, as are the schooling initiatives put into place by legislation that recognizes it as a special educational need.

The trend taken by the most recent literature on the theme of Gifted students regarding matters of educational inclusion is no longer seen to be directed towards the quest for conquests in public policies and legislation, but rather on the contrary shows clear recognition of the theme and ensuring the legal requirement of specialized schooling.

Notwithstanding, scientific research indicates that in practice this process faces many obstacles to the effective inclusion and schooling needed by these subjects being fully achieved. Pérez & Freitas (2011) point out that:

> The invisibility of HA/G students is closely linked to lack of information about the theme and about legislation that provides for their schooling, as well as to lack of academic and teacher training, as well as to the cultural representation of High Ability/Gifted People (HA/GP). (Pérez & Freitas, 2011, p. 111).

In general the research we consulted indicates that teachers fail to identify and fail to attend to the need of these students, given that according to Bahiense & Rosseti (2014), the role played by schools and teachers in identifying them is very important. Identification occurs through daily contact with them. Failure to identify them is a consequence of lack of knowledge on the part of teachers, not about legislation, but rather a lack of clear understanding about what giftedness is.

Martins & Alencar (2011) indicate that the obstacles to providing these students with special schooling arise especially from teacher training whereby this lack of knowledge happens owing to outdated initial and continuing teacher training. Satisfactory training is not being provided to support teachers in identifying and working with these students.

Another factor facilitating failure to recognize these students, according to authors such as Azevedo & Mettrau (2010), Bahiense & Rosseti (2014), Barreto & Mettrau (2011), Cianca & Marquezine (2014), Mori & Brandão (2009), Pérez (2003), Pérez &Freitas(2011),

Rech& Freitas (2005a), Soares, Arco-Verde & Baibich(2004) and Vieira (2010), are myths surrounding Gifted students. These influence the view teachers have of these subjects and prevent them from identifying and referring these students to specialized schooling, both within and outside of regular education. Martins & Alencar (2011) also highlight that,

> In order for schools to become places that promote talents, teachers need to be better guided and to let go of longstanding paradigms, by showing attitudes and using teaching strategies that are attentive to the needs of their students. (Martins & Alencar, 2011, p. 33).

Our literature review found that the theoretical discussion fails to approach the issue of whether Giftedness is of an innate or an environmental character. It places more focus on the fact that there is still no single definition of Giftedness, as well as stressing the existence of Giftedness in several areas, either separate or together, in both academic and creative spheres, thus implying that their identification is not based solely on *IQ tests* (Soares, Arco-Verde & Baibich, 2004; Rech & Freitas, 2005b). The Brazilian literature we examined was found to cite various authors, although Joseph Renzulli stands out among them as his theory of the *Three Rings* stating that Gifted students are those having interrelated above-average ability, creativity and involvement with the task was used as a reference in the majority of the works we reviewed. As a rule the papers take Renzulli as the theoretical basis for their studies. Some papers go into Renzulli's theory itself in further depth, such as the studies of Barreto & Mettrau (2011), Fleith (2006) and Pérez (2009).

The majority of research was found to be based on the spoken interviews of teachers and only a few on the interviews of school administrators and students, so that what students who have gone through this process have to say has been very little explored thus far.

Taking into consideration that "identification will make sense if there is a teaching proposal in line with the needs of students with specific characteristics" (Azevedo & Mettrau, 2010, p. 34), the relevance of our study lies in the fact that the focus of most studies of Giftedness is more directed towards identifying these students than the quality of schooling in multifunctional resources classrooms. Our study also examines the social and affective interaction of these students which is a subject little explored by the research we consulted.

Materials and methods

This is a qualitative and exploratory study. Its methods comprise semi-structured interviews with teachers who work in a multifunctional resources classroom for Gifted students, as well as observation in that classroom which was recorded in a field diary. The subjects taking part in the study are teachers working in a multifunctional resources classroom attended by Gifted students during their free periods and provided by the Education Department of a municipality in the metropolitan area of Curitiba, Paraná, Brazil. Aguiar & Ozella's (2013) Meaning Cores method was used to analyze the data in the attempt to seek, through fluid reading, pre-indicators as well as to understand how the social and affective interaction of these students occurs in the space known as the multifunctional resources classroom, including from the point of view of teachers who work directly with these students.

The resource classroom teacher: a look at social and affective interaction.

All three education professionals working at the multifunctional resources classroom of a municipality in the metropolitan area of Curitiba were interviewed. The interviews took place over a one-month period based on six questions about social and affective interaction in the resources classroom. The study was authorized by the Municipal Education Department by means of an official letter. Each teacher agreed to take part by signing a Free and Informed Consent form. The identity of the Municipality and the participants is not revealed in the study.

Characterization of study participants

Teacher 1, referred to in this paper as Julia, has worked for four years in the resources classroom. She has specific training in giftedness and also has a gifted child of her own. Prior to this she worked as part of the special education evaluation team at the Municipal Education Department. She also teaches at a regular school when she is not working at the resources classroom. Teacher 2, referred to in this paper as Sheila, has a graduate degree in psychology and a master's degree and Ph.D. in education in the specific area of autism. When she worked at the Municipal Education Department she set up the multifunctional resources classroom for high ability students. She has worked for four years in this classroom. Teacher 3, referred to here as Celia, has worked for five months in the resources classroom. Although she does not have specific training, she states that she has vast knowledge of typical practices.

Analysis and discussion

The data collected through the interviews was analyzed by forming Meaning Cores as per the method proposed by Aguiar & Ozella (2006). As such, the speech of each teacher underwent fluid reading in order to identify pre-indicators based on meaningful aspects of their speech. Analysis of pre-indicators led to the identification of indicators by joining pre-indicators together and, finally, the indicators were agglutinated into Meaning Cores. The following sections discuss the meaning cores with the aim of understanding the social and affective interaction of the students who attended the multifunctional resources classroom for Giftedness. The observations undertaken in the classroom contributed to verifying the speech of the interviewed teachers and to structuring the meaning cores.

Meaning Core 1: resources room configuration and activity organization

This meaning core is defined by the way in which the multifunctional resources classroom is structured and by the dynamics of the activities proposed in that classroom. Different to regular education, the multifunctional resources classroom offers an environment that not only provides cognitive development, but also a space for interaction.

The resources classroom is offered to students at inclusive education centers. The municipality has two such centers, one of which operates in the morning and in the afternoon, whilst the other only operates in the afternoon. The municipality has a total of 50 students attending these facilities, plus a further seven students who opted not to attend them and five who are on the waiting list to attend them. The municipality provides transport for students to and from these centers.

The structure of the resources classroom is better than that of a common classroom, having large tables, chairs, cupboards and computers. It is in this simple but welcoming context that the teachers work on the development and accompaniment of these students.

The work undertaken in the resources classroom begins with choosing the composition of each class. The first criterion established by the Education Department is to separate students according to stage, separating initial grade students from final grade students.

> The first criterion we use is an Education Department directive to separate them according to the grade they are in, separating initial grades from final grades (Teacher Julia).

Nevertheless this Education Department criterion is a source of discontent for the teachers:

> We are no longer able to define our own strategy for organizing classes. This stifles our work a great deal, it makes my job much harder, because prior to this I put together students with study assignments that had more in common or were related and this enabled a greater degree of interaction. (Teacher Sheila).

The second criterion used to define class composition is area of interest. When students are grouped together by area of interest, a process of social and affective interaction is ensured, enabling a plurality of different abilities based on similar interests in order to build knowledge sharing, exchange points of view and build wisdom. This situation can be seen in the example put forward by Teacher Celia:

> There's a student who comes for the last classes on Monday and Thursday, he ends up being on his own, and I find it very hard to work with him, because he doesn't want to record things and interaction is difficult when there's only the two of us. On Thursday a new student started and the other student changed. They got on well together right from the start, they're the same age and have the same interests. So what did I do? I reorganized their timetables, so that they can work together. When I showed the project to the new student, he became interested, enthusiastic, whereas the other student who used to be on his own wasn't interested, although I encouraged and stimulated him, but on his own he wasn't interested at all. Now we're going to start over again with the two of them together and I think it's going to work. So at times we need to make changes so that this social and affective interaction between them happens. (Teacher Celia).

The words of the teacher show the importance of working with social and affective interaction and just how much she needs to pay attention to the needs and concerns of her student when organizing class composition. It is evident in this speech that the first student only began to develop after he began to interact with another student. Even though stimulating activities had been presented, interaction with peers was seen to be essential for this student's development.

All three education professionals interviewed consider that the second criteria for organizing class composition, by area of knowledge, should be the first, as ensuring the possibility of these exchanges transforms the exercise into something differentiated and valid.

> This makes my job much harder, because prior to this I put together students with study assignments that had more in common or were related and this enabled a greater degree of interaction. (Teacher Sheila).

According to the teachers, in previous years the criterion for selecting by school grade did not exist and as such it was easier for them to organize their students. Teacher Julia also highlights that the age difference between initial and final grades is not an obstacle to promoting interaction, on the contrary she states there are students from different grades who get on very well together (Teacher Julia).

These students attend the multifunctional resources classroom once a week during their free periods. In order to access the classroom the student must present a report, prepared based on an indication made by their regular education teacher and pedagogical team, whereby the student undergoes a series of tests and assessments with a multidisciplinary team. Following this diagnosis, these students get the attention they need in the resources classroom both as a stimulus to their abilities and also through the process of providing support in the subjects with which they need help.

> Identification of gifted students (...) enables educational activities to be scheduled and which will indeed raise these students to the level of specialist in the area in which they are talented, whatever it may be, whilst also facilitating the development of more complex forms of thinking which will enable students to reconceptualize their existing knowledge or create new knowledge. (Gama, 2014).

Initially the activities proposed in the resources classroom are games. Based on these games, the teachers observe the characteristics of each student, their potentials, difficulties and interests.

> Initially I gave them a lot of games to play. They are games that enable challenges and logical reasoning in addition to interaction, as they all play together. So, the first activities proposed were games, some of them were sequence games, not only because of this but also so that I could talk with them and get to know them. Following this they have to write a text, because I need to perceive how their writing is, a jig-saw puzzle to perceive how the visuomotor question functions, you know, and then you use games involving logical and mathematical reasoning, to see how that is as well. This way you get an all-round view at the beginning (Teacher Celia).

Games are used intentionally at this time, not in relation to contents to be given in different areas of knowledge, but as a way for the teachers to get to know their students, as well as enabling them to observe how the other members of the group relate to each other.

At this initial moment, the teachers seek to get to know the student and propose activities involving playing, especially games in view of their collective nature, not just to promote interaction but also in order to get closer to their students. It is noteworthy the importance given by these teachers to the students getting to know each other:

> We work a great deal with self-knowledge, this year we have worked in particular on the issue of multiple

Taking this speech it is evident that these teachers are concerned about student self-knowledge, so that students can get to know themselves and understand that they are not good at everything, and so that they can also understand the reality of others.

During the second stage of their work in the resources classroom, the teachers start to work with individual interests in order to prepare individual study assignments. To help them to do the assignment, students are encouraged to seek information from several sources and to share and interact with the group based on the information they find. Sizeable activities that are not of interest to the students are not undertaken, as they need to be motivated to seek knowledge to include in their assignment.

> How are we going to create a robot if no one understands anything about it? You have to propose things that meet their interests and build on that, that's how it is, they work together on assignments with each of them providing their contribution. (Teacher Celia).

The teachers seek to plan these strategies together. When they are not able to meet personally, they exchange notes and emails to ensure that the multifunctional resources classroom for High Ability/Giftedness works well, in the quest for inclusion and meeting the needs of the students who attend it in the most appropriate manner.

Meaning Core 2: resources classroom vs. regular education: possibilities

This meaning core is defined by differentiation and possibilities of interaction between multifunctional resources classrooms and regular education classrooms.

> The advantage of the resources classroom is that there are greater possibilities of interaction through the activities themselves, because they do games, they work with assignments and studies, and so they end up helping each other. In a regular classroom, where a teacher has thirty or forty students, interaction does take place, but its takes place during the break, even working in groups is more difficult there, so there's no doubt that the resources classroom makes much more possible. (Teacher Celia).

Based on this statement, we can understand how regular education is currently configured, in classrooms with large numbers of students, often with too many students per class, which makes it difficult for teachers to use different methodologies with the different students comprising the class. Another factor we can highlight is the physical structure of schools to accommodate this large amount of students. This factor is emphasized in the speech of the interviewed teacher:

> As there are fewer students we can get closer to them and also perceive in greater detail difficulties and possibilities, so it is very favorable and I really believe in this work. (Teacher Sheila).

Teachers do not consider themselves to be ready to deal with inclusion. The research of several authors, such as Azevedo & Mettrau (2010), Pérez & Freitas (2011) among others, demonstrates that teachers know nothing or little about Giftedness, in addition to having absorbed myths about these subjects, which not only affect the indication of these students for special education, but also the efforts to include them in regular education.

Regular education currently has a configuration that is peculiar to it, not only because of crammed classrooms, but also because of traditional teaching methods, exacerbated concern about contents to the detriment of methods; placing marks before learning and quantity before quality.

This context is prejudicial to the development process of any subject, as well as having great impact on gifted students who in cognitive terms have great learning ability and feel discouraged by the education system. In view of this, taking the words of the interviewed teacher, we can see the possibilities provided by the resources classroom:

> We have more time and knowing that they have the possibility of talking with each other, they talk all the time, they don't stop, and that's good because they perceive themselves through each other's differences and they often give accounts of how things are in the regular classroom and they are able to understand here why certain things happen there, it makes it easier. (Teacher Julia).

The smaller number of students, working based on games and activities aimed at self-knowledge and areas of interest stimulate the development of students with Giftedness. The multifunctional resources classroom for Gifted students is therefore an environment with greater freedom for social and affective interaction, as it enables students to dialogue about diverse themes and about knowledge they have, as well as providing an opening for exploring possible curiosities and queries that arise. Nevertheless the teachers also stress that the resources classroom also has its limitations:

> Now, with regard to the physical space, it doesn't offer us much, it's a classroom practically the same as the rest, and we have few resources for this, each teacher does their best to ensure what they think is fundamental. (Teacher Julia).

Despite these differences, it is important to highlight that these two areas of teaching, regular education and the resources classroom, need to be interconnected for the full development of gifted students to be achieved. The "exchange" between the regular class teacher, who spends most of the time with the gifted student, but often does not know how to act in relation to him/her, and the more specialized teacher who has closer contact with him/her, is fundamental for sharing knowledge and preparing strategies for the inclusion and development of gifted students.

> This space has other possibilities, different to those of regular education, it has many possibilities, so much so that there are often times when I talk with regular education teachers. I know this student much better than the regular class teacher because my group is smaller, because I have the opportunity to do different activities and get closer to this student, so I often know why he is behaving in a particular way in the classroom, why his performance is low in a given subject. The regular classroom teacher is not able to get this all-round

view. This space is fundamental for him, it couldn't be otherwise. (Teacher Julia).

This exchange can however be compromised to the extent that the resources classroom teacher, who works four days with his/her group of students and has one day to prepare lessons when he/she could talk with the regular classroom teacher, but their lesson preparation days do not coincide, thus hindering dialogue between teachers.

In the accounts of the interviewed teachers it can be clearly seen that all of them who have experience of regular education are convinced that the resources classroom is essential and is an important contribution to these students.

Meaning Core 3: interpersonal relations in the resources classroom.

This core meaning looks at the interactions in the resources classroom between students and their teacher based on the discourse of the interviewed teachers. In the preceding cores we looked at the configuration of the multifunctional resources classroom for Gifted students, ranging from its organization, activities proposed and how, from the point of view of the interviewed teachers, this work is differentiated from regular education. It can be seen that the multifunctional resources classroom is a differentiated space, but how do social and affective interactions take place there?

The literature shows us that these students are often depicted as being solitary, having little interaction with other students and having difficulty in relating socially. However, the discourses of the interviewed teachers reveal the opposite of this statement.

When asked how social and affective relations occur in the space called the multifunctional resources classroom, the teachers are convinced that:

> I think these moments happen all the time, as you can see, they are interactive, they talk incessantly, they talk about their feelings, this moment here in the high abilities classroom happens all the time, they repeatedly digress and talk about their study assignments, curiosities, these moments are happening all the time. (Teacher Sheila).

The classroom work proposal and all the factors listed above enable social and affective interaction to take place. According to Teacher Celia, it is something that happens naturally, it is the situations and configurations created there that enable these relations to occur. Notwithstanding, this process is not always harmonious.

> Usually they get on well, but problems happen in particular because many of them have leadership characteristics, so there is a lot of conflict and so we have to resolve these conflicts between them, so that they accept differences, perceive their own individual characteristics, and that at times they think they are better than someone else because they performed better in a given activity, so we frequently have to mediate these conflicts, but as a rule they relate well with each other, interact well, they take part in the activities. (Teacher Julia).

The efforts of the teacher to mediate these conflicts are essential. The teacher needs to pay attention in order to prevent possible cases of *bullying* and peer exclusion in the group. When there are fewer students, conflict mediation is seen to be more effective. This aspect can be found in the words of Teacher Julia,

> We try, at least I try, to carry outmost of the activities in a collective manner, to deal with what I know arises a lot as a difficulty in regular education, but even so I have cases of students who aren't able to work in groups in the regular classroom, that's why we focus more here on working as a group, so that students learn to accept the opinion of others. (Teacher Julia).

The relationship between multifunctional resources classroom students and teachers is quite smooth.

> In my case it's fine, I've never had problems and that's how it is all the time, I am very affectionate and that draws them to me, it makes them open up to me and tell me about their personal lives, their school lives, they feel at ease to talk about any problem they might have and during the activities we end up talking a lot, the space itself, the way the classroom is organized favors good interaction. (Teacher Julia).

This openness enables gifted students to form ties and this factor is intensified above all through the possibility of the same teacher working for several years with the same student.

> There are students who have been with us for a long time, they were diagnosed as having high abilities and they continue here, what happens most is that in the final years they change classes, but they have been with us for quite some time and interaction with them

is smooth, they are students we have known for years. Owing to the fact that there is now only one class in the morning and two in the afternoon, there are not many vacancies, so it's always the same students who are here because there are no new vacancies because these students continue in the process, so we know each other for longer. (Teacher Sheila).

The teachers' work, through the activities they propose, is in keeping with a more collective way of working that enables social and affective interaction between students. As such, we can see in what the teachers say that interactions in the resources classroom are not always harmonious and that there are interpersonal conflicts. Nevertheless, the way the resources classroom is organized provides possibilities for mediating these conflicts in different and quicker manners, owing to the closeness of the teacher, as well as the differentiated activities proposed, thus promoting more moments of interaction between these students than in the regular classroom.

Our observations of the school context revealed that the regular education classrooms are small. One of them has a lot of material and furniture stored in it, but few of these resources are useable for the activities.

Different to the regular education classroom, the resources classroom offers large round tables and this facilitates group interaction. On the days we carried out observation, the teachers worked on different activities, related to the stage of the study assignment built by each student. We were able to observe that in the resources classroom interaction takes place all the time and naturally, the students feel at ease to talk to each other, not just about the activity, but also about the most diverse themes. We observed that the teacher, as part of the group, dialogues with the students and it can be seen that they are always open to talking with her, telling her about the most diverse subjects. The resources classroom has an atmosphere of respect and freedom, the students talk all the time and are only brought into order when they exceed themselves.

Final considerations

In order to understand how social and affective interaction occurs in the resources classroom, we needed to go beyond just looking at relationships and also get to know the factors that promote them. The *Meaning Core* method enabled in-depth observation of the discourses of the interviewed teachers and the agglutination of these elements so as to be able to better understand the space called the resources classroom and the elements that promote interaction. The following cores were identified: *Resources room configuration and activity organization, Resources classroom vs. regular education: possibilities and Interpersonal relations in the resources classroom.*

After having got to know better the work developed in the classroom and its differential in relation to regular education, it was possible to understand that its space enables interactions, and that the activities are devised and proposed with this purpose. Based on the discourse of the interviewed teachers and our field diaries we were able to understand that social and affective interaction in this space is frequent, as there is an opening for such interactions to take place. The classes are organized with the aim of promoting exchange of knowledge between students and this occurs both in the games proposed and also in the exchange of knowledge arising from the individual study assignments. Even though Education Department rules are followed, an attempt is made to group these students together by area of interest and this enables them to interact and talk with each other in a more relaxed manner.

The strategies presented by the teachers, both with regard to classroom organization and the activities proposed, always aim to promote social and affective interaction between students. This interaction was found to be necessary for the development of these students. It is valued by the teachers and occurs between peers of different age groups who have things in common with regard to their interests.

Within this context, the field diaries helped us to verify the facts mentioned in the speech of the teachers. Through our observations we found that social interaction is very much present in the resources classroom and occurs in a natural and constant manner, both in the relations between students and also in the teacher/student relationship.

We observed that the students dialogue about the most diverse subjects, which may or may not be related to the activities they are working on, and that this dialogue is not forbidden or restricted by the teacher, but rather enriched and valued. The resources classroom is however also marked by conflicts between students, often owing to diverging opinions about different subjects and owing to disrespecting other students. Nevertheless the proximity of the teacher, owing to the reduced number of students, enables adequate mediation in the event of conflicts.

The resources classroom teacher is, in this context, one who continuously assesses their students, organizes the space, relations and the activities that promote interaction and development, whilst also being one who mediates conflicts arising from situations of disrespect. It is also this teacher who accompanies the gifted student and makes the link between regular education teams in the municipality studied.

As such, social and affective interaction in the multifunctional resources classroom in the municipality studied is directly related to the organization of the classroom, the activities proposed and mediation by the teacher in charge of the resources classroom.

As a proposal for future studies, the impacts of this form of teaching on regular education could be examined, as to whether it is really possible, based on quality inclusion, to provide gifted students with full development and that meets their educational needs.

References

Aguiar, W. M. J. & Ozella, S.(2006). Núcleos de significação como instrumento para a apreensão da constituição dos sentidos. *Revista Psicologia, Ciência e Profissão*. São Paulo, 26 (2), 222-245.

Aguiar, W. M. J. & Ozella, S.(2013). Apreensão dos sentidos: aprimorando a proposta dos núcleos de significação. *Revista Brasileira de Estudos Pedagógicos*. Brasília, 94 (236). Jan/Abr. 299-322.

Azevedo, S.M.L. & Mettrau, M.B.(2010). Altas habilidades/superdotação: mitos e dilemas docentes na indicação para o atendimento. *Psicologia, Ciência e Profissão*. 30, 32-45.

Bahiense, T.R.S. & Rossetti, C.B. (2014). Altas habilidades/ superdotação no contexto escolar: percepções de professores e prática docente. *Revista Brasileira de Educação Especial,* 2 (20), 195-208.

Barreto, C.M.P.F.& Mettrau, M.B. (2011). Altas habilidades: uma questão escolar. *Revista Brasileira de Educação Especial,* 17 (3), 413-426.

Cianca, F.S.C. & Marquezine, M.C.A.(2014). Percepção dos coordenadores de licenciaturas da UEL sobre altas habilidades/superdotação. *Revista Brasileira de educação Especial,* 4 (20), 591-604.

Fleith, D.S. (2006). Criatividade e altas habilidades/ superdotação. *Revista Educação especial.* Santa Maria. (28). 219-232.

Gama, M. C. S. S. (2014). As teorias de Gardner e de Sternberg na educação de superdotados. *Revista Educação Especial.* Santa Maria, 27 (50), set/ dez, 665-673.

Martins, A. C. S. & Alencar, E. S. (2011). Características desejáveis em professores de alunos com altas habilidades/ superdotação. *Revista Educação Especial*, Santa Maria, 24 (39), 31-46.

Mori, N.N.R. & Brandão, S. H.A. (2009). O atendimento em salas de recursos para alunos com altas habilidades/superdotação: o caso do Paraná. *Revista Brasileira de Educação Especial*, 3(15), 485-498.

Pérez, S. G. P. B. (2003). Mitos e crenças sobre as pessoas com altas habilidades: alguns aspectos que dificultam o seu atendimento. *Revista Educação Especial*, Santa Maria. 22, 45-59.

Pérez, S. G. P. B; (2009). A identificação das altas habilidades sob uma perspectiva multidimensional. *Revista Educação Especial*, Santa Maria, 22(35), 299-328.

Pérez, S.G.P.B. & Freitas, S.N. (2011). Encaminhamentos pedagógicos com alunos com altas habilidades/superdotação na educação básica: o cenário brasileiro. *Educar em revista*. 41. Editora UFPR: Curitiba, jul/set, 109-124.

Rech, A. J. D. & Freitas, S.N.(2005a). O papel do professor junto ao aluno com altas habilidades. *Revista Educação Especial*. Santa Maria, (25). 59-71.

Rech, A. J. D. & Freitas, S.N. (2005b). Uma análise sobre os mitos que envolvem os alunos com altas habilidades: a realidade de uma escola de Santa Maria/RS. *Revista Brasileira de Educação Especial*, 11 (2). Marília, mai/ago, 395-314.

Renzulli, J.S. (2004). O que é esta coisa chamada superdotação, e como a desenvolvemos: uma retrospectiva de vinte e cinco anos. *Revista Educação*, 27(1).

Soares, A.M.I., Arco-Verde, Y.F.S & Baibich, T.M. (2004). Superdotação: identificação e opções de atendimento. *Educar em Revista*, 23. Editora UFPR: Curitiba, 125-141.

Vieira, N. J. W. (2010). Políticas públicas educacionais no Rio Grande do Sul: indicadores para discussão e analise na área das altas habilidades/ superdotação. *Revista Educação Especial*, 23(37), 273-286.

Winner, E. (1998). *Crianças Superdotadas: mitos e realidades*. (S. Costa, Trad.). Porto Alegre: Artes Médicas.

6.

EMPATHETIC COMPASSION: EMPATHY, MORAL SENSITIVITY, AND OVEREXCITABILITY IN GIFTEDNESS

Alberto Rocha

President of the Board of the National Association for the Study and Intervention of Giftedness (A.N.E.I.S), Portugal.

ORCID: 0000-0002-5570-9872

Natanael Matos

Post-graduate in Clinical Psychology and Health from Fernando Pessoa University, Portugal.

ORCID: 0000-0003-1526-7368

Abstract: *This Chapter show us how compassion, altruism, decentration, defense of others, empathy, solidarity and affective and moral sensibility are features of emotional overexcitability. Moreover, different standards and intensity of overexcitability play a decisive role in the development of human potential and should be valued in the conception and intervention of giftedness in all its richness. The authors explain how further research on the potential of empathy, affective sensibility and moral sensitivity is needed due to all the growing risks humanity faces, and the inherent necessity to make* *good use of intelligence along with moral development. Most of the research in this domain is unempirical and the results are largely considered to be inconsistent, thus reinforcing the need for more in-depth studies on empathetic compassion.*

Keywords: Compassion; Altruism; Overexcitability; Moral Sensitivity.

Introduction

Empathetic compassion, as the highest state of empathy, raises the need to value this potential in giftedness, as well as a much needed and deeper investigation and reflection of the gifted exhibiting characteristics of emotional overexcitability, for whom these necessities have been imperative from an early age.

Emotional intensity and curiosity, early features in a large part of the gifted and talented (Piechowski, 2009), reveal this potential for compassion, empathy, and moral sensibility, manifested in a sense of justice or in concern with global human problems.

The call for research on the potential of empathy (affective sensibility) and moral sensitivity has been deemed urgent by the growing risks humanity faces, and the inherent necessity to make good use of intelligence along with moral development (Cross & Ambrose, 2009; Tannenbaum, 2000). A review of the available literature reveals a scarcity of articles on empirical investigation about empathy in giftedness (Lovecky, 2009). The results of investigations on the social development of gifted children have been considered largely inconsistent (Rinn, 2018).

Theory of Positive Disintegration and Overexcitability

Overexcitability, a fundamental concept of Dabrowski's (1972) Theory and Positive Disintegration (TDP), allows for the specific understanding of the socio-emotional development in the gifted and talented (Piechowski, 1997), with a greater relevance in the context of psychotherapy with the gifted (Mendaglio, 2007), as well as on the empirical investigation of giftedness (Mendaglio, 2012).

Dabrowski (1972) identified five areas in which gifted children and adolescents exhibited high intensity and intense behaviors, known as overexcitabilities, or supersensibilities. Psychomotor intensity (high levels of energy), sensory intensity (high awareness of the five senses), emotional intensity (exceptional emotional sensibility), intellectual sensitivity (intense mental activity, the most recognized in the gifted), or imaginative intensity (they play actively and freely with imagination). Psychotherapy with the gifted exhibiting these characteristics of intensity or overexcitability, raises relevant questions which allow for a better understanding of their needs, the emotional processes they undergo from an early age, and the emotional development which differentiates them.

Overexcitability has a decisive role in the potential for human development and clearly excels in the aforementioned five standards of overexcitability: Psychomotor, Sensory, Emotional, Intellectual, and Imaginative (Piechowski, 1986). These different standards of overexcitability display good independent dimensions from the psychometric point of view (Ackerman, 2009; Falk et al., 1999). Various instruments have been developed for the purpose of measuring and identifying overexcitabilites (Bouchard, 2004; Chang & Kuo, 2013; Falk, Lind, Miller, Piechowski, & Silverman, 1999). Some of the most used instruments in investigation are the *Me Scale* (Chang & Kuo, 2009), the *ElemenOE* (Bouchard, 2002), or the *Overexcitability Questionnaire Two* (OEQ-II; Falk et al., 1999). OEQ-II is the instrument which has proven the most effective in identifying giftedness (Carman, 2011; Oliveira, 2013; Siu, 2010; Tieso, 2007; Wirthwein & Rost, 2011, and has been translated and adapted in approximately 20 countries. Despite its international relevance, it has not yet been translated and adapted for the Portuguese-speaking population.

Intelligence, Overexcitability, and Cognitive Neurosciences

According to Gottfredson (1997), intelligence "reflects a broader and deeper capability for comprehending our surroundings – "catching on", "making sense" of things, or "figuring out" what to do". (pp.13), a view which is the basis for a definition of intelligence agreed upon by fifty-two notable researchers in the field of cognitive ability. In line with this definition, high intelligence is a risk factor for psychological and physiological overexcitability (Karpinski, Kinase, Kolb, Tetreault, & Borowski, 2018). Those with a sharp cognitive ability tend to central nervous system hyperreactivity (Chang & Kuo, 2013), which can lead to several other psychological and physiological consequences. Studies show that overexcitability has been considered a strong predictor of giftedness (Ackerman, 1997; Al-Onizat, 2013; Carman, 2011; Piechowski, 2009; Siu, 2010; Tieso, 2007).

Empathy and Emotional Overexcitability

Emotional intensity and curiosity, precocious characteristics in a large part of the gifted and talented (Piechowski, 2009), reveal this potential for compassion, empathy, and moral sensibility, manifested in a sense of justice, or in concern with human problems. In the field of giftedness, empathy has been studied mainly as an affective sensibility (Lovecky, 2009). In his theory of giftedness, overexcitability, and positive disintegration, Dabrowski (1964) argues that a precocious development of moral sensibility is intrinsic to the development of gifted individuals with emotional overexcitability. According to some studies, many gifted display low or common levels of empathy, but is important to pay attention to those who manifest the potential of affective and moral sensibility (Lovecky, 2009).

Empathetic Compassion

Empathetic Compassion is a designation made by Blum (1980), the target of ethical education and the development of moral in education (Maxwell, 2008), and is considered as the highest state of empathy. The affective and moral sensibilities manifested in some gifted display components of empathetic compassion because they include altruism translated into actions. Currently, there is a growing interest in empathy in the area of giftedness, and more relevance has been placed in the areas of social and emotional intelligence, because of the necessity to differentiate this important component.

Empathy has been approached from different perspectives. It is an essential faculty forliving in society, and it facilitates social interaction skills (Eisenberg et al., 1996; Saarni, 1990). Empathy is the ability to "understand another person's inner frame of reference with accuracy and with its belonging emotional components as if one were that person, without ever losing the condition of "as if one were" (Rogers, 1959, p. 210). Empathy motivates helping others and wanting justice for others (Koller, Camino, & Ribeiro, 2001).

Some researchers have included a behavioral component which refers to moral and pro-social human development (Koller, Camino, & Ribeiro, 2001). According to Strayerand Eisenberg (1987), this behavioral component is derived from the reaction to situations in which an affective mobilization and an active behavioral answer exist. According to Rodrigues & Silva (2012), empathy integrates these three components: the cognitive, the affective, and the behavioral, which correspond to Blum's concept of empathetic compassion (1980).

Empathy and Decentration

Kohlberg (1992) considered that not enough attention was given to the performance of empathy and compassion on moral development, and that decentration was the main cognitive component for its study. Decentration is the capacity of putting oneself in the place of the other and experiencing situations through the other's perspective. Without decentration it would be very hard to feel empathy, to be altruistic and caring, to defend the other's position and seek cooperation. Various instruments have been proposed, and the most used is the *Experiences Questionnaire – Decentering subscale* (EQ-D) (Fresco et al., 2007). Decentration is a central component in psychopathology and psychotherapy. Empathic acuity is one of the main indicators of good understanding in a couple after 4 years in a relationship, as well as being one of the main competencies of a psychotherapist.

Empathy and Socioemotional Development in Giftedness

The results of research about social development of gifted children are largely inconsistent (Rinn, 2018). In some studies, gifted children pose problems in the development of social competencies when compared to their non-gifted peers (Freeman, 2006; Silverman, 1993). Due to their advanced cognitive competencies, gifted adolescents have been shown to have different approaches when creating and maintaining close friendships. In a study of 1465 gifted adolescents, aged between 14 and 18 years old, more than half of them stated that they felt they were not able to be themselves at school (Cross, Coleman, & Stewart, 1993). Another study was unable to find differences in social development between gifted and non-gifted subjects (López & Sotillo, 2009). It has been precisely the component of empathy which has gained study-relevance in the areas of emotional and social development (Baron-Coren & Wheelwright, 2004).

Empathy and Moral Development in Giftedness

According to Daniels and Piechowski (2009), the gifted who exhibit compassion and altruism as imperatives are characterized by emotional overexcitability. Such compassion and altruism are also studied in giftedness as an affective and moral sensibility. According to Webb, Gore, Amend, & Devries (2007), the characteristics which stand out the most in moral sensibility are, in ascending order, the following: decentration, defense of others, empathy and altruism/solidarity.

It should be noted that not all gifted show an advanced moral sensibility, in fact, some are not very empathetic. In spite of this, a high percentage of gifted show uncommon levels of empathy, and care for others from an early age (Lovecky, 2009). Lovecky considers that further research on this aspect is necessary, in order to make the most of the specific potential of these gifted people.

The relevance of empathy in the area of moral development has emerged in a more theoretical way because it was originally dedicated to the cognitive and structural aspects of development. But in early studies, Piaget (1977) and Kohlberg (1971) alerted as to the necessity of understanding a non-cognitive factor, which was precisely empathy, and a cognitive factor, namely decentration ability. The relevance of moral development has emerged in the area of education as well as more recently in the area of giftedness, in a theoretical and empirical platform focusing on moral development in the gifted (Cross & Ambrose, 2009). These concerns with moral development had already been well defined by Tannenbaum (2000), who alerted as to the danger of bad use of intelligence, giving examples of cases in which giftedness was used in ways that are nefarious to humanity. This entire need to develop consciousness arises from the dilemmas which the area of intelligence is facing. In the theories of moral development, empathy and compassion are approached as an affective and moral sensibility or empathetic compassion. Moral sensibility is related with the consciousness one has in the face of ethical dilemmas, being one of the components of moral development (Bebeau, Rest & Narvaez, 1999).

The study of moral development has focused on moral reasoning with authors such as Kohlberg and Piaget (Fleming, 2005). The research undertaken by Kohlberg (1992) forms part of the group of cognitive-evolutionary theories, just like those of Piaget. The most utilized instrument to determine the state of development, according to Kohlberg's model of moral development, is the Defining Issues Test (DIT), created by James Rest (Lourenço & César, 1991; Rest, 1979). Rest (1979) considered that moral reasoning was insufficient to explain moral functioning, proposing the essential components for the production of moral behaviors in his Four Component Model. These are: moral reasoning, moral motivation, moral sensibility and moral character (Bebeau, Rest & Narvaez, 1999). Both empathy and decentration are two very important pillars in the characterization of children with moral sensibility (Silverman, 1993). According to Webb (1998), these characteristics are, in order of reference, the following: altruism and solidarity, empathy for others, defense of others, and decentration.

Hoffman (1994) considers that it is empathy which influences moral reasoning, allowing us to choose the most important moral principles of justice in each moral dilemma (necessity, equality, and equity). For Hoffman (1991), the quest for the well-being of others is derived from empathy.

Hoffman (1991) highlighted the importance of affections on moral development but did not disregard the cognitive aspect. In Hoffman's theory (1991, 2000), the development of a cognitive sense occurs through the differentiation of the *self*, in the understanding of the *self* of others. Kohlberg (1992) acknowledges that not enough attention is given to the role of feelings of empathy and compassion, which would permit a morality theory not restricted by the cognitive processes of decentration.

Through the concepts of reciprocity and decentration, Piaget (1965) implies empathy in education and moral development. Namely, decentration ability is associated with the development of autonomy and the highest states of moral development. There is a consensus about the relevance of empathy on moral development (Camino, 2009; Hoffman, 1991), confirmed in empirical studies as having a positive relationship with moral judgment (Williams Orpen, Hutchinson, Walker, & Zumbo, 2006), a positive relationship with distributive reasoning (Sampaio, Monte, Camino, & Roazzi,

2008), as well as its importance for pro-social moral development (Berenguer, 2010; Eisenberg et al., 1996).

Moral sensibility is the ability to act while taking into account the feelings of others and their necessities. It requires awareness of the other's suffering and the desire to do something to relieve such suffering. It begins at birth and develops throughout life. Moral sensibility, in its more complex form, requires compassion and a sense of justice to decide how to relieve the suffering of an individual or a group (Lovecky, 2009). Moral sensibility has been researched in an exploratory study with Portuguese gifted (Ferreira, 2016).

The majority of research with gifted children has focused on moral reasoning, with moral tasks or dilemmas designed to measure advanced moral reasoning (Kohlberg 1984; Piaget 1965; Rest 1979). Moral reasoning requires a high level of abstract reasoning, as well as the ability to decentralize self-centered concerns in order to appreciate the other's perspective. In this model, moral identity is built over time as children learn to decentralize. There is very little research on how gifted children differ from non-gifted same age peers in terms of moral sensibility and empathy (Lovecky, 2009).

The study of the development of moral sensibility since infancy is based on the study of empathy and compassion. Hoffman's (1991) theory of moral sensibility based on empathy and compassion, or Blum's (1980, 1991) conception of empathetic compassion as an advanced state of moral sensibility, allow for a better understanding of the influence of these non-cognitive components. Moral sensibility not only involves noticing and being receptive to morally relevant problems, but also imagining possibilities of action, as well as their consequences in time in terms of results and reactions from others (Power, Nuzzi, Narvaez, Lapsley, & Hunt 2008).

Questions and Reflections

The study of the potential of empathetic compassion and moral development in giftedness requires research of empathy and moral sensibility on gifted with characteristics of overexcitability, particularly those with emotional overexcitability. The various conceptions and models of giftedness exhibit both advantages and limitations. The Model of Positive Disintegration has been useful in the psychophysiological comprehension of giftedness, as well as in psychotherapy for gifted with characteristics of overexcitability. We need to deepen our understandingof the emotional processes through which these gifted go from an early age, and the emotional development that sets them apart. Does emotional intensity make the empathy and moral sensibility observed in the gifted from an early age an imperative? Can this intensity and the underlying processes of disintegration and integration through which they go be supported and facilitated? How do these processes of positive disintegration occur, and how do they manifest themselves? How can their personal expression and realization be facilitated? In what way can the realization of this potential be facilitated?

The different patterns of overexcitability, or intensity, display a decisive role in the development of human potential and need to be differentiated more specifically, not only with regards to empathy and moral sensibility (which this chapter addressed) but in all other aspects of overexcitability. Otherwise we are at risk of not valuing giftedness in all its richness and intensity.

References:

Ackerman, C. M. (1997). Identifying gifted adolescents using personality characteristics: Dabrowski's overexcitabilities. *Roeper Review, 19*, 229-236.

Ackerman, C. M. (2009). The essential elements of Dabrowski's theory of positive disintegration and how they are connected. *Roeper Review, 31*, 81-95.

Al-Onizat, S. H. (2013). The psychometric properties of a Jordanian version of Overexcitability Questionnaire-Two, OEQII. *Criative Education, 4*(1), 49-61.

Baron-Cohen, S., & Wheelwright, S. (2004). The Empathy Quotient: An investigation ofadults with Asperger Syndrome or High Functioning Autism, and normal sex differences. *Journal of Autism and Developmental Disorders, 34*(2), 163-175.

Bebeau, M., Rest, J., & Narvaez, D. (1999). Beyond the promise: A perspective of research in moral education. *Educational Researcher, 28*, 18-26.

Berenguer, J. (2010). The effect of empathy in environmental moral reasoning. *Environment and Behavior, 42*(1), 110-134.

Blum, L. (1980). *Friendship, altruism and morality.* London: Routledge & Kegan Paul.

Blum, L. (1991). Moral perception and particularity. *Ethics, 101*(3), 701-725.

Bouchard, L. L. (2002). Un instrumento para la medición de sobrexcitabilidades para identificar estudiantes excepcionales de primaria. *Revista del InstitutoAlberto Merani, 2, 5*(1), 40-49.

Bouchard, L. L. (2004). An instrument for the measure of dabrowskian overexcitabilities to identify gifted elementary students. *Gifted Child Quarterly*, 48(4), 339-350. doi:10.1177/001698620404800407

Camino, C. (2009). *A empatia na psicologia do desenvolvimento humano.* In Anais do VI Congresso Norte Nordeste de Psicologia. Retirado de http://www.conpsi6.ufba.br/.

Carman, C. A. (2011). Adding personality to gifted identification: Relationships among traditional and personality-based constructs. *Journal of Advanced Academics, 22*, 412-446.

Chang, H. J., & Kuo, C. C. (2009). Overexcitabilities of gifted and talented studentsand its related researches in Taiwan. *Asia-PacificJournal of Gifted and TalentedEducation, 1*(1), 41-74.

Chang, H. J., & Kuo, C. C. (2013). Overexcitabilities: Empirical studies and application. *Learning and Individual Differences, 23*, 53-63.

Cross, T., & Ambrose, D. (2009). *Morality, Ethics, and Gifted Minds*. Boston, MA: Springer US.

Cross, T. L., Coleman, L. J., & Stewart, R. A. (1993). The social cognition of gifted adolescents: An exploration of the stigma of giftedness paradigm. *Roeper Review, 16*, 37-40.

Dabrowski, K. (1964). *Positive disintegration*. London: Little, Brown.

Dabrowski, K. (1972). *Psychoneurosis is not an illness: Neuroses and psychoneurosesfrom the perspective of positive disintegration*. London: Gryf.

Daniels, S., & Piechowski, M. M. (2009). *Living with intensity: Understanding the sensitivity, excitability and emotional development of gifted children, adolescents and adults*. Scottsdale, AZ: Great Potencial Press

Eisenberg, N., Fabes, R. A., Karbon, M., Murphy, B. C., Wosinski, M., Polazzi, L. ... Juhnke, C. (1996). The relations of children's dispositional prosocial behavior to emotionality, regulation, and social functioning. *Child Development, 67*, 974-992.

Falk, R. F., Lind, S., Miller, N. B., Piechowski, M. M., & Silverman, L. K. (1999). *The Overexcitability Questionnaire Two (OEQ II): Manual, scoring system, and questionnaire*. Denver, CO: Institute for the Study of Advanced Development.

Fleming, J. S. (2005). Piaget, Kohlberg, Gilligan, and Others on Moral Development. *Psychological Perspectives on Human Development*, 1-25.

Ferreira, B. F. L. (2016). *A sensibilidade moral em crianças sobredotadas: um estudo exploratório* (Dissertação de doutoramento). Faculdade de Psicologia da Universidade de Lisboa, Lisboa

Freeman, J. (2006). The emotional development of gifted and talented children. *Gifted and Talented International, 21*(2), 20-28.

Fresco, D. M., Moore, M. T., van Dulmen, M. H. M., Segal, Z. V., Ma, S. H., Teasdale, J. D., & Williams, J. M. G. (2007). Initial Psychometric Properties of the Experiences Questionnaire: Validation of a Self-Report Measure of Decentering. *Behavior Therapy, 38*, 234-246.

Gottfredson, L. S. (1997). Mainstream science on intelligence: An editorial with 52 signatories, history, and bibliography. *Intelligence, 24*(1), 13-23.

Hoffman, M. (1991). Empathy, social cognition, and moral action. In W. M. Kurtines, & J. L. Gerwirtz (Eds.), *Handbook of moral behavior and development* (pp. 275-301). Hillsdale, NJ: Erlbaum.

Hoffman, M. L. (1994). Empathy, role taking, guilt, and development of altruistic motives. In B. Puka (Ed.), *Reaching out: Caring, altruism and prosocial behavior* (pp. 196-218). New York: Garland.

Hoffman, M. L. (2000). *Empathy and moral development: Implications for caring and justice.* New York: Cambridge University Press.

Karpinski, R. I., Kinase Kolb, A. M., Tetreault, N. A., & Borowski, T. B. (2018). High intelligence: A risk factor for psychological and physiological overexcitabilities. *Intelligence, 66*(2018), 8-23.

Kohlberg, L. (1971). *Moral judgment interview and procedures for scoring.* Cambridge, MA: Harvard School of Education.

Kohlberg, L. (1984). *Essays on moral development – The pychology of moral development: Moral stages, their nature and validity.*San Francisco: Harper & Row.

Kohlberg, L. (1992). *Psicología del desarrollo moral.* Bilbao: Biblioteca de Psicología, Desclée de Brouwer.

Koller, S., Camino, C., & Ribeiro, J. (2001). Adaptação e validação interna de duas escalas de empatia para uso no Brasil. *Estudos de Psicologia, 18,* 43-53.

Lovecky, D. V. (2009).Moral Sensitivity in Young Gifted Children. In T. Cross, & D. Ambrose (2009). *Morality, Ethics, and Gifted Minds* (pp. 161-176). Boston, MA: Springer US.

Lourenço, O., & César, M. (1991). Teste de definição de valores morais de Rest: Pode ser usado na investigação moral portuguesa? *Análise Psicológica, 2*(9), 185-192.

López, V., & Sotillo, M. (2009). Giftedness and social adjustment: evidence supporting the resilience approach in Spanish-speaking children and adolescents. *High Ability Students, 20,* 39-53.

Maxwell, B. (2008). *Professional Ethics Education: Studies in Compassionate Empathy.* The Netherlands: Springer

Mendaglio, S., & Peterson, J. S. (2007). *Models of counseling gifted children, adolescents, and young adults.* Waco, TX: Prufrock Press.

Mendaglio, S. (2012). Overexcitabilities and giftedness research: a call for a paradigm shift. *Journal for the Education of the Gifted, 35* (3), 207-219.

Oliveira, J. C. (2013).*Sobre-excitabilidade e talento: evidências de validade da versão brasileira do Overexcitability Questionnaire Two* (Dissertação de mestrado não-publicada), Instituto de Ciências Humanas da Universidade Federal de Juiz de Fora, Juiz de Fora.

Piaget, J. (1965). *The moral judgment of the child*. New York: Free Press.

Piaget, J. (1977). *O julgamento moral na criança*. São Paulo: Mestre Jou.

Piechowski, M. M. (1986). The concept of developmental potential. *Roeper Review, 8*, 190-197.

Piechowski, M. M. (1997). Emotional giftedness: The measure of intrapersonal intelligence. In N. Colangelo & G. A. Davis (Eds.) *Handbook of gifted education* (pp. 366-381), Boston, MA: Allyn and Bacon.

Piechowski (2009). The Inner World of the Young and Bright. In T. Cross & D. Ambrose (Eds.), *Morality, Ethics, and Gifted Minds* (pp. 177-194). Boston, MA: Springer US.

Power, C., Nuzzi, R., Narvaez, D., Lapsley, D., & Hunt, T. (2008). *Moral education: A handbook*. London: Praeger.

Rest, J. (1979). *Development in judging moral issues*. Minnesota: University of Minnesota Press.

Rinn, A. N. (2018). Social and Emotional Considerations for Gifted Students. In S. I. Pfeiffer, E. Shaunessy-Dedrick, & M. Foley-Nicpon (Eds.), *APA handbook of giftedness and talent* (pp. 453-464). Washington, DC: American Psychological Association.

Rogers, C. (1959). A theory of therapy, personality and interpersonal relationships as developed in the client-centered framework. In S. Koch (Org.), *Psychology: a study of science. Study I. Conceptual and systematic* (pp. 184-256). New York: Holt, Rinehart and Winston.

Rodrigues, M., & Silva. R. (2012). Avaliação de um programa de promoção da empatia implementação na educação infantil. *Estudos e Pesquisas em Psicologia, 12*(1), 59-75.

Saarni, C. (1990). Emotional competence: How emotions and relationships become integrated. In R. A. Thompson (Ed.), *Socioemotional development* (pp. 115-182). Lincoln: University of Nebraska Press.

Sampaio, L. R., Monte, F. C., Camino, C., & Roazzi, A. (2008). Justiça distributiva e empatia em adolescentes do nordeste brasileiro. *Psicologia: Reflexão e Crítica, 21*(2), 275-282.

Silverman, L. K. (1993). *Counseling the gifted and talented.* Denver, CO: Love.

Siu, A. F. Y. (2010). Comparing overexcitabilities of gifted and non-gifted school children in Hong Kong: Does culture make a difference? *Asia Pacific Journal of Education, 30*(1), 71-83.

Strayer, J., & Eisenberg, N. (1987). Empathy viewed in context. In N. Eisenberg & J. Strayer (Eds.), *Empathy and its development* (pp. 389-398). New York: Cambridge University Press.

Tannenbaum, A. J. (2000). A history of giftedness in school and society. In K. A. Heller, F. J. Mönks, R. J. Sternberg, & R. F. Subotnik (Eds.), *International handbook of giftedness and talent* (pp. 23-53). Oxford: Elsevier.

Tieso, C. L. (2007). Patterns of overexcitabilities in identified gifted students and their parents: A hierarchical model. *Gifted Child Quarterly, 51*(1), 11-22.

Webb, J. (1998). Existential depression in gifted Individuals. *Communicator, 29*(3), 62-69.

Webb, J. T., Gore, J. L., Amend, E. R., & DeVries, A. R. (2007). *A parent's guide to gifted children.* Scottsdale, AZ: Great Potential Press.

Williams, K. M., Orpen, S., Hutchinson, L. R., Walker, L. J., & Zumbo, B. D. (2006). Personality, empathy, and moral development: examining ethical reasoning in relation to the Big Five and the Dark Triad. Trabalho apresentado no 67th Annual meeting of the Canadian Psychological Association. Retrieved from http://www.psych.ubc.ca/~dpaulhus/research/DARK_TRIAD/ PRESENTATIONS/ CPA06.D3&morality.pdf.

Wirthwein, L., & Rost, D. H. (2011). Focussing on overexcitabilities: Studies with intellectually gifted and academically talented adults. *Personality and Individual Differences, 51,* 337-342.

7.

NURTURING CREATIVITY AND PRODUCTIVE GIFTEDNESS IN HIGH-ABILITY STUDENTS

Susan J. Paik

Associate Professor at the School of Education at Claremont Graduate University, USA.

ORCID: 0000-0002-3273-5402

Charlina Gozali

PhD candidate in education at Claremont Graduate University, USA.

ORCID: 0000-0002-2827-8309

Abstract: *Using the Productive Giftedness Model (PGM) as a guiding framework, the purpose of this chapter is to discuss the key factors and conditions found to cultivate creativity. Creative productivity requires a comprehensive approach, as illustrated in PGM; the model delineates key psychosocial and environmental factors that influence creativity and "productive giftedness" (defined as mastery, expertise, or excellence) (Paik, 2013, 2015). The ten-factor model includes individual factors (ability, motivation, development), instructional factors (learning climate, quality and quantity of instruction), and environmental factors (home, mentors, peers, and extracurricular time), all of which affect creative and productive outcomes. Embedded in the model are also alterable (direct influences) and contextual* *(indirect influences) factors; both factors influence access to opportunities, support, and resources for students (Paik, 2013, 2015; Paik et al., 2019). In summary, the chapter illustrates the importance of creativity and productive giftedness, synthesizes related literature on school and other learning environments, and provides implications for improving creativity. Nurturing creative productivity encompasses multiple factors and the collaborative efforts of key stakeholders – parents, teachers, mentors, peers, and others in conducive learning climates.*

Keywords: *Creativity, Productive Giftedness, Motivation, Psychosocial Factors, Instructional Factors, Environmental Factors.*

Introduction and Purpose

In 1972, the *Marland Report*, the first national report on gifted education in the United States, officially recognized creativity as an essential part of giftedness (J. C. Kaufman, Kaufman, Beghetto, Burgess, & Persson, 2009). Despite the public's positive sentiment toward creativity, however, Kim (2011) found that creative thinking has fallen since 1990, particularly in the U.S. Based on the *Torrance Tests of Creative Thinking* (TTCT) of nearly 300, 000 scores from all ages, the study revealed a "creativity crisis", especially among younger children (Kim, 2011). Using the Productive Giftedness Model (PGM) as the guiding framework, the current chapter will explore the factors and conditions found to cultivate creativity among students (Paik, 2013, 2015).

The purpose of this chapter is to: 1) briefly define and discuss the practical importance of creativity and productive giftedness; 2) present the Productive Giftedness Model (PGM), a theoretical framework, that delineates the key factors (individual aptitude, instruction, and environment) that influence creativity; 3) synthesize key literature specifically on school and environmental factors and creativity; and 4) provide research and practice implications for improving creative productivity among students.

Significance of Creativity and Productive Giftedness

Defining Creativity and Productive Giftedness

Early conceptions of creativity were often tied to the idea of genius, divine inspiration, and great ability. However, while examinations on genius and talent can be traced as far back as Plato's early writings on "divine madness", research on creativity was not introduced until the 20th century (Albert, 1992; Schlesinger, 2009). It is not surprising then that, in the last few decades, researchers have sought to define creativity.

In 1967, Vygotsky claimed that, "any human act that gives rise to something new is referred to as a creative act, regardless of whether what is created is a physical object or some mental or emotional construct that lives within the person who created it and is known only to him" (Vygotsky, 2004, p. 7). Csikszentmihalyi (1996) stated that creativity was not only a novel product or idea, but something that also changed or transformed the existing domain. On the other hand, Plucker, Beghetto, and Dow's definition of creativity emphasized "the interaction among aptitude, process, and environment" that enabled individuals to produce new products that were also useful to that societal context (2004, p. 90).

While various definitions exist, the common emphasis is on productivity or what might be referred to as "productive giftedness" (Paik, 2013, 2015). Productive giftedness is defined as having more than just creative potential; it is the ability to *actualize* potential in the form of creative and productive outcomes (e.g., achievements, accomplishments, or even eminence later in life) (Paik, 2013, 2015). At its most basic, creativity is "the ability to *produce* work that is novel (original, unexpected), high in quality, and appropriate (useful, meets task constraints)" (Sternberg, 2003, p. 89). However, Sternberg et al. (2011) further elaborates that terms such as "gifted" or "creatively gifted" must be accompanied by a product. The creative individual needs to move beyond potential and produce something, not for the sake of any production, but for the sake of talent actualization (Paik, 2013, 2015). To have creative influence and impact, Cassandro & Simonton (2003) take it further and state that productivity is the key predictor to a creator's reputation. In other words, creativity is necessary, but its greatest expression and impact must be actualized in productive form. All students have potential, but how can we help them to actualize their creative potential into productive giftedness?

Benefits of Creativity and Productive Giftedness

On an individual level, creativity is important because it has been associated with numerous positive physical, psychological, and cognitive benefits. Creativity, in general, has been linked to better physical health (Lepore & Smyth, 2002; Pennebaker, 1997; Pennebaker, Kiecolt-Glaser, & Glaser, 1988), improved well-being and mood (Amabile, Barsade, Mueller, & Staw, 2005; Carson, Bittner, Cameron, & Brown, 1994; Nicol & Long, 1996; Plucker et al., 2004), higher resilience (Metzl, 2009), and better social harmony (King & Pope, 1999). Creativity can also result in higher academic achievement and motivation (Grigorenko et al., 2009; J. C. Kaufman, Davis, & Beghetto, 2012). Furthermore, creativity is not only useful in creative domains such as the arts, but is a requirement for success in any talent domain (Pfeiffer & Thompson, 2013; Sternberg, 2003). Athletes, for instance, require creativity during training in order to develop strategies and skills to win competitions (Durand-Bush & Salmela, 2002). Similarly, scientists and other academics also utilize creativity in making new discoveries, solving scientific and mathematical problems, and writing research reports (Paik, 2012). Some researchers even argue that creative productivity is what separates expertise from competence in the field (Pfeiffer & Thompson, 2013; Paik, 2013).

The importance of studying creative productivity first started as early as 1835 when Adolphe Quetelet (1796-1874) studied the production of French and English playwrights ("Adolphe Quetelet (n.d.)", 2011). Since then, productivity has been studied in almost every field. On a societal level, creativity and productive giftedness propel new ideas and innovations that can improve the quality of life (Csikszentmihalyi, 1996; Paik, 2012, 2013, 2015; Sternberg, 2003; Sternberg, Jarvin, & Grigorenko, 2011). Advances in well-drilling and water filtration technology, for instance, have helped to address the lack of access to clean water faced by millions in developing countries (Charity Water, 2017). An innovative infant warmer developed by a group of students at Stanford University has helped save more than 200, 000 babies from premature death in rural areas around the world (Embrace Innovations, 2017). New products and services ultimately lead to the creation of jobs that enhances the economy (Sternberg, 2003). In fact, creative productivity has been identified as "the most important economic resource of the 21st century" (Florida, 2002; J. C. Kaufman, 2016, p. 320) and an essential component to organizational success (Agars, Kaufman, & Locke, 2008).

Theoretical Framework

Despite concerns of the looming creativity crisis, given optimal experiences and conditions, creativity can be cultivated (Csikszentmihalyi, 1996; Paik, 2015; Pfeiffer & Thompson, 2013; Runco & Cayirdag, 2013). The Productive Giftedness Model (PGM) is a comprehensive ten-factor model that examines how key environmental and psychosocial factors influence creative and productive outcomes (creative accomplishments – e.g., award-winning paintings, sculptures; high achievement – e.g., exceptional performance in school or other programs; see Figure 1) (Paik, 2013, 2015). The model includes individual aptitude, school, and environmental factors that are largely alterable (Paik, 2015). Based on an effort-ability model, one of the major tenets of the model is that children can achieve, and in the current case, demonstrate creativity, when provided with favorable conditions of opportunity, support, and resources (Paik, 2013, 2015; Paik & Walberg, 2007; Paik, Gozali, & Marshall-Harper, 2019). Both effort and ability are essential to developing creative talent. Embedded in the ten PGM factors are also Alterable Factors (direct influences that can be optimized – e.g., parent, teacher, and student practices, attitudes, time) as opposed to Contextual Factors (indirect influences that cannot be altered – e.g., historical, cultural, political, demographic, other factors); both factors help us to better understand access to different opportunities, support, and resources for students (Paik, 2013, 2015; Paik et al, 2019; Paik, Marshall-Harper, Gozali, & Johnson, 2020).

To help the reader understand the overall model (Figure 1), brief definitions are provided for each of the factors. However, for the purposes of this chapter, a review of literature will be provided only for *school factors* (quality of instruction, quantity of instruction, and school-classroom climate) and *environmental factors* (home, mentoring, peers, and extra-curricular time) as research shows conducive learning environments are key for talent development (Bloom, 1985; Csikszentmihalyi, 1996).

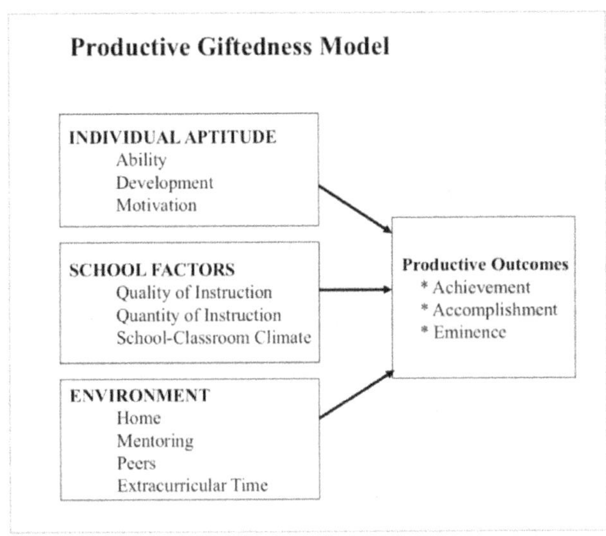

FIGURE 1: Productive Giftedness Model (Paik, 2013[3]) Individual Aptitude

In PGM, Individual Aptitude factors include *development*, *ability*, and *motivation* (Paik, 2013, 2015). *Development* highlights the continuous nature of learning and achievement (Paik, 2015). Previous research, for example, has demonstrated the cumulative effects of learning and thus, the importance of early investments and interventions (Heckman, 2000; Merton, 1968). *Ability* includes any indicator of achievement and other measurable outcomes such as GPA, standardized test scores, creative products, or other

---

[3] Paik, S. J. (2013) Nurturing Talent, Creativity, and Productive Giftedness: A New Mastery Model. In K. H. Kim, J. C. Kaufman, J. Baer, and B. Sriramen (Eds.) *Creatively Gifted Students Are Not Like Other Gifted Students: Research, Theory, and Practice.* Boston, MA: Sense Publishers.

accomplishments in different talent areas (Paik, 2013). *Motivation*, or more specifically *focused motivation*, is defined as "undeterred, intentional perseverance with an end goal or product in mind" (Paik, 2013, p. 106). This factor includes intrinsic and extrinsic motivation, as well as individual traits and characteristics (e.g., perseverance, resilience, self-regulation) (Paik, 2015).

School (or Instructional) Factors

School factors in the model include *quality of instruction, quantity of instruction,* and *school-classroom climate* (Paik, 2013, 2015). The *quality of instruction* factor refers to teaching, curriculum, assessment, and other instructional factors related mostly in schools and classrooms; however, certain talent areas require more training outside of school. The *quantity of instruction* factor covers the amount of time spent learning skills in school or out of school. This factor also includes time spent on domain-specific instruction. Finally, the *school-classroom climate* (or learning climate) refers to "school or classroom experiences or characteristics that affect the overall morale" of that learning climate (Paik, 2015, p. 276).

Environmental Factors

Environmental factors in the model include the *home, mentoring, peers,* and *extracurricular time* (Paik, 2013, 2015). The *home environment* comprises home-related information such as parental beliefs and practices, relationships with family members, availability of learning materials and opportunities, and other demographic information such as family structure, culture, race, language, socioeconomic status, and parental educational attainment (Paik, 2015). *Mentoring* involves formal or informal coaching or guidance, especially in the specific field or talent area (Paik, 2015). *Peers* refer to an individual's networks and interpersonal relationships and how it influences their attitudes, beliefs, and experiences (Paik, 2015). *Extracurricular Time* covers how time is spent outside of formal schooling (e.g., academic, recreational, social, skill-building, technology usage, or domain-specific activities) (Paik, 2015).

Creativity and Instructional Factors

The following sections briefly synthesize key literature related to creativity and how to encourage more creative productivity in school, classroom, and other learning climates.

School-Classroom Climate (or Learning Climate)

In his seminal book, *Creativity: Flow and the Psychology of Discovery and Invention*, Csikszentmihalyi (1996) highlighted the influence of the environment on creative productivity. A supportive climate can be key in influencing motivation, learning, and creativity. Positive school and classroom climates emphasize learning over performance and self-improvement over competition, promoting a joy of learning in students (Ommundsen, 2001). Within the classroom, creativity is also enhanced by establishing norms and high expectations for learning. Effective classroom management, student engagement, relationship and community building are all initiated and mediated by the teacher. Best practices for teachers include the ability to: 1) convey knowledge but also "spark the joy of learning" (Csikszentmihalyi, Rathunde,

& Whalen, 1993, p. 195); 2) capture student attention, curiosity, and anticipation for learning through engaging activities such as anecdotes, storytelling, and real-life examples (Rief & Heimburge, 2006); and 3) create positive learning experiences that are enjoyable, rewarding, and encourage further participation and involvement (Csikszentmihalyi et al., 1993).

Despite the well-documented importance of learning environments, creative and talented individuals often endure sub-optimal school-classroom conditions. For example, published poets were found to have varied school experiences, ranging from positive teacher encouragement and support to feeling depressed and self-destructive because of the constraints placed upon their self-expression and freedom (Piirto, 2004). In general, supportive learning environments need to be safe spaces, both physically and psychologically. Teachers can also promote a safe environment for creativity by assessing their own attitudes towards unconventional thinking and behaviors in themselves and in others (Hong & Milgram, 2011). In order to create such an environment, educators should encourage students to express themselves and their differences, as well as identify and reward demonstrations of risk-taking, divergence, and curiosity (Richards, 2010a; Runco, 2010). Educators should also foster a cooperative (rather than competitive) climate, provide periods of activity and self-reflection, encourage divergent thinking, and allow flexibility in learning and completing tasks in order to nurture creativity (Cropley & Urban, 2000). Since creative students often have novel and unconventional ways of thinking, learning, and behaving, it is also vital that classrooms provide challenge, freedom, and opportunities for exploration. Additional strategies for stimulating creativity include asking more open-ended questions, soliciting students' ideas, incorporating group work and collaboration, and exposing students to a wide variety of cultures and ideas (Cropley

& Urban, 2000; Hong & Milgram, 2011; Pfeiffer & Thompson, 2013; Skiba, Tan, Sternberg, & Grigorenko, 2010).

Quality of Instruction

The quality of instruction received in educational settings is critical to cultivating creativity and talent. Unfortunately, researchers argue that creativity has become increasingly marginalized in schools as a result of standardized curriculum, high stakes testing, and centralized education systems (Bloom & Sosniak, 1981; Csikszentmihalyi et al., 1993; Pfeiffer & Thompson, 2013). Beghetto (2010a) similarly asserts that "creativity occupies a conflicted space in many K-12 classrooms" (p. 458). Although educators acknowledge the importance of creativity, nurturing creativity is often neglected as teachers are forced to juggle a plethora of other curricular goals (J. C. Kaufman et al., 2012). In many instances, creativity is not only neglected, but its appearance in the classroom is often punished by teachers focused on meeting curricular demands (J. C. Kaufman et al., 2012; Skiba et al., 2010). Instead of encouraging creative behavior, teachers may also perceive creativity as a liability, hindrance, handicap, or problem behavior (Baudson & Preckel, 2013; Beghetto & Kaufman, 2010; Hong & Milgram, 2008). The encouragement of creative expression by teachers is even more crucial since studies have shown that gifted children often display creative and non-conformist tendencies (Goertzel, Goertzel, Goertzel, & Hansen, 2004; Piske, Stoltz, Vestena, et al., 2016).

Moreover, creativity is a skill and habit that is needed for success in any domain. Hence, instructors in all domains – in and outside of schools – would benefit from practicing strategies that promote creativity in students. Instructional practices that promote creativity include 1) providing time and opportunities for students to be creative (Runco, 2010; Sternberg, 2010; Sternberg, Jarvin, & Grigorenko, 2009); 2) providing developmentally appropriate challenges (Pfeiffer & Thompson, 2013); 3) using nontraditional activities such as brainstorming, drawing cartoon strips, or writing riddles (Sternberg et al., 2009); and 4) utilizing more interactive teaching methods (Beghetto, 2010b). Instructors can also nurture creativity by encouraging and tolerating students' imagination and creativity (Armstrong, 1998; Runco, 2010), welcoming interruptions (Beghetto, 2010b), incorporating multidisciplinary perspectives (Neu, Baum, & Cooper, 2004), and teaching flexibly (Armstrong, 1998; Skiba et al., 2010). Instructors should also encourage intellectual risk-taking by respecting all ideas and helping students connect those ideas to the broader curriculum (Pfeiffer & Thompson, 2013; Richards, 2010a; Runco, 2010; Russ & Fiorelli, 2010; Skiba et al., 2010). Most importantly, instructors should nurture creativity by modeling creativity in their own lives (Hong & Milgram, 2008; J. C. Kaufman et al., 2012; Pfeiffer & Thompson, 2013; Richards, 2010a). As Sternberg (2010) rightly asserts, "students develop creativity not when they are told to, but when they are shown how" (p. 409).

Quantity of Instruction

The amount of instruction one receives combined with the amount of time dedicated to talent development are strong determinants of eventual accomplishments. Often, creatively accomplished individuals demonstrate a strong will to follow through on their goals. Their use of time and commitment to deliberate practice were also deemed critical to their achievement (Paik, 2003; Paik et al, 2019). For instance, concert pianists in Bloom's (1985) study on highly talented young people demonstrated that time for weekly piano lessons and daily practice was routinely scheduled and prioritized before involvement in any other school or social activities. Pianists' time spent on the piano eventually became a habit and parental monitoring became unnecessary (Bloom, 1985).

Researchers have found that reaching a level of expertise in any field takes about ten years, or ten thousand hours, of preparation involving deliberate practice (Ericsson, Krampe, & Tesch-Römer, 1993). Deliberate practice is a highly structured activity that includes careful monitoring of one's progress, relevant and timely feedback from instructors, and opportunities for practicing learned strategies and skills (Ericsson et al., 1993; Seider, 2013). Since deliberate practice requires sustained effort over extended amounts of time, intrinsic and extrinsic motivation are both necessary. Intrinsic motivation levels, oftentimes, separate those who become experts from those who remain novices (Ericsson et al., 1993).

For those in creative fields, from fiction writers and music composers to Scrabble players and entrepreneurs, this "ten-year rule" certainly applies. A study of fiction writers revealed that after their first publication, 10.6 years passed before they produced their best publication (S. B. Kaufman & Kaufman, 2007). Similarly, a study on the creative achievement of eminent composers confirmed that their masterworks were linked to improvement over their lifespan (Kozbelt, 2008). Another study found expert Scrabble players to have engaged in more practice and study time compared to average players – 3, 541 hours of Scrabble-related activities in the past ten years for experts compared to 1, 318 hours for average players (Tuffiash, Roring, & Ericsson, 2007).

Creativity and Environmental Factors

The following sections briefly synthesize key literature related to creativity and productive giftedness with regards to parents, mentors, peers, and how time is spent outside of school.

Home

Families can play a significant role in developing a person's creativity and talent. In fact, children spend approximately 92% of their time in the home, while the remaining 8% is spent within a school setting (Walberg & Paik, 1997; Paik et al, 2020). Therefore, it is not surprising that highly creative people benefit from supportive and stimulating home environments (Bloom, 1985; Stariha & Walberg, 1995). Parents often serve as children's first teachers and they can provide resources or experiences that can help to stimulate learning. For example, taking children to museums, reading to them, or providing other opportunities or resources can help motivate creativity (Bradley, Corwyn, McAdoo, & Coll, 2001). Eminent sculptors reported feeling supported by their parents in childhood and were often encouraged to try new tools or participate in special art or craft projects with older family members (Bloom, 1985).

Csikszentmihalyi (1997) emphasized parents' role in guiding and encouraging children's creative endeavors. Creative adults often recalled childhoods in which parents treated and spoke to them like adults. This simple act of speaking to a precocious child like a peer not only helped to quicken cognitive development, but also left a significant impression as they developed their creativity. Establishing clear and high expectations was another way that parents supported creative learning (Csikszentmihalyi, 1997;

Gould, Dieffenbach, & Moffett, 2002). These high expectations help to develop a disciplined practice, build self-confidence, and encouraged passion for the talent domain (Csikszentmihalyi, 1997; Paik et al, 2019).

Studies on eminent creative individuals have also shown that different home environments may breed different kinds of success (Albert, 1996; Bloom, 1985; Goertzel et al., 2004). For example, families of academically gifted individuals tend to emphasize interdependent family relationships, while families of creatively gifted children stress independence (Olszewski, Kulieke, & Buescher, 1987). A study of over 700 eminent individuals found that creative persons often came from "less conventional homes" that were "troubled – by poverty; by a broken home; by rejecting, over-possessive, estranged, or dominating parents; by financial ups and downs; by physical handicaps; or by parental dissatisfaction" (Goertzel et al., 2004, p. 282). These types of experiences may reflect findings that highly creative children tend to come from families with less expectations of conformity and generally more freedom from parental supervision (Olszewski et al., 1987). However, Simonton (2010) emphasized that different kinds of environments affect creativity. For example, eminent artists may come from less stable, heterogeneous backgrounds, while eminent scientists may grow up in more stable, homogeneous backgrounds. These different patterns in home life reinforce the varying pathways to creativity.

Peers

Parents play a much more pivotal role in social engagement in the early years, but peer influence increases as an individual matures. As children enter adolescence, peer interactions account for more than 30% of their social interactions (Gifford-Smith & Brownell, 2003). Understanding the role of peers in development is important because positive peer relationships can significantly influence academic and creative talent development (Lee, 2002).

In the adolescent years, peers may also influence individual commitment to talent development in the areas of arts or sports (Patrick et al., 1999). The level of commitment to and motivation for talent development depended on the nature of the peer relationships. Social engagement with peers within the talent domain reinforced positive relationships, motivation, and commitment to talent development. However, peer relationships may also negatively influence talent development if related activities negatively impact social interaction goals (Csikszentmihalyi et al., 1993; Patrick et al., 1999). In particular, students involved in non-school related talent activities reported feeling torn between their talent activity and their friends (peers); some choose to stop pursuing talent development in favor of improved relationships (Csikszentmihalyi et al., 1993; Patrick et al., 1999).

However, creativity itself is not always encouraged or welcomed in social or educational settings (Richards, 2010b). Peers, teachers, or other adults may have negative views of unconventional styles or behaviors. However, Claire (1993) found that peer interactions through mutual work and collaboration allows for more creativity in social contexts. For example, children first learning to create art benefit from being around other young artists (Boyatzis & Albertini, 2000). Though they may not be directly interacting, often choosing to draw by themselves, young artists "benefit from hearing the internalized questions, evaluations, and suggestions of peers" (Boyatzis & Albertini, 2000, p. 46)

Mentoring

Aside from familial and peer influences, a relationship with a supportive adult, particularly those who are also eminent in the child's area of interest, can be fundamental to developing talent and creativity (Bloom, 1985; Stariha & Walberg, 1995; Walker, 1986). Kaufman and Beghetto (2009) describe the important role of teachers, parents, and mentors in nurturing creativity particularly in the early stages of personal discovery. Students in the process of exploring creative paths can especially benefit from the support of a mentor. Through a mentoring relationship, a young person can gain a general sense of purpose and direction on life and career plans, and also receive emotional support during key stages of transition and development (Ambrose, Allen, & Huntley, 1994).

Kram and Isabella (1985) defined mentorship as a relationship between a senior and more experience individual and a less experienced person, who often is also younger than the mentor. Successful mentoring relationships are based on high quality connections that take into account the diverse experiences and backgrounds of both the mentor and the mentee (Ragins, 2007). Additionally, Johnson and Ridley (2008) describe an excellent mentor as someone who displays dependability and nurtures creativity. A mentor can help fuel passion and enthusiasm for a talent area and inspire outstanding creative productivity and accomplishments in the mentee (Haensly & Parsons, 1993).

Mentoring can take many forms, often in traditional one-on-one relationships, but alternative mentoring relationships may also be beneficial. For example, creative individuals may benefit from multiple mentors throughout different developmental stages (Haensly & Parsons, 1993; Higgins & Kram, 2001). As creative individuals mature, they may also benefit from a triangular mentorship model, in which a mentee has two mentors (Ambrose et al., 1994). In this alternative mentoring format, the mentee may be able to receive different kinds of support from each mentor. Mentors may also benefit from the three-way partnership as they can inspire and support one another through the process of supporting the mentee (Ambrose et al., 1994). In this way, they become partners in the mentoring relationship. Mentors are key to supporting skill-building in creative individuals throughout different stages in life (Paik, 2013, 2015).

Extracurricular Time

Schools are often viewed as the primary sites for learning; however, compared to time spent in the home or in the greater community, students only spend roughly 8% – 13% of their waking periods in school (Redding, 1998; Walberg, Niemiec, & Frederick, 1994; Walberg & Paik, 1997). A greater understanding of how children spend their time when not in school may provide insight into other influences on developing creativity. Activities spent outside of the formal school environment also have greater significance when educational institutions may be unsupportive of talent development or creativity (Bloom, 1985; J. C. Kaufman & Sternberg, 2010; Piirto, 2004). Students who find learning in schools difficult, particularly those who exhibit creative or unconventional tendencies, might thrive under more flexible and favorable conditions offered by after- or out-of-school programs (Danish, 2000).

Researchers have also found that participation in organized extracurricular activities (both school or non-school based) influence psychosocial development (Bartone, Snook, Forsythe, Lewis, & Bullis, 2007). Out-of-school activities, such as sports or other talent programs, may contribute to building higher levels of initiative, emotion regulation, and teamwork (Larson, Hansen, & Moneta, 2006). Developing these skills in the early years may help reinforce essential life skills that are beneficial to future productive outcomes such as creativity, leadership, or eminent accomplishments.

General involvement in creative expressions, like the arts, can help students strive for and achieve higher levels of accomplishments (Chambers & Schreiber, 2007; Heath & Roach, 1999). Activities do not always have to be structured or formally organized in order to provide benefits (Chambers & Schreiber, 2007). Sommerfeld (2011) found that unstructured, spontaneous, and child-initiated play encourages exploration, leadership, and creativity. One key example is the story of innovative business and technology leader Steve Jobs. During high school, Jobs spent much of his out-of-school time in the garage of neighbor and Hewlett Packard (HP) engineer, Larry Lang (Isaacson, 2011). This informal learning time exposed Jobs to opportunities and experts that stimulated his curiosity and innovation. Bloom and his colleagues (1985) found that highly accomplished individuals were often involved in a variety of extracurricular activities in their youth before focusing on a specific talent domain. For instance, eminent sculptors reported being involved in activities such as music, dance, sports, horseback riding, or language lessons. What these activities had in common were high levels of support and encouragement that motivated students' creative expressions and talent development.

Conclusion & Implications

Creativity is not only a life enhancer, but also a life essential. Sternberg (2003), for instance, argues that success in life is achieved through a combination of analytical, creative, and practical abilities. People need creativity to achieve in life because they need to optimize the specific combination of traits, opportunities, resources, and talents available to them (Durand-Bush & Salmela, 2002; Runco & Sakamoto, 1993). Csikszentmihalyi (1996) further states "creativity is a central source of meaning in our lives" (p. 1); it is what makes us human.

Creativity needs to be inspired and motivated first by adults so that children are encouraged to demonstrate it. Further, creativity and productive giftedness need to be developed through practice, and such development takes discipline and commitment. Achieving eminence in creative fields is uncommon; however, actualizing creative talent is the result of constant effort and focused motivation (Paik, 2013, 2015).

Researchers have found that one's conception of effort and ability determines their behavior, particularly when it comes to achievement (Dweck, 2007). The Productive Giftedness Model supports an effort-ability approach to achieving success. While ability is important, effort can play an even greater role in talent development. One way to encourage children's views of effort over ability is to create home and classroom environments that promote learning over performance and competition (Blumenfeld, Pintrich, & Hamilton, 1986). Such teachers create a classroom environment where learning is prioritized, and mistakes are viewed as part of every students' academic development (Espinoza, da Luz Fontes, & Arms-Chavez, 2014). As a result, students may be more willing to embrace challenge and learn from their mistakes.

Creatively gifted students are also often demotivated and discouraged in school if teaching is monotonous and mundane (Piske, Stoltz, & Machado, 2014). The well-being of gifted children is greatly determined by the motivation s/he receives during learning (Piske et al., 2016). Instructional practices that nurture creativity can help alleviate some of the cognitive, social, and emotional challenges creatively gifted students typically experience (Piske, et al., 2016). Ultimately, student interest in what is taught will determine learning, motivation and creativity.

In general, curriculum should be developed with students' long-term development in mind (Drew, 2010) and class content should always have real-world application (Bloom & Sosniak, 1981). A talent development view of schooling, according to VanTassel-Baska (1998), "focuses on the optimal, not minimal, development of each student" (p. 761). Public education should also be designed under the belief that all children are talented and have potential to be developed. Furthermore, since no perfect measure of talent identification has been discovered, schools and educators should treat talent as something to be grown and developed instead of mined (Sosniak & Gabelko, 2008).

In approaching talent development, many researchers have long argued for utilizing a life-span approach towards examining creativity and the development of creative individuals (Paik, 2013; 2015; Piirto, 1998). Creativity can and should be facilitated in the early years (Haensly & Parsons, 1993; J. C. Kaufman & Beghetto, 2009). Supporting creativity early on can help develop future creative endeavors, intellectual accomplishments, and social-emotional development, which can continue well into adulthood (Haensly & Parsons, 1993).

And finally, talent cannot be grown alone. Parents, teachers, mentors, and peers do matter as indicated in the Productive Giftedness Model; key stakeholders in conducive learning environments can significantly help or hinder the opportunities, support, and resources students need for creative productivity.

Acknowledgments

We would like to acknowledge and thank Herbert J. Walberg, John Griesinger, Mae Choe, Anais Janoyan, and Christine Kang for their earlier assistance and careful review of this chapter.

References

Agars, M. D., Kaufman, J. C., & Locke, T. R. (2008). Social influence and creativity in organizations: A multilevel lens for theory, research, and practice. In M. D. Mumford, S. T. Hunter, & K. E. Bedell-Avers (Eds.), *Multi-level issues in organizational innovation* (pp. 3-62). Amsterdam, The Netherlands: JAI Press.

Albert, R. S. (Ed.). (1992). *Genius and eminence* (2nd ed). Oxford, New York: Pergamon Press.

Albert, R. S. (1996). What the study of eminence can teach us. *Creativity Research Journal, 9*(4), 307-315.

Amabile, T. M., Barsade, S. G., Mueller, J. S., & Staw, B. M. (2005). Affect and creativity at work. *Administrative Science Quarterly, 50*(367-403).

Ambrose, D., Allen, J., & Huntley, S. (1994). Mentorship of the highly creative. *Roeper Review, 17*(2), 131-134.

Armstrong, T. (1998). *Awakening genius in the classroom*. Alexandria, VA: Association for Supervision and Curriculum Development.

Bartone, P. T., Snook, S. A., Forsythe, G. B., Lewis, P., & Bullis, R. C. (2007). Psychosocial development and leader performance of military officer cadets. *The Leadership Quarterly, 18*(5), 490-504. doi:10.1016/j.leaqua.2007.07.008

Baudson, T. G., & Preckel, F. (2013). Intelligence and creativity. In K. H. Kim, J. C. Kaufman, J. Baer, & B. Sriraman (Eds.), *Creatively gifted students are not like other gifted students* (pp. 181-212). Rotterdam, The Netherlands:

Sense Publishers. Retrieved from http://link.springer.com/10.1007/978-94-6209-149-8_13

Beghetto, R. A. (2010a). Creativity in the classroom. In J. C. Kaufman & R. J. Sternberg (Eds.), *The Cambridge handbook of creativity* (pp. 447-463). New York, NY: Cambridge University Press.

Beghetto, R. A. (2010b). Nurturing creativity in the micro-moments of the classroom. In K. H. Kim, J. C. Kaufman, J. Baer, & B. Sriraman (Eds.), *Creatively gifted students are not like other gifted students* (pp. 394-414). Rotterdam, The Netherlands: Sense Publishers. Retrieved from http://www.scopus.com/inward/record.url?eid=2-s2.0-84855962078&partnerID=tZOtx3y1

Beghetto, R. A., & Kaufman, J. (2010). *Nurturing Creativity in the Classroom*. New York: NY: Cambridge University Press.

Bloom, B. S. (Ed.). (1985). Developing talent in young people. New York, NY: Ballantine.

Bloom, B. S., & Sosniak, L. A. (1981). Talent development vs. schooling. *Educational Leadership, 39,* 86-94.

Blumenfeld, P. C., Pintrich, P. R., & Hamilton, V. L. (1986). Children's concepts of ability, effort, and conduct. *American Educational Research Journal, 23*(1), 95-104.

Boyatzis, C. J., & Albertini, G. (2000). A naturalistic observation of children drawing: Peer collaboration processes and influences in children's art. *New Directions for Child and Adolescent Development, 2000*(90), 31-48. doi:10.1002/cd.23220009004

Bradley, R. H., Corwyn, R. F., McAdoo, H. P., & Coll, C. G. (2001). The home environments of children in the United States part I: Variations by age, ethnicity, and poverty status. *Child Development, 72*(6), 1844-1867.

Carson, D. K., Bittner, M. T., Cameron, B. R., & Brown, D. M. (1994). Creative thinking as a predictor of school-aged children's stress responses and coping abilities. *Creativity Research Journal, 7,* 145-158.

Cassandro, V. J., & Simonton, D. K. (2003). Creativity and genius. In *Flourishing: Positive psychology and the life well-lived* (pp. 163-183). Washington, DC: American Psychological Association. Retrieved from http://www.researchgate.net/profile/Dean_Keith_Simonton/ publication/247428890_Cognition_Creativity_Genius_and_Truth_in_ Advertising/links/54b696ce0cf2e68eb27ea2f9.pdf

Chambers, E. A., & Schreiber, J. B. (2007). Girls' academic achievement: varying associations of extracurricular activities. *Gender and Education, 16*(3), 327-346.

Charity Water. (2017). Solutions. Retrieved from https://www.charitywater.org/ our-approach/solutions/

Claire, L. (1993). The social psychology of creativity: The importance of peer social processes for students' academic and artistic creative activity in xlassroom Contexts. *Bulletin of the Council for Research in Music Education*, (119), 21-28. doi:10.2307/40318608

Cropley, A., & Urban, K. (2000). Programs and strategies for nurturing creativity. In K. A. Heller, F. J. Monks, R. F. Subotnik, & R. J. Sternberg (Eds.), *International handbook of giftedness and talent* (pp. 481-494). Oxford, UK: Elsevier. Retrieved from https://www.researchgate.net/profile/Arthur_ Cropley/publication/286825058_Programs_and_Strategies_for_Nurturing_ Creativity/links/567616ae08ae502c99ce0f6a.pdf

Csikszentmihalyi, M. (1996). *Creativity: Flow and the psychology of discovery and invention*. New York, NY: Harper Collins Publishers.

Csikszentmihalyi, M. (1997). *Creativity: The psychology of discover and invention*. New York: HarperPerennial.

Csikszentmihalyi, M., Rathunde, K., & Whalen, S. (1993). *Talented teenagers: The roots of success and failure*. Cambridge: Cambridge University Press.

Danish, S. J. (2000). Youth and community development: How after-school programming can make a difference. In S. J. Danish & T. P. Gullotta (Eds.), *Developing competent youth and strong communities through after-school programming* (pp. 275-301). Washington, DC.: Child Welfare League of America, Inc.

Drew, D. E. (2010). America's wasted talent : A Karplus lecture. *Science Education, 7*(4), 287-295.

Durand-Bush, N., & Salmela, J. H. (2002). The development and maintenance of expert athletic performance: Perceptions of world and olympic champions. *Journal of Applied Sport Psychology, 14*(3), 154-171. doi:10.1080/10413200290103473

Dweck, C. S. (2007). *Mindset: The new psychology of success* (Reprint edition). New York: Ballantine Books.

Embrace Innovations. (2017). About Us. Retrieved from https://www.embraceinnovations.com/

Ericsson, K. A., Krampe, R. T., & Tesch-Römer, C. (1993). The role of deliberate practice in the acquisition of expert performance. *Psychological Review, 100*(3), 363-406.

Espinoza, P., da Luz Fontes, A. B. A., & Arms-Chavez, C. J. (2014). Attributional gender bias: Teachers' ability and effort explanations for students' math performance. *Social Psychology of Education, 17*(1), 105-126.

Florida, R. (2002). *The rise of the creative class and how it's transforming work, life, community, and everyday life.* New York, NY: Basic Books.

Gifford-Smith, M. E., & Brownell, C. A. (2003). Childhood peer relationships: Social acceptance, friendships, and peer networks. *Journal of School Psychology, 41*(4), 235-284. doi:10.1016/S0022-4405(03)00048-7

Goertzel, V., Goertzel, M. G., Goertzel, T. G., & Hansen, A. (2004). *Cradles of eminence: Childhoods of more than 700 famous men and women* (2nd edition). Scottsdale, AZ: Gifted Psychology Press.

Gould, D., Dieffenbach, K., & Moffett, A. (2002). Psychological characteristics and their development in olympic champions. *Journal of Applied Sport Psychology, 14*(3), 172-204. doi:10.1080/10413200290103482

Grigorenko, E. L., Jarvin, L., Diffley, R., Goodyear, J., Shanahan, E. J., & Sternberg, R. J. (2009). Are SSATS and GPA enough? A theory-based approach to predicting success in secondary school. *Journal of Educational Psychology, 101*(4), 964-981.

Haensly, P. A., & Parsons, J. L. (1993). Creative, intellectual, and psychosocial development through mentorship relationships and stages. *Youth & Society, 25*(2), 202-221.

Heath, S. B., & Roach, A. (1999). Imaginative actuality: Learning in the arts during the nonschool hours. *Champions of Change: The Impact of the Arts on Learning, 19-34.*

Heckman, J. J. (2000). *Invest in the very young.* Chicago, IL: Ounce of Prevention Fund: The University of Chicago Harris School of Public Policy Studies.

Higgins, M. C., & Kram, K. E. (2001). Reconceptualizing mentoring at work: A developmental network perspective. *Academy of Management Review, 26*(2), 264-288.

Hong, E., & Milgram, R. M. (2008). *Preventing talent loss.* New York: Routledge.

Hong, E., & Milgram, R. M. (2011). School personnel and climate. In *Preventing talent* loss (pp. 113-122). New York, NY: Routledge.

Isaacson, W. (2011). *Steve Jobs.* New York, NY: Simon and Schuster.

Johnson, W. B., & Ridley, C. R. (2008). *The elements of mentoring.* Macmillan Publishers.

Kaufman, J. C. (2016). Creativity 101 (second edition). New York, NY: Springer.

Kaufman, J. C., & Beghetto, R. A. (2009). Beyond big and little: The Four C model of creativity. *Review of General Psychology, 13*(1), 1-12. doi:10.1037/a0013688

Kaufman, J. C., Davis, C. D., & Beghetto, R. A. (2012). Why creativity should matter, why it doesn't, and what we can do about it. In D. Ambrose & R. J. Sternberg (Eds.), *How dogmatic beliefs harm creativity and higher-level thinking* (pp. 145-156). New York, NY: Routledge.

Kaufman, J. C., Kaufman, S. B., Beghetto, R. A., Burgess, S. A., & Persson, R. S. (2009). Creative giftedness: Beginnings, developments, and future promises. In *International handbook on giftedness* (pp. 585-598). The Netherlands: Springer.

Kaufman, J. C., & Sternberg, R. J. (Eds.). (2010). *The Cambridge handbook of creativity.* Cambridge: Cambridge University Press. Retrieved from https://books.google.com/books?hl=en&lr=&id=1EBT3Qj5L5EC&oi=fnd&pg=PR7&dq=cambridge+handbook+of+creativity&ots=7LboCzXA0q&sig=UAWWgyYrzzqfUMAYr0zF5XDFk4k

Kaufman, S. B., & Kaufman, J. C. (2007). Ten years to expertise, many more to greatness: An investigation of modern writers. *The Journal of Creative Behavior, 41*(2), 114-124.

Kim, K. H. (2011). The creativity crisis: The decrease in creative thinking scores on the Torrance Tests of Creative Thinking. *Creativity Research Journal, 23*(4), 285-295. https://doi.org/10.1080/10400419.2011.627805

King, B. J., & Pope, B. (1999). Creativity as a factor in psychological assessment and healthy psychological functioning: The assessment of psychological health: Optimism, creativity, playfulness, and transitional relatedness. *Journal of Personality Assessment, 72*, 200-207.

Kozbelt, A. (2008). Longitudinal hit ratios of classical composers: Reconciling "Darwinian" and expertise acquisition perspectives on lifespan creativity. *Psychology of Aesthetics, Creativity, and the Arts, 2*(4), 221-235.

Kram, K. E., & Isabella, L. A. (1985). Mentoring alternatives: The role of peer relationships in career development. *Academy of Management Journal.* Retrieved from http://amj.aom.org/content/28/1/110.short

Larson, R. W., Hansen, D. M., & Moneta, G. (2006). Differing profiles of developmental experiences across types of organized youth activities. *Developmental Psychology, 42*(5), 849.

Lee, S.-Y. (2002). The effects of peers on the academic and creative talent development of a gifted adolescent male. *The Journal of Secondary Gifted Education, 14*(1), 19-29. doi:10.4219/jsge-2002-387

Lepore, S. J., & Smyth, J. M. (2002). *The writing cure: How expressive writing promotes health and emotional well-being.* Washington, DC.: American Psychological Association.

Merton, R. K. (1968). The Matthew effect in science. *Science, 159*(3810), 56-63.

Metzl, E. S. (2009). The role of creative thinking in resilience after hurricane Katrina. *Journal of Psychology of Aesthetics, Creativity, and the Arts, 3*, 112-123.

Neu, T. W., Baum, S. M., & Cooper, C. R. (2004). Talent development in science: A unique tale of one student's journey. *Journal of Secondary Gifted Education, 16*(1), 7. doi:10.4219/jsge-2004-467

Nicol, J. J., & Long, B. C. (1996). Creativity and perceived stress of female music therapists and hobbyists. *Creativity Research Journal, 9,* 1-10.

Olszewski, P., Kulieke, M., & Buescher, T. (1987). The influence of the family environment on the development of talent: A literature review. *Journal for the Education of the Gifted, 11*(1), 6-28. doi:10.1177/016235328701 100102

Ommundsen, Y. (2001). Students' implicit theories of ability in physical education classes: The influence of motivational aspects of the learning environment. *Learning Environments Research, 4,* 139-158. doi:10.1023/A:101249 5615828

Paik, S. J. (2003). Ten strategies that improve learning. *Educational Horizons, 81*(2), 83-85.

Paik, S. J. (2012). From dogmatic mastery to creative productivity. In D. Ambrose & R. Sternberg (Eds.) *How dogmatic beliefs harm creativity and higher-level thinking,* 185-191. New York: NY: Routledge.

Paik, S. J. (2013). Nurturing talent, creativity, and productive giftedness: A new mastery model. In K. H. Kim, J. C. Kaufman, J. Baer, & B. Sriraman (Eds.), *Creatively gifted students are not like other gifted students,* 101-119. Rotterdam, The Netherlands: Sense Publishers.

Paik, S. J. (2015). Educational productivity. In J. D. Wright (Ed.), *International encyclopedia of the social and behavioral sciences,* 2 (7), 272-278. Oxford, UK: Elsevier. doi:10.1007/s10531-013-0544-y

Paik, S. J., Gozali, C., & Marshall-Harper, K. R. (2019). Productive giftedness: A new mastery approach to understanding talent development. In R. F. Subotnik, S. G. Assouline, P. Olszewski-Kubilius, H. Stoeger, & A. Ziegler (Eds.), *The Future of Research in Talent Development: Promising Trends, Evidence, and Implications of Innovative Scholarship for Policy and Practice. New Directions for Child and Adolescent Development,* 168, 131-159.

Paik, S. J., Marshall-Harper, K.R., Gozali, C., & Johnson, T. (2020). The life and success of Sonia Sotomayor: Perseverance and productive giftedness. In S. J. Paik, S. M. Kula, J. J. González, & V. V. González (Eds), *High-Achieving Latino Students: Successful Pathways Toward College and Beyond.*

Paik, S. J., & Walberg, H. J. (Eds.). (2007). *Narrowing the achievement gap: Strategies for educating Latino, Black, and Asian students.* New York, NY: Springer.

Patrick, H., Ryan, A. M., Alfeld-Liro, C., Fredricks, J. A., Hruda, L. Z., & Eccles, J. S. (1999). Adolescents' commitment to developing talent: The role of peers in continuing motivation for sports and the arts. *Journal of Youth and Adolescence, 28*(6), 741-763.

Pennebaker, J. W. (1997). Writing about emotional experiences as a therapeutic process. *Psychological Science, 8,* 162-166.

Pennebaker, J. W., Kiecolt-Glaser, J. K., & Glaser, R. (1988). Disclosures of traumas and immune function: Health implications for psychotherapy. *Journal of Consulting and Clinical Psychology, 56,* 239-245.

Pfeiffer, S. I., & Thompson, T. L. (2013). Creativity from a talent development perspective: How it can be cultivated in schools. In K. H. Kim, J. C. Kaufman, J. Baer, & B. Sriraman (Eds.), *Creatively gifted students are not like other gifted students* (pp. 231-255). Rotterdam: The Netherlands.

Piirto, J. (1998). *Understanding those who create.* ERIC. Retrieved from https://eric.ed.gov/?id=ED420961

Piirto, J. (2004). *Understanding creativity.* Scottsdale, Ariz: Great Potential Press.

Piske, F. H. R., Stoltz, T., & Machado, J. (2014). Creative Education for Gifted Children. *Online Submission, 5,* 347-352.

Piske, F. H. R., Stoltz, T., Machado, J. M., Vestena, C. L. B., de Oliveira, C. S., de Freitas, S. P., & Machado, C. L. (2016). Working with Creativity of Gifted Students through Ludic Teaching. *Online Submission, 7,* 1641-1647.

Piske, F. H. R., Stoltz, T., Vestena, C. L. B., de Freitas, S. P., de Fátima Bastos Valentim, B., de Oliveira, C. S., Machado, C. L. (2016). Barriers to Creativity, Identification and Inclusion of Gifted Student. *Creative Education, 7*(14), 1899-1905. doi:10.4236/ce.2016.714192

Plucker, J. A., Beghetto, R. A., & Dow, G. T. (2004). Why isn't creativity more important to educational psychologists? Potential, pitfalls, and future directions in creativity research. *Educational Psychologist, 39,* 83-97.

Quetelet, A. (n.d.). (2011). In *Encylopedia.com*. Retrieved from http://www. encyclopedia.com/topic/Adolphe_Quetelet.aspx

Ragins, B. R. (2007). Diversity and workplace mentoring relationships: A review and positive social capital approach. In T. D. Allen & L. T. Eby (Eds.), *The Blackwell handbook of mentoring: A multiple perspectives approach* (pp. 281-300). Malden, MA: Blackwell Publishing Ltd.

Redding, S. (1998). *Parents and learning.* International Academy of Education. Retrieved from http://www.orientation94.org/uploaded/MakalatPdf/ Manchurat/prac02e.pdf

Richards, R. (2010a). Everyday creativity in the classroom: A trip through time with seven suggestions. In R. A. Beghetto & R. J. Sternberg (Eds.), *Nurturing creativity in the classroom* (pp. 206-234). New York, NY: Cambridge University Press.

Richards, R. (2010b). Everyday creativity: Process and way of life- four key issues. In J. C. Kaufman & R. J. Sternberg (Eds.), *The Cambridge handbook of creativity* (pp. 189-215). Cambridge: Cambridge University Press.

Rief, S. F., & Heimburge, J. A. (2006). *How to reach and teach all children in the inclusive classroom: practical strategies, lessons, and activities* (2nd ed). San Francisco: Jossey-Bass.

Runco, M. A. (2010). Education based on a parsimonious theory of creativity. In R. A. Beghetto & J. C. Kaufman (Eds.), *Nurturing creativity in the classroom* (pp. 235-251). New York, NY: Cambridge University Press.

Runco, M. A., & Cayirdag, N. (2013). The development of children's creativity. In O. N. Saracho & B. Spodek (Eds.), *Handbook of research on the education of young children* (3rd ed., pp. 413-465). New York, NY: Routledge.

Runco, M. A., & Sakamoto, S. O. (1993). Reaching creatively gifted students through their learning styles. In R. M. Milgram, R. Dunn, & G. E. Price (Eds.), *Teaching and counseling gifted and talented adolescents: An international learning style perspective* (pp. 103-115). Westport, CT: Praeger Publishers.

Russ, S. W., & Fiorelli, J. A. (2010). Developmental approaches to creativity. In J. C. Kaufman & R. J. Sternberg (Eds.), *The Cambridge handbook of creativity* (pp. 233-249). New York, NY: Cambridge University Press.

Schlesinger, J. (2009). Creative mythconceptions: A closer look at the evidence for the "mad genius" hypothesis. *Psychology of Aesthetics, Creativity, and the Arts, 3*(2), 62-72. doi:10.1037/a0013975

Seider, S. (2013). Effort determines success at Roxbury Prep. *Kappan*, (October), 28-33.

Simonton, D. K. (2010). Creativity in highly eminent individuals. In J. C. Kaufman & R. J. Sternberg (Eds.), *The Cambridge handbook of creativity* (pp. 174--188). Cambridge: Cambridge University Press.

Skiba, T., Tan, M., Sternberg, R. J., & Grigorenko, E. L. (2010). Roads not taken, new roads to take: Looking for creativity in the classroom. In R. A. Beghetto & J. C. Kaufman (Eds.), *Nurturing creativity in the classroom* (pp. 252-269). New York, NY: Cambridge University Press.

Sommerfeld, A. (2011). The Role of Parents in Students' Structured and Unstructured Out-of-School-Time Activity Participation. In H. Kreider & H. Westmoreland (Eds.), *Promising Practices for Family Engagement in Out-of-School Time*. Charlotte, N.C.: Information Age Publishing, Inc.

Sosniak, L. A., & Gabelko, N. H. (2008). *Every child's right: Academic talent development by choice, not chance*. New York, NY: Teachers College Press.

Stariha, W. E., & Walberg, H. J. (1995). Childhood precursors of women's artistic eminence. *The Journal of Creative Behavior, 29*(4), 269-282.

Sternberg, R. J. (2003). *Wisdom, intelligence, and creativity synthesized*. Cambridge: Cambridge University Press.

Sternberg, R. J. (2010). Teaching for creativity. In R. A. Beghetto & J. C. Kaufman (Eds.), *Nurturing creativity in the classroom* (pp. 394-414). New York, NY: Cambridge University Press.

Sternberg, R. J., Jarvin, L., & Grigorenko, E. L. (2009). *Teaching For Wisdom, Intelligence, Creativity, and Success*. Thousand Oaks, Calif: Corwin Press.

Sternberg, R. J., Jarvin, L., & Grigorenko, E. L. (2011). Creativity and giftedness. In *Explorations in giftedness* (pp. 82-101). New York, NY: Cambridge University Press.

Tuffiash, M., Roring, R. W., & Ericsson, K. A. (2007). Expert performance in SCRABBLE: implications for the study of the structure and acquisition of complex skills. *Journal of Experimental Psychology: Applied, 13*(3), 124-134.

VanTassel-Baska, J. (1998). The development of academic talent: A mandate for educational best practice. *Phi Delta Kappan, 79*(10), 760-763.

Vygotsky, L. S. (2004). Imagination and creativity in childhood. *Journal of Russian & East European Psychology, 42*(1), 7-97.

Walberg, H. J., Niemiec, R. P., & Frederick, W. C. (1994). Productive curriculum time. *Peabody Journal of Education, 69*(3), 86-100.

Walberg, H. J., & Paik, S. J. (1997). Home environments for learning. In H. J. Walberg & G. D. Haertel (Eds.), *Psychology and educational practice* (pp. 356-368). Berkeley, CA: McCutchan Publishing.

Walker, W. J. (1986). Creativity: Fostering Golden Environments. *The Clearing House, 59*(5), 220-222. doi:10.2307/30186518

8.

MOTIVATED OR UNMOTIVATED FOR THE CREATIVE: APPROACH VALUES FROM A HIGHLY ABLE LEARNER'S POINT OF VIEW

Éva Gyarmathy

Senior researcher at the Institute for Cognitive Neuroscience and Psychology of the Hungarian Academy.

ORCID: 0000-0002-3882-9397.

Abstract: *I present the main factors that play a role in the development of creativity and its relationship to outstanding skills by analyzing the processes that make creative functioning effective. In many cases, some essential elements of creative thinking, such as the inner drive, the motivation that does not allow the creative person to let go of the task, appear as a disturbance, a neurological difference in the unusual processing of information. The relationship of creativity identified with integration disorders seems necessary. However, disturbances can be reduced or even prevented. Environmental factors can influence the development of characteristics necessary for creative thinking in many ways. Awareness of characteristics and environmental factors, as well as their relationship,*

and conscious application of the procedures leading to the solution are an important tool not only in talent management but also in the treatment of integration disorders.
Keywords: *Creativity, Talent, School Atmosphere.*

"Common sense is the collection of prejudices
Acquired by age eighteen."Albert Einstein

Introduction

Creativity is a wonderful thing, and it is recognized everywhere and by everyone, but a breakthrough is still to come in everyday practice, particularly in school. Despite all the scientific results and promoting materials, the school still fails to view creativity as an inseparable part of learning.

The inability of education to change is manifest not only in the question of creativity, as there is hardly an area where education has been able to move away from the practices of the previous centuries. One key reason for this could be the fact that of all professions, the socialization, and as such, the preparation of teachers is one of the most thorough and most profound. Learning the role of teacher begins in childhood, without this being conscious. During their socialization, the pattern is rammed home for teachers each day, at the level of personal experience. Teachers are basically the good students, who were successful at school and who then carry on the values, solutions and behavior patterns they learned as children.

And if the school failed to consider creativity as a part of learning, then teachers have been carefully prepared not to be motivated for creative solutions, activities and behavior. It thus obviously takes special effort for teachers to change their point of view and to be able to convert their method from one focusing on ready-made knowledge to teaching how to find solutions. A lot of theoretical and practical knowledge is needed for this task.

Why should I be creative?

The adult world very much values the outstanding skills development of children. Children who can read, write and count at a kindergarten age, while doing nothing special that anyone could not do a few years later, receive general acknowledgement and even get a talent label for their achievements beyond their age.

Children, on the other hand, who show outstanding creativity, are at best treated to a forbearing indulgence by their environment. Creating a channel system capable of regulating water flow, designing protection for foxes or composing a song are true creative achievements, still, they are not taken seriously if done at age five. Indeed, if children engage in such non-school-related activities, say, age ten, let alone if they do so instead of reading and counting, they may downright come off badly. This is so despite the fact that in terms of intellectual investment, a creative act far surpasses the acquisition of reading skills.

Smart children thus learn early on that it is better to stay smart and not engage in risks. They haven't heard about creativity, yet, but they know already that asking something about which adults don't know the answer is generally regarded as silliness. If they let their imagination run free, they will be told off for not paying attention, and if they tell adults what they were thinking of, the reaction they get is very probably one of "you're talking nonsense". If they are inquisitive and ask questions, they disturb others and are sometimes even called impertinent. If they quench their curiosity by taking the computer apart, wanting to learn how it works, then they really get into trouble and get "you've ruined something again".

Smart children often arrive at school hiding inside their shell. They may make a few additional attempts at asking questions and finding tasks for themselves, or maybe bombarding the teacher with their own ideas, but they soon learn the most important lesson of all: at school, tasks are set by the teacher, and questions are asked by the teacher. Smart, imaginative children turn into even smarter, but less imaginative youths. They win academic competitions, even though they don't know what those are good for. Then they find out that if they perform well, they get into institutions providing even more knowledge so that they may learn even more of what we already know.

Meanwhile, children who failed to grasp the rules of the game, slowly drop behind. They are unable to draw orderly circles in their exercise books. Circles invariably become cherries or car tires, and they get scolded by the teacher. Later on, they would tinker away at home and miss days of school. They would frequent shady places, dance, play music or whittle away. They would write computer programs instead of doing homework. If the teacher confronts them, they behave impudently, saying how school tasks are boring.

Intelligent children know what they are allowed to do, and as a result they will make it into talent education programs, but not the little rascals who produce amplifiers at home (and, God forbid, even sell them), or invent new food supplements and go to the pharmacy to find out how pills are made. Intelligent children go to university and become smart adults, maybe even researchers, who will always play safe and do research in areas and bring results that never lead to surprises. Everyone understands them, everyone agrees with them, and they get accolades by the dozen.

Big surprises and risks do not belong to their world. Knowledge is their bastion, and they look down on the insecurities and ramblings of the creative. They cannot fathom why some of their peers would leave a successful career simply because of an interest in a new area, and because of wanting to do something they are intrigued by. Good students become good scholars and will loathe and despise "lazy bon vivants" because the good students themselves never dared to venture into the unknown.

The essence of creativity is that even the un-connectable can be connected, the insolvable solved, only not in the ways we already know and have learned about in school and can simply whip out from inside our heads, or from a book/the internet. This is why imagination, risk-taking, probing of the boundaries, viewpoint change and associative looseness all form part of creativity.

Talent, intelligence, creativity, motivations – vectors and origins of forces

The concepts in the section title are heavily interrelated. They are inseparable and would invariably crop up when any of them comes under scrutiny. For instance, ever since Guilford came up with the expression "creativity" in 1950, the concept has been intertwined with the concept of talent. It was used for a long time as a synonym of genius, although ever since the beginning it was apparent that creativity in and of itself is insufficient for outstanding achievements.

Talent education came to appropriate creativity and its development, even though it is a basic ability for everyone, and an integral part of learning and coping with everyday situations. Then, fortunately, creativity became everyone's property, and humanistic psychology celebrated it as the highest level of mental health.

However, the concept of creativity did not get linked to learning, although Guilford (1950) explicitly noted this connection when creating the concept: *"a creative act is an instance of learning"* (p. 446). Several other outstanding thinkers regard creativity as an important element of human thinking and learning, which should be mirrored in school learning, as well.

Vygotsky, Piaget, Steiner, Morin, and many other professionals working on learning and teaching have written insightfully about the problem (Piske et al., 2016; Piske et al., 2017), and even authors from different starting points arrive at the conclusion that creativity needs to get a prominent place in learning, and, by extension, at school.

It is, of course, not only creativity that has been linked with the concept of talent. Talent was linked, at the beginning of the 20th century, with intelligence (Terman, 1926), then, towards the end of the century, with motivation (Gyarmathy, 2014) by scholars working on the subject, while especially multi-factor theories like the classical three-circle theory of Renzulli (1986) put forward that talent is a complex phenomenon the related concepts of which are heavily intertwined.

According to Gyarmathy (2014), we can study ability, creativity and motivation separately when thinking about talent, but we would continuously come up against the problem that none of them stands up on its own.

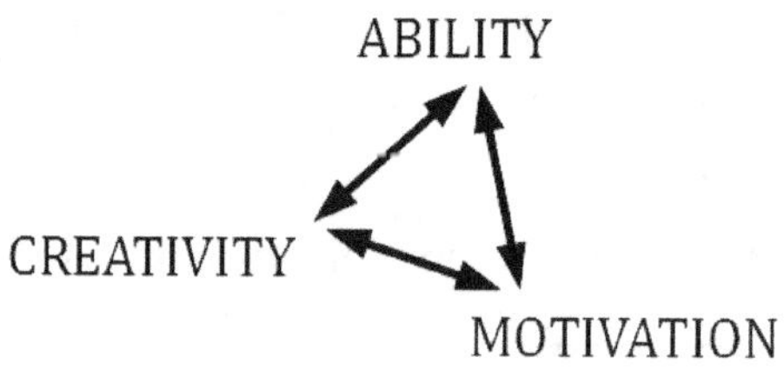

FIGURE 1: The attitude characteristic of talent is not simply the sum of three characteristics, but the interplay of three vectors, three directions of force (Gyarmathy, 2014)

MacKinnon (1962) states, there is a slight correlation between intelligence and creativity up until an IQ of about 120, but above this point, neither the intelligence quotient nor school performance is able to predict the individual's level of creativity. In other words, high intelligence is no guarantee for creativity, while low intelligence provides no room for it. Therefore, if we select the top 1-5% most intelligent as the talent population, a high proportion of creative individuals will certainly be left out from this group.

Landau (1980) emphasizes that creativity is the joint manifestation of logic, knowledge and imagination. At the point where knowledge becomes insufficient, ideas are needed, and imagination kicks in, looking for, and ideally finding, new solutions. Next, we again need methodical knowledge, and thus it is the elaboration of the idea that makes new knowledge usable.

Intelligence looks for an answer within the body of existing knowledge and arrives at a solution using convergent thinking. Creativity uses divergent thinking to mobilize knowledge from different areas and find diverse answers (Landau, 1980).

According to Getzelz and Csikszentmihalyi (1975), in order to understand creativity, we need to regard human beings as not only problem solvers but also problem finders. A problem-finding behavior is a form of stimulus seeking. Creative thinking incorporates problem finding. Our thinking about intelligence should be broadened to include creativity.

The motivational aspect of creativity – self-rewarding and autonomous

While Guilford (1950) identified divergent thinking as an element of intelligence, Amabile (1983) regarded intelligence as an element of creativity, which is a necessary, but not sufficient component of the creative process. She emphasized that several factors belonging to creativity, such as motivation for exploration or intellectual risk-taking, cannot be measured using intelligence tests.

The difference between creative-intelligent and merely intelligent students lies in characteristics of personality, motivation and behavior. It lies not in a difference in abilities, but in a predisposition to creative thinking, according to Davis and Rimm (1985).

When existing knowledge is insufficient, that is when exploration, seeking out the new becomes necessary. Arriving at a solution often requires uncovering extra resources, and motivation can initiate exploration and risk-taking. The power of striving for success can also strengthen the creative ability if the necessary behavior has a prominent role in the individual's coping arsenal.

The disadvantage of highly intelligent students lies in their knowledge because the tasks at school or even in competitions fail to reach the level at which their knowledge at hand proves insufficient. They don't get socialized to find creative solutions. Freeman's (1990) study also revealed that driving intellectual talents towards attaining school excellence can lead to a reduction in their creative potential.

Intelligent students trust knowledge, rather than imagination, although both are necessary for creative thinking. However, while knowledge is certain, imagination is knowledge not yet confirmed, it is more of a possibility. Only an individual who tolerates uncertainty and indeterminateness will be able to trust imagination. Creative individuals can do this, and are not content with the usual solutions, which would keep problem-solving at the old level. The process is self-rewarding, and so once someone can experience the creative approach, that experience will become a motivating force.

Besides being self-rewarding, creative thinking is also autonomous and self-controlled, because it doesn't simply use others' knowledge, it creates new knowledge itself. As such, measuring creativity is an odd process, because it is impossible to be creative on command since creative thinking has a significant amount of unconscious content.

The usual reward-based motivation methods are unsuitable. External reinforcement typically lowers the internal drive. Also, it is impossible to grade and evaluate fairly the result of a creative task, and this should not, in fact, be done, because it leads to the loss of the joy that comes with solutions born from imagination. In the case of creative tasks, the feedback should be neutral: "This is also an interesting solution" "This is also a way to do it". "I didn't think of that."

The controlling atmosphere, which still enjoys priority at school, is not conducive to experiencing autonomous, self-controlling and self-rewarding behavior, including creative solutions. Intelligent students will thereby experience success not through the mobilization of imagination, but of knowledge.

The factors of a creative climate (Ekvall, 1996) – challenge, dynamism, playfulness, humor, freedom, risk taking, time and support for ideas, trust, openness, debate – are downright contrary to the factors of the school atmosphere. Children with outstanding abilities in an environment not supporting the creative approach have no other option than to develop even more outstanding abilities.

However, even a creative climate encourages knowledge acquisition. There is indirect evidence that creativity and mastery motivation[4] are closely related. Support from this comes from the creative climate study of Szilvia Péter-Szarka (2012), who

---

[4] According to Barrett and Morgan (1995), mastery motivation is multidimensional and self-rewarding and encourages the individual to persevere in situations requiring at least a small amount of challenge, when skills acquisition and task solving is needed.

found that mastery motivation test results were a much better indicator of the effect of the creative climate than creativity test results. In other words, a suitable environment may be able to initiate the motivational aspect of creativity.

According to Gyarmathy (2014), talent is a greater than normal internal drive directed towards change: it is directed towards development and effecting improvement. Talent is not interested in whether something is attainable, but in how it can be attained. A consequence of this motivation is obsessed preparation, practice, work and divergent thinking, which is directed at finding ways outside of the usual ones if the usual solutions are insufficient.

Children with outstanding abilities and creative children

Siegler and Kotovsky (1986) differentiate two different concepts of giftedness:

1. Schoolhouse giftedness can be identified and assessed at school age;
2. Creative-productive giftedness is to be studied, they claim, in adulthood.

Achievement realization and the period of goal attainment is associated in the case of the schoolhouse gifted with a time interval varying between minutes and months (e.g., from tests to exams), while in the case of the productive gifted, this tends to take between months to years. The schoolhouse gifted do well at school, of course, as this is their primary characteristic; they are excellent at obtaining and storing knowledge; in contrast, the productive gifted use knowledge to discover new things, and prefer that which can be discovered over that which can be learned.

The problem of gifted education favoring abilities is that those who perform well in education are not necessarily identical to the talented who will later be capable of outstanding creations. Schoolhouse or lesson-learning giftedness is, however, easy to assess and can even be gauged through school grades. These children are excellent at storing and regurgitating information, while the creative-productive gifted are capable of new, original creations. Their thinking is analogous to that of a researcher, an explorer, or an artist. They use their knowledge to bring a new product about, while the former type exploits what is at hand.

Naturally, the two types are not mutually exclusive. Individuals who are successful at school may also be creative-productive gifted, capable of new creations, in which venture their knowledge acquisition ability may be of help. Even if schoolhouse giftedness does not come with sufficient creativity, it can be a valuable contribution to humanity by handing down culture. Simplifying things a little, we could say that the creative-productive gifted shape culture, while the schoolhouse-testing, or lesson-learning gifted use and maintain culture.

However, creative solutions fail to grow in an education system in which the goal is clear-cut knowledge and convergent thinking, and learning is externally controlled and defined. Creative energy will "dry up under the relentless impact of 'serious' academic schooling" (Eisner, 2002, p. 5). Indeed, creative children are at a disadvantage at school. They do not easily tolerate monotony, they get bored, they generally confuse the teacher with unusual questions and humor, their behavior is unpredictable, non-conforming, and irritating for the teacher.

Due to their characteristics and special performance, the creative-productive gifted must face the fact throughout their lives that they don't fit into the world that builds on predictable achievers and those who meet expectations. Even despite the myriad evidence for the power of creativity. Professionals who do well at school and then cling to certain knowledge throughout their lives do not look favorably on "unreliable" creative solutions.

This approach of persecution is not new, and is not confined to those with average abilities; in fact, the highly-able are especially loathe to accept "geniuses", who were regarded as pariahs in earlier times, too: "In this persecution men of genius have no fiercer or more terrible enemies than the men of academies, who possess the weapons of talent, the stimulus of vanity, and the prestige by preference accorded to them by the vulgar, and by governments which, in large part, consist of the vulgar" (Lombroso, 1891, p. 36).

Incorporating creativity into school education would protect the creative, and would make the development of divergent thinking and imagination available to everyone, but this requires accepting that creativity necessitates a different-from-normal thinking and nervous system.

Creativity is deviance

Creativity had not even been named as such when it was already linked to insanity and lunacy by professionals, and this approach still endures in thinking about creative talent. The form of insanity called a genius by Lombroso (1891), which he described using biographical anecdotes, received further scientific support from Nisbet (1893).

> "... apparently at the opposite poles of the human intellect, genius and insanity are, in reality, but different phases of a morbid susceptibility of, or want of balance in, the cerebrospinal system" (Nisbet, 1893, in Mula, Hermann, Trimble, 2016).

Cesare Lombroso (1891) cites Mirabeau in the preface of his book: "Good sense is the absence of every strong passion, and only men of strong passions can be great". He subsequently writes: "Good sense travels on the well-worn paths; genius, never. And that is why the crowd, not altogether without reason, is so ready to treat great men as lunatics."

Lombroso discloses much about his view of geniuses in chapter II with the following keywords: "The signs of degeneration: Height, Rickets, Pallor, Emaciation, Physiognomy, Cranium and Brain, Stammering, Lefthandedness, Sterility, Unlikeness to Parents, Precocity, Delayed development, Misoneism, Vagabondage, Unconsciousness, Instinctiveness, Somnambulism, The Inspiration of Genius, Contrast, Intermittence, Double Personality, Stupidity, Ilypernesthesia, Paroesthesia, Amnesia, Originality, Fondness for special words" (Lombroso, 1891, p. 5).

Motivation towards creative solutions is rooted in a different-from-normal neural functioning. Mula et al. in their 2016 work 125 years after Lombroso arrive at the conclusion supported by numerous scientific data that creativity requires some amount of neuropsychological deviance. Their keywords are: frontotemporal dementia, bipolar, cyclothymic mood disorder. Kéri (2010) collected some further psychiatric categories often characterizing the creative personality: schizophrenia, schizotypal personality disorder, autism, ADHD, and cerebral abnormalities, such as low latent inhibition, hyperconnectivity and hypofrontality, cognitive dysmetria, racing thoughts, an expansion of conceptual boundaries, "overinclusive" thinking.

All this may sound frightening, but only because the psychiatric nomenclature foregrounds the illness and disorder aspect of irregular traits. Neurological functions and neurochemical mechanisms indicating psychosis are also a precondition of creative associations, but these neurological factors of creative development are not overly attractive for an education oriented toward intellectual coping.

Some traits also characterize creativity that often leads to learning and behavior problems, this time not so much from a medical point of view:

Oversensitivity: Creative individuals are often characterized by extreme sensitivity already as small children. Smells, colors, materials and sounds may have an extremely strong effect on them. This incurs a disadvantage in everyday life in many respects, but at the same time, this sensitivity makes one capable of getting a feel for fine details, with small differences and nuances possibly becoming significant; oversensitivity thus contributes to creative thinking through fine-tuning.

We learned from Andersen's tale (The Princess and the Pea) that princesses can be identified from their sensitivity. Problem sensitivity, that is, discovering problems, can be an initiator of change and creation. This is furthered by a sensitivity to nuances and fine differences. Small children still react to everything, and if the world is not narrowed down to the "smart things" by their environment, then they may retain sufficient sensitivity for divergent thinking.

Weak latent inhibition: A weakness of mental inhibition can cause a lot of problems in integration, but at the same time, some amount of laxity is necessary to arrive at previously not obvious associations. The studies of Carson (2014) proved that if weak latent inhibition, otherwise linked to schizotypal traits and psychosis, is present in individuals with high intelligence, then high creativity ensues. Creative performance increases with lower latent inhibition in individuals with average intelligence, as well, but it is lower in comparison to individuals with high intelligence. It seems a deviant neurological functioning would be most worthwhile in the case of intelligent individuals.

Perfectionism: A good student sets the bar according to the teacher's expectations, while creative students do so according to their own expectations, which doesn't always correspond to what the school regards as important. Creative children often want to perfect in a different way and in a different area than what the adult world would like.

Striving for perfection can lead to a lot of trouble in a world content with imperfections. Creative minds find it unacceptable if something that is important to them is not perfect. If they find the solution wanting, they will begin anew, even at the cost of destroying the creation they regard as not good enough.

Sequential weakness: The holistic processing style associated with the right hemisphere is an enormous advantage in discovering connections, but there is also a need for the detail-oriented, analytical functioning of the left hemisphere. The right hemisphere produces wholes, images, concepts and ideas from the details at hand. Its functioning is intuitive and less conscious. It produces a whole even when details are sparse, but often a mistaken one. As a result, a weaker role of the left hemisphere in information processing can lead to specific learning difficulties.

While the school does its best to confine thinking to the left hemisphere, Australian researchers (Chi and Snyder, 2011) have developed a "cap" that stimulates the right hemisphere and blocks the functioning of the left hemisphere so as to strengthen creative performance. By blocking knowledge, imagination gets the chance to work in lieu of memory, and the brain thus influenced can approach problems in an open-minded way without bias. However, individuals born with such a "thinking cap" might easily receive a label of learning difficulty. School expectations and creative functioning stand rather wide apart.

Strong stimulus-seeking behavior: Divergent thinking is manifest in exploration. A strong exploratory behavior, however, is often identified as hyperactivity by the environment. At the same time, hyperactivity can in fact in many respects even be an advantage. Neurotransmitters are produced at lower than average levels in the stimulus processing system of hyperactive individuals. Stimuli create less tension in them, and they therefore live in a constant state of experience seeking. They easily tolerate the tension caused by uncertainty and equivocality, indeed, it is almost necessary for them to maintain the appropriate neurological state. They seek out such situations, and therefore have a greater chance of being able to deal with the tension-producing stages of the creative process.

Daydreaming: A typical element of lists identifying creativity, but mostly gets identified as a sign of attention disorder when manifest at school. Such individuals are unable to pay attention to what is directly before them and is obvious, because they get distracted by other stimuli or get immersed in their own internal imagery. Their attention wanders and they spot things others don't. At other times, they are hyper-focused and everything else ceases to exist around them. Thomas Alva Edison was dismissed as unteachable by his teacher because he would be immersed in observing how a spider was weaving its web instead of paying attention to his teacher. Learning can take many forms. A spider's web offers up so many mysteries that one could weave a whole school year's material out of it. It's quite understandable for a child with a different-from-normal thinking who is hungry for knowledge to get caught up in it.

The different forms of learning are the different forms of creativity

Creativity denotes the elusive phenomenon when elements in the mind are arranged differently from before and something new and original is created, and it likewise denotes the behavior of the individual resisting the known and the conventional, even seeking out ambiguity, uncertainty and disorder, from which a new order may arise.

The creativity of small children is a natural form of free imagination, mostly still unconstrained by knowledge. Mature creative thinking, however, must grapple with the conventional and the established. We should differentiate child and adult giftedness. Adult giftedness is not simply the continuation of child giftedness. Few of the apparently gifted children go on to become outstanding creators. Adult creativity entirely requires abilities and personality. Early childhood, school-age and mature creativity are different, as these constitute different stages of development.

The following are three stages of the development of creativity:

1. The pre-conventional stage lasts until about the age of eight years. Imagination can soar freely, not yet being constrained by knowledge and experience. Children learn about the world through play. Play allows for making mistakes, and everything may happen, so there is an enormous opportunity to learn and fantasize about the world.

2. In the conventional stage, the goal is discovering reality. Children wish to learn and desire challenges and develop their skills and abilities. Should this not seem so, that is due to the school failing to offer learning opportunities in the appropriate way.

3. The post-conventional stage is the stage of creation. After about the age of twelve to thirteen, youngsters start looking for real tasks. At this point, a child's playful imagination must be mobilized while in possession of previous knowledge, and reality and knowledge must be reconciled and integrated with imagination. Knowledge must thereby be recreated. This is the level of expert learning when the learner no longer simply knows the rules but creates them.

When all goes well, everyone goes through the first two stages. However, individuals will only enter the third stage once they have enough experience with the first two stages and possess the power needed to tolerate the uncertainty of knowledge-recreation.

People become motivated to creativity when they start believing that they are capable of creating something new. This is supported by education following the natural knowledge acquisition process. The three forms of learning are the three stages of development:

1. Free exploration, trial-and-error learning, play – all learning should start with this.
2. Methodical learning, acquisition of rules and methods – without this, there is no secure understanding.
3. Comprehensive knowledge, the overview of regularities, the creation of an individual knowledge system – the autonomous thinking of adults, created not through education but by the individual.

Education should establish the first two levels of learning in order for the third, creative adult thinking to emerge. Irrespective of whether a learner has a nervous system that is open to creativity or one that is less open to it, the above will support the optimal development of thinking.

For a creative personality, the environment is a repository of experience. For these individuals, everything seems novel, and novelty is as good as a basic need for them. As such, creative minds cause a disturbance in a narrow education system. At the same time, the majority, that is, the children whose nervous system can only tolerate creative tension to an average extent, will at best only obtain knowledge in a rigid education, and are unable to even fathom the associated possibilities of improvisation.

However, once children have had a chance to experience learning through free exploration and being able to probe the world without serious consequences, just like in playing, they will be able to approach novelties without anxiety. Non-organized learning, when children play with the learning material, automatically advances to methodical learning, when the learner wants to look at the material in a logical system. If the school provides these, then it lays the most important foundation stones for creativity: it develops imagination and logic. The third stage, when individuals need to assemble knowledge themselves, perchance in some new system of order, happens automatically.

Children with outstanding knowledge, even child prodigies, will often fail to become outstandingly creative adults, because they turn to knowledge too early on, and fail to experience the free, playful manipulation of the elements of the world to a sufficient extent. In cognitive development, the dividing line is teenage age. This is when it gets determined, whether an individual with even extremely outstanding early abilities and knowledge will become a creative talent. If they fail to experience free, commitment-free play that surpasses even their own desire for knowledge, then they may become excellent professionals, but not creative talents. They fail to make it to the post-conventional stage, and will only excel conventionally.

The environment socializing for creativity

What hasn't been, should be brought about, if everything points towards its fundamental necessity. Creative school learning is such a thing. It is not creativity lessons that we need, but an approach, building up creative processes. The greatest task falls on teachers, who need to refresh their views about learning and behavior in some respects.

A characteristic of creative solutions is reconciling the irreconcilable, that is, producing, or "creating", something that hasn't been. This is exactly the task at hand for teachers, and so they can, in fact, obtain some new experience by taking on what creative people do.

A creative personality emerges from a background of a special brain physiology, but its essence, tolerating uncertainty-induced tension, can be developed. To this end, situations are suitable in which one must resist the conventional and tolerate the tension induced by the unconventional and the ambivalent, from which new solutions are born.

Everyday experience shapes neurological functions, which is why the environment is definitive in the development of creativity, as well. There are some further key aspects of creative functioning over and above an excellent associative ability, which, through awareness, can be used to as ammunition in the development of creativity. Here are two examples, illustrated with practical tasks:

Pushing the boundaries: Probing the boundaries is important for mental health, too, as it may uncover non-existing obstacles. Still, the environment mostly fails to appreciate this behavior. On the other hand, if there are no rules to probe and push, children fail to learn how to constructively tackle barriers and obstacles. Children need rational boundaries and flexible rules to learn that there are rules which can be changed through mutual agreement. We can encourage the probing of boundaries even through school materials and small tasks and questions, and show that things are not immutable or finite:

- What does multiplication mean in life? Does nature do multiplication? In what ways can we do multiplication?
- What could be possible directions of evolution? Will the human brain merge with machines, or is the world of machines coming?
- The fate of some characters before the beginning or after the end of a literary work.

Viewpoint change: We can gain strikingly new knowledge by looking at something from a different viewpoint, from afar, from the outside, or from the inside:

- The location of historical events helps us get a feel for situations or battles.
- The process of photosynthesis can be depicted looking out from inside of a leaf.
- The age of enlightenment from the point of view of the historian and the literary expert.
- Self-characterization, but written as if from the point of view of a friend.

Conclusion

Fish is Fish.[5] From the point of view of a fish, a bird is a fish with wings, a cow is a fish with horns giving milk, and so on.

---

[5] In the story of Leo Lionni, the tadpole, once matured into a frog, explores the land, and then goes back into the pond to tell its friend, the fish, about what it has seen. The fish, however, only knows the fish world and translates everything to its own point of view.

The same is the case with smart children and teachers, who see the world from the confines of their own socialization. In order to obtain experience, they must step out of their comfort zone and learn how not to be "fish", which may seem difficult and dangerous. This is why it would be much better, if creative thinking belonged to the comfort zone, that is, were part of socialization: we shouldn't educate only from the perspective of a fish.

A creative personality emerges from a special neurological arrangement. Those who are born with such traits don't have many choices, and can mostly choose between creativity or psychological disorders, and for the time being, the latter seems too often the direction individuals take. For a highly-able child, at this point it is not worth taking on the mental burden that comes with creativity, but it is easier to gather knowledge and depend on what already is.

Introducing the creative climate into education can facilitate the integration of children born creative, as well as taking on the risk of the creative way in general.

In order for someone to be creative, they don't need to be "different". It's quite enough for them to be themselves, because they will then certainly differ from everyone else. If they are accepted, they will be able to accept both themselves, and those who are different. If they have the choice and the decision, then they can experience dealing with uncertain situations and this in-congruency induced tension becomes natural, and the tension induced by creative processes will tolerable, or perhaps even agreeable. All the while, children can be autonomous through their choice and get to know themselves.

Creative functioning can be bolstered by a culture which treats diversity and different solutions as values, which offers freedom and alternatives, which regards in-congruency as natural, and which looks at speciality, not as a disorder, but as a challenge, a task to solve.

References

Amabile, T. M. (1983) *The Social Psychology of Creativity.* Springer, New York.

Carson, S. (2014) Leveraging the "mad genius" debate: why we need a neuroscience of creativity and psychopathology. *Front. Hum. Neurosci.* 8-771.

Chi R. P., Snyder A. W. (2011) Facilitate Insight by Non-Invasive Brain Stimulation. *PLoS ONE* 6(2): e16655. doi:10.1371/journal.pone.0016655

Davis, G. A., Rimm, S. B. (1985) *Education of the gifted and talented.* Prentice Hall Inc., Anglewood, Cliffs, New Jersey.

Eisner, E. (2002). *The arts and the creation of mind.* NewHaven, CT: Yale University Press.

Ekvall, G. (1996). Organizational climate for creativity and innovation. *European Journal of Work and Organizational Psychology* 5 (1), 105-123.

Freemann, J. (1990) The intellectually gifted adolescent. In: M. J. A. Howe (Ed.) *Encouraging the Development of Exceptional Skills and Talent.* British Psychological Society, 89-108.

Getzels, J. W., Csikszentmihalyi, M. (1975) From problem solving to problem finding. In I. A. Taylor & J. W. Getzels (Eds) *Perspectives in Creativity.* Aldine Publishing Company, Chicago.

Guilford, J. P. (1950) Creativity. *American Psychologist* 5, 444-454.

Gyarmathy, E. (2014) The talent's netting way of thinking. *Gifted Educational International Online,* 2 Dec., 1-17.

Kéri, S. (2010) Kreativitás és pszichopatológia az újabb neurobiológiai kutatások tükrében. [Creativity and psychopathology in the light of recent neurobiological research]. *Magyar Pszichológiai Szemle* 65(2), 243--272.

Landau, E. (1980) *Mut zur Begabung. [Courage towards giftedness.*] Reinhardt: München.

Lombroso, C. T. (1891) *The man of genius.* London: Walter Scott

MacKinnon, D. W. (1962) The nature and nurture of creative talent. *American Psychologist,* 17, 484-495.

Mula, M., Hermann, B., Trimble, M. R. (2016) Neuropsychiatry of creativity. *Epilepsy & Behavior* 57, 225-229

Nisbet J. F. (1893) *The insanity of genius.* London: Ward and Downey. In M. Mula, B. Hermann, M. R. Trimble (2016) Neuropsychiatry of creativity. *Epilepsy &Behavior,* 57, 225-229.

Péter-Szarka, Sz. (2012): Creative climate as a means to promote creativity in the classroom. *Electronic Journal of Research in Educational Psychology,* 10, 1011-1034.

Piske, F. H. R., Stoltz, T., Guérios, E., de Camargo, D., Vestena, C. L. B., de Freitas, S. P., de Oliveira Machado Barby, A. A., & Santinello, J. (2017). The Importance of Teacher Training for Development of Gifted Students' Creativity: Contributions of Vygotsky. *Creative Education,* 8, 131-141. doi:10.4236/ce.2017.81011

Piske, F. H. R., Stoltz, T., Guérios, E., de Freitas, S. P. (2016). Creativity and Complex Thoughts of Gifted Students from Contributions of Edgar Morin and Rudolf Steiner. Creative Education, 7, 2268-2278. doi:10.4236/ce.2016.715221

Renzulli, J. (1986) The three-ring conception of giftedness: a developmental model for creative productivity. In R. J. Sternberg & J. E. Davidson (Eds.) *Conceptions of Giftedness.* Cambridge: Cambridge University Press.

Siegler, R. S., Kotovsky, K. (1986). Two levels of giftedness: Shall ever the twain meet? In R. J. Sternberg, J. E. Davidson (Eds.) Conceptions of giftedness. Cambridge, England: Cambridge University Press. 417-435.

Terman, L.M. (1926) Mental and Physical Traits of Thousend Gifted Children. *Genetic Studies of Genius*, I (2) Stanford University Press, California.

9.

COMMITMENT, CREATIVITY AND BRAINS: PERSPECTIVES ON GIFTED EDUCATION

Daiana Yamila Rigo

Professor of University of Río Cuarto degree and postgraduate courses, Argentina.

ORCID: 0000-0003-0312-6429

Romina Elisondo

Associate Professor at the Department of Education Sciences of the University of Río Cuarto, Argentina.

ORCID: 0000-0002-7841-9878

María Laura de la Barrera

PhD in Psychology from the Faculty of Psychology of the University of San Luis, Argentina.

ORCID: 0000-0002-2096-0741

Abstract: *This chapter presents three current perspectives that come together to think about the educational practices of gifted children. The theoretical advances regarding commitment, creativity and the brain are discussed, lines of research that show the importance of promoting the configuration of instructional contexts that highlight differences in ways of learning, respecting* *the times and styles of each person, from the socio-constructivist perspective. From a sociocultural approach, arguments are put forward for understanding that giftedness is the result of the joint interaction of multiple contextual and personal factors, resulting in the value of practices found in the model of the three rings.*

Keywords: *Commitment; Creativity; Brain; Education.*

This chapter presents three current perspectives relevant to gifted education: progress in relation to commitment, creativity studies and neurosciences. Currently, theses lines of research refer to the importance of promoting instructional contexts that highlight the differences in ways of learning, respecting the time and styles of each person.

Based on the socio-constructivist model, the importance of developing situated practices and interactions with a wide variety of symbolic, physical and social resources is highlighted. There are several theoretical models that contemplate these topics which we intend to discuss in this chapter. From a sociocultural perspective, we find Tannenbaum and Mönks and Van Boxtel, who mention that giftedness is the result of the interaction of multiple contextual and personal factors. Specifically, from the model of the three rings, three components are emphasized: commitment to the task, creativity and evolutionary aspects, which together interrelate under certain educational circumstances (Renzulli, 1978; Renzulli and Gaesser, 2015).

This chapter is organized into three sections which, from a pedagogical perspective, approach in more depth commitment to academic tasks, creativity and neurosciences, as educational contributions towards giftedness.

Possibilities and alternatives for commitment

Boredom is an emotion that is frequently cited in literature about giftedness.Despite gifted students tending to have great persistence, commitment and improvement in relation to school tasks, boredom is an emotion that usually emerges as a result of faster learning rhythms, or perceived lack of cognitive challenge in tasks. Relationships between high skills and boredom should not be understood as a cause-effect relationship, but rather as a feeling that can appear in every student facing activities that are outside their zone of proximal development (Feldhusen and Kroll, 1991; Guirado, 2015).

Boredom is defined as an affective state composed of unpleasant feelings, lack of stimulation and low physiological activation. Boredom provokes the sensation that time does not pass, so people want to escape from that situation. It is characterized by postures or gestures that denote dismotivation, low involvement, lack of interest and little appreciation of the activity. Therefore, boredom can be described as an emotion that involves five dimensions, namely: affective, cognitive, physiological, expressive and motivational dimensions (Preckel, Götz & Frenzel, 2010; Perkrum, Göetz, Daniels, Stupnisky & Perry, 2010).

Boredom is characterized as a negative feeling against something repetitive, as the opposite of academic commitment and one of the main reasons for disengagement.

Commitment generates great academic interest in various disciplinary fields, including Educational Psychology; because it has a double function: preventing student dropout and general disinterest. A considerable number of models and definitions have been offered about this construct. In general, commitment is the level to which students are involved, connected and actively engaged to learn and perform. More specifically, commitment to academic tasks refers to the intensity and emotion with which students are involved to initiate and carry out learning activities. Commitment is an energy in action that connects the person with the activity. There is a consensus that commitment is a constructive goal that includes affective, cognitive and behavioral aspects (Appleton, Cristenson, Kin & Reschly, 2006; Fredriscks, Blumenfeld & Paris, 2004; Rigo, 2017).

Landis & Reschly (2013) state that student commitment can be an essential construction for understanding, predicting and preventing school dropout and disinterest among gifted students. There are contextual factors that connect these students and other features that disengage them. That is to say, a multitude of factors, such as lack of structure and clarity in the assignment, lack of support towards having greater autonomy in decision making, low perception of the usefulness of what has been taught, or continuing absence of challenges, can influence the learning experience of the students, who end up assuming a more passive participation, decreasing their levels of involvement and self-regulation (Tze, Klassen & Daniels, 2014).

In this sense, some educational barriers for the promotion of enriched contexts are identified by Piske, et al. (2016), referring mainly to repetitive teaching, uniformity of knowledge and teaching practices that are rarely oriented towards designing a class that encourages curiosity and students' interest in learning. In part, as noted by Reis & Renzulli (2010), difficulties in adapting the curriculum derive from lack of teacher training, which makes it difficult to carry out modifications to instruction practices in order to respond adequately to the needs of students in general, and to the needs of students with high intellectual abilities in particular.

In particular, taking Renzulli & Gaesser's (2015) model of the three rings, we return to the dimension relating to commitment to the task in order to understand giftedness. These authors mention that intrinsic motivation is not always present or absent, but rather that it comes and goes in relation to the characteristics and features of some contexts and circumstances that are the result of educational experiences linked to a form of teaching that promotes it. From this point of view, two elements are key:school tasks on the one hand and the teaching role on the other. Studies on commitment show that challenging tasks are those that involve students to start the task, find information to solve it, participate in class discussions and maintain interest in the work proposal. On the contrary, tasks that are too easy tend to produce feelings of boredom and those that are too complex generate frustration.

Also, among the initial studies on academic tasks, some factors synthesized in the acronym TARGET proposed by Epstein (1989, in Huertas, 1997) are pointed out, i.e. the tasks that most generate motivation are those characterized by their variety and diversity, significance, authenticity, moderate level of difficulty and possibility of choice and control. Likewise, the model highlights the importance of feedback generated in the context of a class and the use of rewards, both to encourage group work and also to undertake evaluation based on criteria of achievement, whereby this is understood as a process; respecting individual learning times and promoting time management by offering guidance for planning, monitoring and reflecting during the development of the task (Rigo, 2017; Gentry, Gable & Springer, 2010; Piske, Stoltz & Machado, 2014).

More current contributions continue to highlight the importance of such features in the activities that are formulated to promote commitment, moving towards new aspects that should be reflected in the formulation of instructional design and class planning (Rigo & Donolo, 2014). In this regard, there are contributions that emerge from the field of Neurosciences, which show the importance of novelty and estrangement in the formats and academic proposals for promoting not only what we understand as affective and behavioral commitment, i.e. to capture students' interest and participation, but also what we know as cognitive commitment, which implies long-term, lasting and meaningful learning (Acaso, 2015; Ballarini, 2015).

The role of the teacher in the classroom is to guide, rather than deliver information to children; to formulate open tasks, in order to monitor the learning process that students are taking, offering help to locate content, methodological techniques, or to help them understand how to use certain resources. These possibilities are enabled when research assignments are being carried out, using inductive logic, discovering and investigating problems that have a strong relationship with daily life (Renzulli, 2010; Rigo & Donolo, 2017).

In this framework, in order to formulate educational practices in line with inductive learning, the proposal put forward by Rigo & Donolo (2016; 2017) and defined as Problematic Situations, is promising for engaging students, as it makes propositions that at the same time are challenging, interesting and related to daily life, which are not solved in an hour, but involve a process that includes and is carried out along with instructional practices. These are problematic situations, because students need not only their previous knowledge to solve it, but also face the challenge of looking for new information to completely solve the problem formulated, while also being associated with circumstances arising in their lives outside school. It does not evaluate content or data, but rather the understanding of putting into play the central concepts of the curriculum to analyze a daily situation. It has the strength to understand instruction and evaluation as recursive moments, enriched by formative feedback, understood as a dialogue through which the student not only receives information about their performance, but also has the possibility to participate in reflection about it; at the same time, the teacher receives feedback as a basis for modifying instruction.

We understand that student commitment and especially commitment of gifted students, is the result of the opportunities, the resources and supports that are provided through the school in order to develop it. This involves the challenge of thinking of the school beyond a place where information is simply received, towards a context for developing new and richer experiences to enhance the talents and capacities of children and young people, contributing to more authentic and less monotonous learning.

Proposals from creativity

Creativity is one of the components that integrates this complex phenomenon of giftedness (Renzulli & Gaesser, 2015; Piske, Stoltz & Machado, 2014). Sak (2016) also highlights the importance of creative skills, the analysis of giftedness and the design of educational strategies. Authors interested in this area analyze creativity as an important aspect of giftedness and propose guidelines for the construction of creative contexts of teaching and learning. Our proposals are based on sociocultural perspectives of education (Rinaudo, 2014) and creativity (Glăveanu, 2015). We therefore emphasize the importance of mediations between teachers and students, collaborative work and activities that promote interaction with different objects and contents of the surrounding culture.

Our proposals are not limited to promoting learning and creative processes in gifted people, but aim to impact the educational contexts in general through the interactions between the different participants. Although creativity is an aspect that is currently considered in the evaluation of giftedness (Nakano, Primi, Ribeiro & Almeida, 2016), it is not usually a priority issue in the education of people with high skills. We agree with Piske, Stoltz & Machado (2014) in that *"the creative potential of gifted students has not received adequate attention in the school context, most times teachers are not prepared to attend to their needs"* (: 348).

We consider it essential to develop multidimensional evaluations and interventions with gifted people (Almeida et al. 2016; Nakano et al, 2016; Sak, 2016). We understand creativity as the potential of people to generate ideas and innovative and alternative products in different situations and contexts. Likewise, from the perspectives of problem finding and problem solving (Kozbelt, Begheto & Runco, 2010), we define creativity as abilities to formulate and solve problems based on interactions between divergent and convergent thoughts.

Boosting creative processes in the gifted does not appear to be a simple task. Putting forward activities and proposals that challenge students (Piske, Stoltz & Machado, 2014), promote curiosity, motivation and the development of thoughts and creative products is a great challenge for educators.In the field of giftedness, the educational model proposed by Sak (2016) is very interesting and includes three main components: analytical, practical and creative skills. Analytical skills refer to abilities to identify problems, develop plans, organize information, monitor processes, evaluate results and make decisions. Practical skills involve: control of impulses, perseverance, focus on objectives and results, implementation, responsibility, independence, sensitivity, management of thinking styles and definition of priorities. Regarding the creative component, the author mentions seventeen skills to be developed in gifted education: redefine problems; question assumptions; generate ideas; market creative ideas; creative imagination; perceive multiple facets of knowledge; overcome obstacles; take risks; tolerate ambiguity; build self-efficacy; discover self; explore true interests; postpone expectations; model creativity; motivate self; formulate associations; and construct analogies.

We consider that the skills mentioned in Sak's model (2016) can be developed in different contexts inside and outside the classroom. In the classroom context, it is relevant for teachers to promote learning as a creative act (Beghetto, 2016) that involves novel personal interpretations (subjective moment) that are put into discussion with other students and teachers (intersubjective moment). According to Beghetto (2016) it is essential that teachers pay attention to the moments of the class where questions, comments and unexpected and original contributions emerge, offering aids, orientations and interventions that stimulate divergent thinking, originality and discussion among participants. Glăveanu and Beghetto (2017) propose stimulating creativity in the classroom based on dialogue and openness to different perspectives, that students and teachers put their different points of view into play in order to arrive at more creative positions.

Teachers can also promote creativity by designing activities, resources and teaching and learning strategies. Current studies indicate that the promotion of autonomy, the free choice of alternatives in solving tasks, the analysis of different resources and collaborative work are conducive to creativity (Davies et al., 2013; Lin, 2011; Beghetto, 2016). Regarding content, activities that promote relationships between disciplines and analysis beyond the areas of knowledge, borders and enigmas not solved by isolated disciplines seem propitious. Creativity emerges from undisciplined knowledge that is related in a complex way (Elisondo, 2015). Likewise, creative thoughts and products stimulate those activities and educational proposals that generate surprise and are unexpected for students (Elisondo, Donolo and Rinaudo, 2013; Elisondo and Melgar, 2016).

Creativity is a socio-cultural process that implies relations between cultural subjects and objects, whereby promoting interactions with diverse persons, contents and artifacts is a way of fostering creativity. Research indicates that tasks outside the classroom (museums, fairs, NGOs, etc.), extracurricular activities and visits from unexpected teachers and specialists are perceived by students as opportunities for creativity (Chao, Chen & Hwang, 2013; Davies et al, 2013; Melgar, Elisondo, Donolo & Stoll, 2016).

It is also relevant for creativity that teachers offer performance models typical of creative behavior. Root-Bernstein & Root-Bernstein (2017) propose working in the classroom with creative examples, whether they be people, products or problems. According to these authors, exploring ways of solving and forming problems, strategies and situations involved in creative processes developed by other people or groups, is a way of stimulating creativity in the classroom. In short, in gifted education and education in general, it is important to build teaching and learning contexts that promote different skills and performances not only in the cognitive field but also and especially in the area of emotions and intersubjective links. There are agreements among specialists which consider it to be essential to develop creative educational proposals within the framework of respect, tolerance for diversity and cooperative dialogue between students and teachers (Beghetto & Kaufman,

2014). The development of ludic activities (Piske et al., 2016) is one of the ways to enhance cognitive, creative, emotional and social skills. Gifted education has the challenge of stimulating students and enhancing learning, without neglecting vital areas in human development such as intersubjective links and emotions.

Giftedness: some approaches from the neurosciences

In the psychopedagogical field, it is common to find studies and approximations around subjects with learning difficulties or disorders. That is to say, there seems to be a predominant tendency of focusing on what is missing, on what is not incorporated or learned. The concept of giftedness emerges, however, when the issue is the existence of a surplus, rather than something that is missing.

Since its inception, this notion has been linked directly with intelligence. The interesting thing is that it is possible to agree on how we understand and define it. We can assure, as affirmed by Passer & Smith (2007), that intelligence provides the ability to acquire knowledge, think and reason effectively, and to manage the environment in an adaptive way. This last aspect is fundamental in relation to the subject we are dealing with.

From the perspective of neurosciences, Clark (2007) proposes that the brains of gifted people have more neurons, with more integrated and complex connections; a greater number of dendrites that create new and diverse connections, also glia that grow allowing greater myelination of axons, enriching the speed and quality of transmission of neural information. This is related to what Geake (2004) calls greater activity of the prefrontal lobes, which are responsible for the most complex functions of human beings, such as the coordination of information from various sources, the elaboration of goals and plans, among others.

Jausovec (1998, 1996) presented evidence of a wider use of alpha waves in young people with high IQ during the performance of specific activities which would indicate a change in frequency, based on the electrical activity of the neurons, which would manifest states of concentration being able to adapt quickly to certain tasks. That is to say, they manage to be more flexible to attentional changes, compared to young people without giftedness.

Simonetti (2001) returns to these investigations in neuroscience and emphasizes that in our nervous system, especially in the relationship between brain and intelligence, it becomes necessary to deepen, both structurally and functionally, aspects related to physical, emotional, cognitive and intuitive issues in relation to giftedness. He states that studies have shown that the level of intelligence achieved by a subject is the result of an advanced and integral process within the brain. For this reason, he asserts that the concept of intelligence and, therefore, that of giftedness understood as intelligence development, must include all brain functions and, in particular, its efficient and integrated use. Based on this we could therefore assume that those people who present what we could call more intelligent behaviors, would necessarily have to manifest greater integration and use of the diverse functions of the brain. The author thus concludes that low frequency high amplitude alpha percentage is predominant, and that the frontal lobe plays a preponderant role in the cognitive processes of giftedness as well as speed in the resolution of tasks and the establishment of relationships.

These considerations allow us to affirm that it is not just a matter of predisposition or genetics, but that strength, integration, flexibility and complexity, around the brain development characteristic of giftedness, needs opportunities to achieve such a construction, that is to say, a stimulating environment that collaborates with this particular dynamic.

In addition, when studying giftedness, there are authors who have related it for years with what they call dyssynchrony or theory of positive disintegration and who have even alluded to psychic over-excitability, as being responsible for advanced development (Ramiro Oliver, Marcilla Fernández & Navarro Guzmán, 1999; Gur, 2011).

Gur (2011) reviews various investigations and concludes that the main differences between people with and without giftedness lie in certain physical characteristics, or in characteristics of linguistic, cognitive and social development. With respect to the former, the investigations reviewed indicate that certain differences in size and weight can be found, that these people may have extra energy, but there is no evidence of psychomotor skills or superior physical development. In relation to the latter, they deploy a different language around the creative use of words, ask reflective questions, discuss problems and ideas, make broad descriptions, have a rich vocabulary, handle humor, and easily understand the figurative meaning of language. Regarding the development of cognition, their curiosity, their power to question, ask questions and solve problems stand out. They seek in-depth and detailed information about their own interests, with preferences for individual work without depending on others, as a challenge, showing some rejection of routines that sometimes become boring at school. They can understand abstract concepts and learn to read and write early before starting school. Finally, regarding the sociability of these children, some are rather withdrawn with their peers while others become leaders, are followed by others and often tend to make friends with adults at their chronological age. They may be more sensitive to values and moral issues, to the expectations and points of view of others, but others are carried away by an almost natural hyperactivity that makes them distracted or leads them to doubt their decisions.

Therefore, although the first thing that stands out is the relationship with the high levels of intelligence that are usually present (Lubart, Holling & Ushakov, 2016; Arffa, 2007), over the years further issues have been determined in relation to aspects of personality of those subjects. Some studies come to interesting conclusions. For example, in relation to gender, although similar profiles can be identified, some differences between girls and boys show that the former are more sociable, open, affectionate and participative, as well as more enthusiastic, optimistic, self-confident, enterprising, spontaneous, socially daring, serene, peaceful and confident. While boys appear as smarter, quicker in the understanding and learning of ideas, conscious, persevering, moralistic, sensible, subject to the rules, with great force of the superego, manifesting good assimilation and adaptation to the rules and values that govern the world of the elderly, of soft and impressionable sensibility (Ramiro Oliver, Marcilla Fernández & Navarro Guzmán, 1999).

Therefore, it is essential not to speak of giftedness in general, but to pay attention to the particularities of each case. If we think about school contexts, the figure of the tutor or mentor is highlighted as fundamental, who collaborates closely from a pedagogical perspective, knowing the profile of each case, thus being able to intervene, whether by rethinking the curriculum, the methodologies, the academic results, favoring to a greater extent self-regulated and metacognitive behaviors in relation to peers and teachers in the various school situations. Promoting among gifted students (or not) a shared science of language, practicing and internalizing the habit of reflection, will help them become more aware of their own metacognitive knowledge and the strategies they use to learn. Shared evaluation, between others and with others, providing motivating feedbacks, becomes fundamental.

Therefore, it is clear that a quality curriculum for the gifted should improve higher order thinking skills.We are referring here to metacognition, focusing on authentic interdisciplinary themes, addressing the needs of gifted students, being dynamic, flexible and including challenges. We continue to insist that it should not be a question only to be considered for students who have these characteristics, but for classes in general (Miedijenskya &Tal, 2016; Kelemen, 2010)

Final considerations

To summarize, this chapter shows three dimensions that interrelate in the development of giftedness, which will take place only when the individual interacts actively and dynamically with the educational, social and cultural context. In this regard, Blumen (2008) mentions that currently research suggests that its development is the result of reciprocal interactions between subjects and the environment, through which the genetic potential of the organism is updated. In such a way that, the greater the interaction between people and the environments -formal, non-formal and informal- as stimulating educational experiences, the greater realization of the genetic potential. Therefore, people need not only a supportive environment that offers them opportunities to grow and develop their genetic potential, but also a commitment to interact with the environment and develop creative thinking.

In conclusion, we present arguments aimed at understanding that if we offer opportunities to participate in varied experiences, students will have more possibilities to develop their talents at school in a creative and committed way; in this direction, the social environment is converted from a socio-cultural perspective into an important factor for maximizing the potential of the subjects in the process of development. For that reason, institutional design is a central aspect of educational experiences.

References

Acaso, M. (2015). *Reduvolution. Hacer la revolución en la educación*. Paidós Contextos: Buenos Aires.

Almeida, L., Araújo, A., Sainz-Gómez, M., & Prieto, M. D. (2016). Challenges in the identification of giftedness: Issues related to psychological assessment. *Annals of Psychology*, 32(3), 621-627.

Appleton, J., Christenson, S., Kin, D., & Reschly, A. (2006). Measuring cognitive and psychological engagement: validation of the student engagement instrument. *Journal of School* Psychology, 44, 427-445.

Arffa, S. (2007). The relationship of intelligence to executive function and non-executive function measures in a sample of average, above average, and gifted youth. *Archives of Clinical Neuropsychology*, 22(8): 969-978.

Ballarini, F. (2015). *REC. Por qué recordamos lo que recordamos y olvidamos lo que olvidamos.*Sudamericana: Buenos Aires.

Beghetto, R. A. (2016). Learning as a creative act. In T. Kettler (Ed.). *Modern Curriculum for Gifted and Advanced Learners*. Routledge: New York.

Beghetto, R., & Kaufman, J. (2014). Classroom contexts for creativity. *High Ability Studies*, 25(1), 53-69.

Blumen, S. (2008). Motivación, sobredotación y talento: un desafío para el éxito. *Revista de Psicología*, XXVI (1), 147-184.

Chao, J., Chen, M., & Hwang, M. (2013). Vitalizing creative learning in science and technology through an extracurricular club: A perspective based on activity theory. *Thinking Skills and Creativity*, 8, 45-55.

Clark, B. (2007). *Growing up Gifted*. Merril/Prentice: Hall Columbus, OH.

Davies, D., Jindal-Snape, D., Collier, C., Digby, R., Hay, P., & Howe, A. (2013). Creative learning environments in education. A systematic literature review. *Thinking Skills and Creativity*, 8, 80-91.

Elisondo, R. (2015). La creatividad como perspectiva educativa. Cinco ideas para pensar los contextos creativos de enseñanza y aprendizaje. *Revista Electrónica Actualidades Investigativas en Educación, 15*(3), 1-23.

Elisondo, R., Donolo, D. & Rinaudo, C. (2013). The Unexpected and Education: Curriculums for Creativity. *Creative Education*, 4(12b). Retrieved from http://www.scirp.org/journal/ce/(10-05-2014).

Elisondo, R., & Melgar, M. (2016). Las ratas y los estudiantes. El poder de la novedad en la educación. *IV Congreso Internacional de Ciudades Creativas.* Universidad Complutense de Madrid, enero de 2016. Retrieved from http://congreso2016.ciudadescreativas.es/Ciudades_Creativas_2016_tomo1.pdf

Feldhusen, J., & Kroll, M. (1991).Boredom or challenge for the academically talented in school. *Gifted Education International*, 7, 80-81.

Fredriscks, J., Blumenfeld, O. & Paris, A. (2004). School Engagement: Potential of the concept state of the evidence. *Review of Educational Research*, 74(1), 59-109.

Geake, J. (2004). How children's brains think: Not left or right but both together. *Education*, 32(3), 65-72. doi: 10.1080/03004270485200351

Gentry, M., Gable, R., & Springer, P. (2010). Gifted and Nongifted Middle School Students: Are Their Attitudes Toward School Different as Measured by the New Affective Instrument, My Class Activities...? *Journal for the Education of the Gifted*, 24(1), 74-96.

Glăveanu, V., (2015). Creativity as a sociocultural act. *The Journal of Creative Behavior,* 49(3), 165-180.

Glăveanu, V. P., & Beghetto, R. A. (2017). The Difference That Makes a 'Creative' Difference in Education. In R. A. Beghetto & B. Sriraman (Eds.). *Creative*

Contradictions in Education (pp. 37-54). Springer International Publishing: Nueva York.

Guirado, A. (2015). *¿Qué sabemos de las altas capacidades? Preguntas, respuestas y propuestas para la escuela y la familia.* GRAÓ: Barcelona.

Gur, G. (2011). Do gifted children have similar characteristics? Observation of three gifted children. *Procedia Social and Behavioral Sciences*, 12, 426-435.

Huertas, J. A. (1997). *Motivación. Querer Aprender.* Aique: Buenos Aires.

Jausovec, N. (1998). Are gifted individuals less chaotic thinkers? *Personality and Individual Differences*, 25(2), 253-267

Jausovec, N. (1996). Differences in EEG Alpha Activity Related to Giftedness. *Intelligence*, 23(3), 159-173.

Kelemen, G. (2010). A personalized model design for gifted children' education. *Procedia Social and Behavioral Sciences*, 2, 3981-3987.

Kozbelt, A. Begheto, R. & Runco M. (2010). Theories of Creativity. In J. Kaufman & R. Sternberg. *The Cambridge Handbook of Creativity* (pp. 20-47). Cambridge: Cambridge University Press.

Landis, R. & Reschly, A. (2013). Reexamining Gifted Underachievement and Dropout through the Lens of Student Engagement. *Journal for the Education of the Gifted*, 36(2), 220-249.

Lin, Y. (2011). Fostering creativity through education. A conceptual framework of creative Pedagogy. *Creative Education*, 2(3), 149-155.

Lubart, T. Holling, H. & Ushakov, D. (2016). Introduction to the special issue Intelligence, Creativity and Giftedness. *Learning and Individual Differences*, 52, 120.

Melgar, F. Elisondo, R. Donolo, D. & Stoll, R. (2016). Estudio exploratorio de experiencias innovadoras con docentes inesperados en la Universidad. *Revista Cuadernos de Investigación Educativa*, 7(2), 31-47.

Miedijenskya, S. & Talb, T. (2016). Reflection and assessment for learning in science enrichment courses for the gifted. *Studies in Educational Evaluation*, 50, 1-13.

Nakano, R., Primi, R., Riberio, W. & Almeida, L. (2016). Multidimensional Assessment of Giftedness: Criterion Validity of Battery of Intelligence and Creativity Measures in Predicting Arts and Academic Talents. *Annals of Psychology*, 32(3), 628-637.

Passer, W. &Smith, E. (2007). *Psychology. The Science of Mind and Behavior* (3. udg.). McGraw-Hill: Boston.

Perkrum, R. Göetz, T. Daniels, L., Stupnisky, R., & Perry, R (2010). Boredom in Achievement Settings: Exploring Control – Value Antecedents and Performance Outcomes of a Neglected Emotion. *Journal of Educational Psychology*, 102(3), 531-549.

Piske, F. H. R., Stoltz, T., Machado, J. M., Vestena, C. L. B., de Oliveira, C. S., de Freitas, S. P., & Machado, C. L. (2016). Working with Creativity of Gifted Students through Ludic Teaching. *Creative Education*, 7, 1641-1647. doi:10.4236/ce.2016.711167

Piske, F. H. R., Stoltz, T., & Machado, J. (2014). Creative Educational Practices for Inclusion of Gifted Children. *Creative Education, 5*, 803-808. doi:10.4236/ce.2014.510093

Piske, F., Stoltz, T., Vestena, C., Perszel de Freitas, S. Valentim, B., Sant'ana de Oliveira, C., Barby, A., & Machado, C. (2016). Barriers to Creativity, Identification and Inclusion of Gifted Student. *Creative Education*, 7, 1899-1905. doi:10.4236/ce.2016.714192

Preckel, F., Götz, T., & Frenzel, A. (2010). Ability grouping of gifted students: Effects onacademic self-concept and boredom. *British Journal of Educational Psychology*, 80, 451-472

Ramiro Oliver, P., Marcilla Fernández, A., & Navarro Guzmán, J. (1999). El alumno superdotado. *Revista Latinoamericana de Psicología*, 31(3), 537-546.

Reis, S. & Renzulli, J. (2010). Is there still a need for gifted education? An examination of current research. *Learning and Individual Differences*, 20, 308-317.

Renzulli, J. (2010). El rol del profesor en el desarrollo del talento. *Revista Electrónica Interuniversitaria de Formación del Profesorado*, 13 (1), 33-40.

Renzulli, J. (1978). What makes giftedness? Re-examining a definition. *Phi Delta Kappan,* 60, 180-184.

Renzulli, J. & Gaesser, A. (2015). A Multi Criteria System for the Identification of High Achieving and Creative/Productive Giftedness. *Revista de Educación*, 368, 92-121. doi: 10.4438/1988-592X-RE-2015-368-290.

Rigo, D. (2017). Docentes, tareas y alumnos en la definición del compromiso. Investigando el aula de nivel primario de educación. *Educação em Revista*, 33, 1-24.

Rigo, D. & Donolo, D. (2014). Entre pupitres y pizarrones. Retos en educación primaria: el aprendizaje con compromiso. *Educatio Siglo XXI*, 32(2), 59-80.

Rigo, D. & Donolo, D. (2016). La evaluación... más de lo mismo, sin libro. Desafiando formatos y modalidades. *Panorama.Revista de Ciencias Sociales*, 10(19), 5-23.

Rigo, D. & Donolo, D. (2017). El valor de utilidad de los contenidos escolares. Percepciones de los estudiantes de nivel primario. *Psicodebate*, 17(1), 35-50.

Rinaudo, M. (2014). Estudios sobre los contextos de aprendizaje: arenas y fronteras. In P. Paoloni, M. Rinaudo & C. González, (Eds). Cuestiones en Psicología Educacional. Perspectivas teóricas y metodológicas orientadas a la mejora de la práctica educativa (pp. 163-206*). Cuadernos de Educación*. Sociedad Latina de Comunicación Social: La Laguna. Retrieved from http://www.cuadernosartesanos.org/educacion.html.

Root-Bernstein, R. & Root-Bernstein, M. (2017). People, Passions, Problems: The Role of Creative Exemplars in Teaching for Creativity. In R. A. Beghetto & B. Sriraman (Eds.). *Creative Contradictions in Education* (pp. 143-164). Springer International Publishing: Nueva York.

Sak, U. (2016). EPTS Curriculum Model in the Education of Gifted Students. *Anales de Psicología*, 32 (3), 683-694. doi:10.6018/analesps.32.3.259441

Simonetti, D. (2001). Alunos com alta capacidade intelectual: indicadores Neuropsicológicos. *Revista FACEVV*, 6, 31-45.

Tze, V., Klassen, R. & Daniels, L. (2014). Patterns of boredom and its relationship with perceived autonomy support and engagement. *Contemporary Educational Psychology* 39, 175-187. doi:10.1016/j.cedpsych.2014.05.001

10.

CREATIVE WAYS TO DEVELOP CREATIVITY IN GIFTED STUDENTS

Otto Schmidt

Education consultant specialized in giftedness and other areas of special education.

ORCID: 0000-0003-2115-9275

Abstract: *Creativity is a highly important element of almost everything found and done in daily life. It is present in all thinkers, communicators, and problem solvers, but at different levels. Creativity makes people more effective within themselves, in life, and in their learning. It can be taught and improved as a skill. This article shows people how to get out of "the box" and think beyond their perceived ordinariness. Some of the common misperceptions or blocks to being more creative are addressed. Creativity-promoting strategies, exercises, and models are presented that provide trigger words and ways to do things that stimulate creative thinking. Powerful consciousness openers are provided. All people will often be more confident in engaging more deeply in what they do if guided to develop their creativity skills. It is not a fixed innate ability or reserved for gifted*

people. Our new and constantly changing world needs creative
people to meet any challenges through creative engagement.
Keywords: Creativity Training; Improving Thinking; Learning to be
Creative; How to be more creative; Thinking outside of the box.

Introduction and Discussion

Creativity training for gifted students is one of the most important responsibilities of their teachers. From this writer's perspective, it should be mandatory to teach creativity to all students, but teaching it to the highly intelligent should be an especially high priority. It is a vital part of their education because it directly affects the well being of all aspects of their lives and learning.

Developing, nurturing, and enhancing creativity helps produce better thinkers, communicators, and problem solvers. Creativity training can improve peoples' abilities when they are planning and developing approaches to independent and self-directed learning. Teachers can encourage gifted students to express themselves more openly in order that their needs are more easily and also more fully met. Their ideas are then exposed for all to see and possibly use. Providing them with creativity skills that challenge and encourage the emergence of the imagination, means students may more likely express themselves more confidently as conceivers and producers of the new and exciting instead of just being the consumers of the old. Many gifted students have exceptional thinking and problem solving abilities. They need to be given the tools to grow and improve their skills, talents, and abilities that will hopefully be used to improve not only their lives but also the world in general. It is important to nurture the most intelligent who have the potential to do great things for themselves, our societies, countries, and national economies.

Creativity lessons can help gifted students overcome some of the emotional issues, frustrations, turmoil, and problems that have been identified as specific to giftedness. Creativity can help students develop interesting and better ways to desensitize themselves. As well, it gives them approaches to others who are intolerant or abusive toward them. Creativity training can also help students become more comfortable with their gift(s) and provide them with different ways to reduce anxiety and stress sometimes caused from being seen as different from the norm.

How to creatively handle problems and issues that arise with teachers and other students helps them to be more effective – within themselves, in life, and in their learning. They will often be more willing to then more confidently show their giftedness.

Most educators are not qualified or specifically trained to deal with gifted students. They usually have curriculum guidelines and their mandate is to teach subjects to the general population and to a norm within schools. Specialized teachers of the gifted – whether in gifted-centered schools or withdrawal programs – can often custom design courses for their students. If so, teachers first learn the processes themselves and then can do creativity training in broader and deeper terms. Gifted students should then be more comfortable and able to go into the various mainstreams of post-elementary and post-secondary institutionalized education with skills that help them cope and even better excel in what are the usual "regular" classes.

If gifted students are forced to remain and work only in regular classrooms, one of the best ways to help them is to teach all their regular classroom teachers the basics of how to teach creativity and then they can pass on the training to all their students. All regular classroom teachers should receive creativity training.

There will be people who will react to this by thinking that any student can learn the techniques that are presented. The answer, very simply is yes, that's true. Students who are not gifted can and should also be taught the skills presented in this article. The difference, however, is gifted students can often learn the concepts and challenges in creativity training more quickly and absorb and use them to deeper and broader levels. Creativity training then becomes vital for highly intelligent people so they can accelerate their learning, excel and learn on their own terms, and meet many of their needs for themselves. Gifted students should not expect that teachers will give them all they need. Creativity training at any age or grade level helps teachers and students develop a more custom, individualized way of educating them. Students become less dependent on teachers and pressure is taken off teachers who no longer have to provide so much of the content/knowledge/facts given to students or dictate what a student learns. Teachers become guides as students become empowered as self-directed (I choose what and how much to learn), independent (I choose to work alone or with others) learners who can study and learn more creatively.

What is Creativity?

One of the best and easiest definitions of creativity is taking the ordinary and doing something unordinary with it. This is something anyone can do if motivated to "stir the creative juices". This definition encourages people to think more beyond the common and more deeply when engaged in any task. The mind loves a challenge.

Another more challenging and highly valuable definition of creativity is open and free-flow thinking. It is the ability to first acknowledge openly and then allow subconscious thinking to surface and show itself without filters, fear, or censorship of any kind. In the former definition, the person is more under control of the thinking. In the latter, it is the opposite. There is risk-taking and overcoming of innate fears of the unknown as a person willingly releases power to the subconscious and becomes a spectator and recorder of free-flow personal thoughts. Proof that there is unabashed, free-flow thinking is the person becomes amazed and awed by what manifests itself from deep within.

In both cases, aversion to risk-taking and openness are the difficult things to overcome. There can potentially be negative consequences to expressing oneself creatively. What manifests may be highly unusual or so unordinary that others then laugh at, make fun of, tease, ridicule, scorn, upset, or put down the ideas. Recipients may consider the idea(s) too far deviant from the level of acceptability. The rebel must pay a price. Many creative people have suffered greatly at the hands of narrow-minded conservative thinkers, and those who prefer that the display of thoughts and ideas be limited to what is considered stereotypically "acceptable" and within limits of acceptability within the "normal" world.

To some degree, every person has creative abilities. People survive by creatively solving problems and issues many times during a day. Gifted students often have the potential to do better than the rest of the population and therefore potentially provide greatly to the world. They need to be shown how to tap into their inner creativity to find and then express their ideas openly.

Many people believe that creativity is simply innate. Either you have it or you don't. Some of us have a lot and others just a little through genetics or chance and the amount can't be changed. This is, however, not the case.

The position is being taken here that creativity is a skill and can be taught and learned. Ordinary people can become more unordinary in their thinking. Given the right conditions and proper instruction, the subconscious of most people can be approached and carefully opened to reveal and release incredible thoughts and ideas that they had no idea were in there.

Why is Creativity Important?

- Helps meet our daily needs and provides ideas for our survival
- It spices up life and makes it more interesting and tolerable
- For effective problem solving in everyday situations
- To satisfy and fulfill a strong basic inner need and desire to express ourselves
- Helps us share our skills, talents, and abilities with rest of the world
- Striving to make new creative ideas alive is exciting, motivating, and enervating

  A person's creativity is called upon regularly throughout a lifetime. Whether one is a child, an entrepreneur at any age, a student, or an employee at any workplace, creativity is a highly desirable quality. Creative people can often:
- Think more innovatively to generate new products or services
- Come up with better solutions to problems
- Overcome difficulties when answers/solutions aren't immediately or readily obvious from available information
- Move away from traditional thinking that previously decided that solutions are based on the way things were done before

- Meet the challenge of something that they have never experienced before
- Deal more effectively with difficult people and related disagreements
- Find ways of dealing with situations when there are financial troubles, low cash situations, or a need for generating or increasing income
- Contribute more effectively within a team effort
- Solve conflicts in more satisfactory ways
- Deal more effectively with pressing or possibly unrealizable deadlines
- Find creative ways to solve problems when all seems lost
- Create ways of finding important things that may have been mislaid
- Solve travel problems that may arise unexpectedly
- Fit in more readily and easily in a job or profession of which they know very little

Two Kinds of Creativity

a) New to the World: "This is brand new. Nobody has ever seen or done this before."

Comment: Most people limit their thinking because they compare what they produce to what has already been produced in the world. Unfortunately and in reality, most ideas that people generate are not original. When they find out that their idea is already in existence, they get disappointed and think they are not creative. People tend to become deflated and gradually believe that only a few chosen ones have been created to be creative – not them. They then slowly shy away from problems and inventive challenges. The preconceived idea is that whatever I produce has probably already been created or done somewhere and there is no point in reinventing something that already exists.

For example: A young person tries to create a new type of car or bicycle that is different from all others in the world. This is obviously a daunting challenge for any amateur or hobbyist! It is a great challenge even for professional engineers or designers. After the excitement of creating a new concept is over and the person finds out that what was designed is already in the world, there is sadness and frustration. With this kind of thinking, people often don't even bother to start at such a task. Comparing what is created to the rest of the world is. However, it is not the only way of thinking about the situation.

b) New to the Self: "I have never ever done this before. What I just produced reallyamazed me. I am very proud of myself."

Comment: A second way of thinking about one's creativity is in relation to the self, not the rest of the world. It can be highly rewarding and satisfying to realize that something has been done creatively new and different within and beyond one's comfort zone or usual personal realm of operation. It may be disappointing to find something has already been invented, discovered, or created but it is important to recognize at some point that "I have never done anything like this before. I have stretched beyond my boundaries of thinking and into new territory. Wow, this is original to me". Originality, in relation to oneself, is as valid as originality in relation to the world.

Great satisfaction can be drawn from such an experience. The motivation to produce the new, accept challenges, and further stretch creative abilities can continue and strengthen but now for self-satisfaction and personal growth. What is produced does not have to be just for the world. It can be just for me.

Positive Approaches to Developing and Nurturing Creativity Establishing the Right Attitude for Creativity.

"I am a creative person". (Notice the words are in the present tense on purpose for a sense of immediacy) This is an excellent self-affirmation to repeat so that it becomes strongly internalized and helps establish an internal positive attitude that reduces inhibitions to expressing creatively.

Be open to the possibility and acknowledge in a loving way that you have creativity to share with the world. Reduce inhibitions, think positively about being more creative and be willing to take the leap of faith in expressing yourself. The subconscious will appreciate that and feel more and more free to perform. There will be a greater incentive to generate better ideas. Think about pushing the boundary to generate one additional possible solution to a problem. Wonder about more details that weren't at first obvious.

It is important that teachers who work on developing creativity with gifted students acknowledge their own creative limitations and make efforts to overcome them. A safe and secure environment to express and communicate freely can be established at any time well before creativity training. Students need to feel secure that their ideas will be accepted and appreciated – no matter how odd, weird, shocking, etc. Teachers can establish a more powerful free and open thinking zone by being free and open themselves.

Fears and Negative Attitudes to Overcome

"I am afraid to do anything that isn't acceptable to others". Change the channel of thinking to do that which you believe

is right for you. Others may or may not like what you produce but that is acceptable and reflects real life. People don't have to like everything that you produce! Embrace the thought that you can give people the free option of liking or not liking what you produce. Be in charge by being ahead of the audience and ask for opinions and criticisms about your work, instead of waiting anxiously for others to give you their criticisms. Accept ALL of what they say. As the song says, "You can't please everyone, so you got to please yourself". Another good way to be more accepting of others' criticisms and opinions is, "Listen hardest to the person who disagrees with you the most". You want to know what those who disagree with you think! It can be valuable information that can be very helpful.

"I don't want to possibly lose control by releasing my inner self". Most people want full control of their lives and thoughts at all times. They often feel uncomfortable when asked to let go and allow unbridled, free-flow thinking. To be a spectator to one's thoughts means giving up the control of one's thoughts. Out of control thinking is often perceived as a negative. However, opening the subconscious in simple, enjoyable steps/stages will not be a negative experience if carefully guided. Salvador Dali, the famous artist, was willing to let his imagination roam uncontrollably into unbelievable extremes and depths of creativity as seen in his many art works. He is an inspirational example of someone willing to take the risk and free his subconscious in order to allow it to take the ordinary and do something highly unordinary with it.

c) "If I let my imagination go, I am afraid that I might get lost somehow and never come back".

The imagination is endless is possibilities and is fathomless. One part of creativity training encourages going deeper and deeper in small stages and comfortable steps during which the subconscious is given increased control.

The subconscious once opened rarely wants to go back to former ways of thinking. The mental charge and creative stimulation are highly exciting and create a desire for more. The door to creativity once opened, cannot be closed. One can then become a spectator to one's thoughts that flow and ebb and change in ways sometimes unimaginable, almost at will and in a conscious state. There is nothing magical or mystical about it. We all have a subconscious that can be tapped – but it does involve a willingness to press past a level of control into the uncontrolled.

The process of opening the subconscious can be intimidating, despite great care in use of words and a very slow approach. I worked with an acclaimed Russian pianist who was sadly unable to go into the untapped zone of her subconscious during a simple experiment. Every cell in her body was full of other people's music except her own. As an exercise, she was asked to sit at the piano and in ready-to-play position. She was then asked to clear her thoughts, relax, and just wait until something inside pushed to move her fingers and start playing on the keys. After a short time, she suddenly did start playing and then stopped just as suddenly. I asked her if she had ever played that music before. She hadn't. It was totally new to her. She was then asked to relax again and continue playing. She surprisingly refused. It made her uncomfortable to play music with which she was totally unfamiliar. It is almost a given that she would not suggest that her students do such impromptu playing for even a short time during her formal lessons with them. What a possibly great lost opportunity for creating new music.

"Everyone else is more creative than me. I'm not very good at it." Low self-esteem, lack of motivation, and poor self-concept can often be reversed when people are shown how to be more creative in an enjoyable and playful setting. It is best to do it in small steps. Do simple, spontaneous creativity exercises that amaze and produce awe. Let the inner imagination slowly express itself.

If we tell ourselves something long enough we will eventually believe it. That is how propaganda and advertising works. We have the ability to change a negative way of thinking about creativity in order to give our minds a greater chance of self-expression. Breaking the negative mind set is vital for change and continued growth and improvement of inner creativity. There must be hope in being able to achieve at a different level especially knowing that there are supportive and expert teachers and fellow students who can help. "I learned to walk and talk. I can learn to be more creative too". Let's do it together in a safe and caring environment.

"I was never very good at doing creative things, so why should that change?"This often suggests that the person has had bad experiences related to being creative. People can easily stifle creativity in others because what comes from it is often so subjective. Children especially, may have their fragile egos shattered by judgmental, controlling adults or classmates who may intentionally or unintentionally think they know what is acceptable or not and what is creative or not.

Opening the Subconscious to Internal Creativity

a) Abstract Triggers

De Bono CoRT Thinking Skills – When solving problems, a novel and creative response may be needed. This is one of the best collections of triggers to creative thinking. Edward De

Bono coined the term "Lateral Thinking" that started a revolution in creative thinking. People learned to approach problems and situations from more indirect perspectives. By focusing on unorthodox approaches and using different lights to view the same problem/situation, new and creative ideas are generated.

In some cases, there may not be a precedent or previous experience that can be used as a starting point. For example, Edward De Bono in his CoRT Thinking Skills has an exercise that challenges people to think of whether all cars should be painted yellow. DeBono challenges participants to think deeply and "out of the box". What are the positives and negatives? Predict the future and determine what might or might not happen? Futurists can readily use Lateral Thinking to make predictions. Innovators and inventors can use the model for developing new products and services.

Guided Fantasies – One of the best ways to help people desensitize to the experience of opening the subconscious to free-flow thinking is through a series of exercises provided during what is called Guided Fantasies. An early pioneer in this approach and an advocating education consultant is Lorraine Plum. To prepare students, they are led through formal relaxation and stress control techniques. The instructions for both can readily be found on the internet, at wellness centers, or spiritual renewal centers. Once fully relaxed – but not asleep – a Guided Fantasy can begin. As suggested by the title, it is a guiding process not directing. Participants are given open-ended, carefully worded instructions that allow them to think freely their way e.g. imagine a piece of paper in front of you. On the back is something that has color and shape. You don't know what it is but you know it is there. We will now turn the page. Look at what is there. Be amazed. You have never seen anything like this before.

A more complex fantasy can involve a journey to a new planet in the universe and creating all the features and inhabitants, etc. In a guided fantasy, it is vital that the thoughts are not controlled. For example, if you were told to think of a dog house, an image would immediately appear. However, if you were told to think of a shelter for a dog, the imagination must go to work in different and more open ways. More creative thoughts are likely to appear. There are many "opening" exercises that can be provided during training that leads up to the more formal and deeply enriching Guided Fantasies. Participants can never copy the ideas of others. Neither can they control their thinking as consciously as in normal situations. Engage the group of participants in an exciting discussion after the experience and hear about the fantastic and unusual new creative ideas they generated. If they willingly engaged and experienced, there will be no going back to the usual ways of thinking. Creativity has been unleashed and will continue to grow. Ah, that's how it is done!

b) Concrete Triggers

TRIZ – This is a Russian-developed forecasting system/template that guides a person in analytical and problem-solving thinking. It was developed after an extensive study of patterns that are found in the patents and processes of inventing. The triggers for active thinking and generating ideas are presented in a very detailed collection of topics, questions and explanations that elaborate and point out the many facets, perspectives, and dimensions of any problem or situation. TRIZ guides and directs people into an awe-inspiring awareness of details, a better understanding of how to go deeper into any topic, and if used effectively TRIZ shows how almost any problem can be solved creatively by almost anyone willing to engage with the analytical templates and also willing to put the time and effort into doing all the expected thinking.

In itself, it is highly concrete and sequential but at the same time TRIZ expands the mind in many ways because it shows possibilities and areas of thinking.Analytical skills, opening of the mind, viewing situations/problems from many different perspectives are the goals of the TRIZ process. Future problem solving will never be the same again for those who learn the system well.

SCAMPER – The letters stand for Substitute, Combine, Adapt, Minify/Magnify, Put to other uses, Eliminate, Reverse, Robert Eberle's model is based on the idea that what is new is done by reconfiguring the old or what already exists and we must learn new ways of doing that. SCAMPER may be considered concrete-based and sequential but leads to creative thinking in a fast and relatively easy way – especially for young people who need simpler guides. It is also less time consuming because it tends to be more general and does not go into the depth of details that TRIZ does. High quality creative ideas can still flow steadily. Like TRIZ, it provides a set of triggers for thinking in many situations and can help people aim for solutions in many different situations.

The Need for Creativity in the New and Changing World

With the world truly becoming a global village, people and countries must become more creative. Competition is no longer with just a neighbor or those in a local community. Competition comes from all directions and is international.

Countries compete for income from their exports and services. Where do these come from? They come from the creativity of the people.

Companies need to diversify sales lines with new products/ services in order to maintain a healthy income for growth and prosperity. Individual entrepreneurs must be able to create and switch jobs requiring perhaps different skills, and rapidly replace the obsolete with new and better ideas.

New approaches and jobs must be created to meet new demands and needs brought about by economic disruptors such as Amazon, Uber, and AirBnB.

Technological advancements make jobs obsolete at an accelerating pace but at the same time they cause regeneration and the creation of other totally new ones.

The above requires creative thinking. How can we humans satisfy new needs and wants, adapt laterally or vertically to losses, or develop new responses to old problems? Creativity is the source of solutions.

Reading List

Anderson, R. F. (1980). Using Guided Fantasy with Children.Alexandria: American School Counselor Association.*Elementary School Guidance and Counseling, 15*(1), 39-47.

De Bono, E. (1971). *New Think: The Use of Lateral Thinking in the Generation of New Ideas*. New York: Avon Books.

De Bono, E. (1973). *Lateral Thinking: Creativity Step by Step*. Toronto: Harper Perennial, 1973.

De Bono, E. (1992). *Serious Creativity*. New York: Harper Business.

De Bono, E. (2004).*De Bono's Thinking Course*. London: BBC Books.

De Bono, E. (2012). *How to Have Creative Ideas*. New York: Random House.

Eberle, B. (1996) *Scamper On: Games for Imagination Development*. Waco: Prufrock Press.

Eberle, B. (2005) *Scamper: Creative Games and Activities for Imagination Development*. Waco: Prufrock Press.

Plum, L. (1986). *Flights of Fantasy*. New York: R.R. Bowker.

Creativity Websites

(Note: Some of these highly creative websites may not be suitable for younger people. Please review each and use at your own discretion.)

Awesome Inventions, www.awesomeinventions.com

Behance: Showcase and Discover Creative Work, www.behance.net

CoRT Thinking (66 Lessons in Thinking), www.cortthinking.com

Creativity Post, www.creativitypost.com

Designorate, www.designorate.com

Instructables, www.instructables.com

Kickstarter, www.kickstarter.com

Neatorama, www.neatorama.com

The TRIZ Journal, www.triz-journal.com

TRIZ 40, www.triz40.com

Futurism and futurists are a stimulating source of ideas to develop and on which to apply creativity:

Futurism, www.futurism.com

Futurist.com, www.futurist.com

World Future Society, www.wfs.org

11.

PROMOTING CREATIVITY WITH GIFTED STUDENTS: FROM PIERRE BOURDIEU'S CONTRIBUTIONS TO PEDAGOGICAL PRACTICES

Fernanda Hellen Ribeiro Piske

Doctor of Education from the Federal University of Paraná (UFPR), Brazil.

ORCID: https://orcid.org/0000-0002-1516-6455.

E-mail: ferhellenrp@gmail.com

Tania Stoltz

Full Professor at the Federal University of Paraná, Brazil.

ORCID: 0000-0002-9132-0514.

Ettiène Guérios

Full Professor at the Federal University of Paraná, Brazil.

ORCID: 0000-0001-5451-9957

Cristina Costa-Lobo

Full Professor at Instituto de Estudos Superiores de Fafe (IESF, Portugal).

ORCID: 0000-0003-4459-8676

Abstract: *The aim of this chapter is to promote creativity in the education of the gifted students from the perspective of Pierre Bourdieu. This chapter makes an analysis of the phenomenon of creative resistance based on Bourdieu's concept of "habitus",* *that is to say, the system of individual representations socially formed by structured arrangements and permanently configured by social functions and actions. For the authors, the school system is a reality composed of many rules that can constitute a barrier that blocks the abilities of the students who attend it. Knowing that development and expression of creativity depend not only on an individual's own efforts but also on the social context in which the person is immersed, it is important to reflect on the possibilities of developing creativity, avoiding resistance to this important attribute in the development of these students. Artistic practices can be an example of the re-signification of the teaching of students with high skills to the extent that the artistic object has in itself the means to instill emotions and culturally rich reactions to appropriation of the world. Thus it is the responsibility of the school to enable freedom of expression and encourage the development of the gifts, talents and potential of students in order to promote more creative and innovative teaching.*

Keywords: *Creativity; Gifted students; Innovative teaching; Education; Pierre Bourdieu.*

Introduction

Rethinking education requires the re-signification of a universe that involves ideas, thoughts, educational paradigms and concepts that remain in society. There are still many education professionals who think that gifted students already know enough, and for this reason, they do not need more attention to their special educational needs (Piske, 2018). Moreover, such professionals end up inhibiting creative potential. In this sense, this article aims to reflect on possibilities of developing the creativity of gifted students, avoiding resistance to this important attribute in their education.

The limited knowledge that many teachers have about the area of giftedness prevents them from understanding that the focus of the specialized service for gifted students is not only to meet cognitive needs but also each dimension of their development. This limited knowledge ends up allowing many myths to enter many schools, making the teaching staff, on the whole, believe that the gifted student is a self-sufficient individual who can deal with his/her own special needs alone.

Among the various myths about the education of gifted students, we can highlight: the belief that somebody is gifted from birth; perfection should be the main goal for the development of the gifted student; the notion that all students can be gifted or that no student is gifted (Cross, 2002). It is necessary to unravel such myths, to understand them and to avoid them so that there are no mistakes regarding the education of the gifted.

Ideas, thoughts, paradigms and concepts are generated when senses and meanings attributed by people in a certain context arise, mostly without much reflection. Thinking creatively requires innovation; however, "it is easier to develop people's creativity by changing environmental conditions than by trying to make them think creatively" (Csikszentmihalyi 1996, p. 1).

For Rudolf Steiner (2003, 2015), the creative environment is fundamental for the integral development of each person, providing the harmonious integration of their thinking, feeling and doing. The conditions of the environment depend on the senses and meanings that are attributed to each thing, including creativity (Piske & Stoltz, 2020).

The role of the teacher is fundamental in an environment conducive to student learning and development. Indeed, Guérios (2002, 2015) shows that the conception that teachers have of the classroom and other components of educational action influences the pedagogical practice that they develop. She observed that by conceiving it as an environment "to create, recreate, think, rethink, give oneself the right to construct, to discuss, regardless of the physical layout of the classroom" (Guérios, 2002, p. 98), the possibility of developing creativity is enhanced. According to the author, "it is amazing what these students are capable of doing" (ibid., p. 98). Conversely, students' creativity may be strangled if teachers conceive of the classroom as being an environment of absolute certainties to be reproduced.

Morin explains why this occurs. "We settle safely in our theories and ideas, and these have no structure to welcome the new. However, new things come unceasingly" (Morin, 2000, p. 30). In the educational context "New things shoot without stopping in interstitial spaces, it is necessary to let new things sprout" (Guérios, 2002, p. 193). Focusing on gifted students, there is an urgent need for teachers to be creative professionals in their pedagogical practices in order to develop their defining characteristics.

What senses and meanings have been given to gifted education? It is up to teachers to rethink their educational practices and review what can be improved so that gifted education has quality and enables inclusion measures. This analysis can be difficult, since many teachers are unable to re-signify their own practices. In other words, for some professionals, teaching has become meaningless.

But what sense should be given to teaching? It is important to think about the teaching that is offered even if this takes a certain amount of time. Immediatism does not meet the needs of the school effectively. Thinking without reflection does not lead to a change in the educational paradigm.

The immediate itself does not allow the act of knowing and this is because a certain distance is always necessary (Morin,

2000). Many individuals are likely to think that transforming the educational context is a utopia; however, a change may occur if there are several individuals who think that it is possible to innovate and reinvent education.

The construct of creativity, due to its complexity and difficult multidimensional definition, means that today there are varied perceptions of creativity (Piske & Stoltz, 2020). Its concept is associated with something complex, multifaceted and with little analysis and exploration. To overcome the many obstacles faced today by educational institutions, instituting a change in methodological and pedagogical paradigms only seems possible with the involvement of all educational actors, in a collaborative perspective, with confrontation of ideas and respect for the other, aiming at significant improvements of the appropriations made by students (Piske, 2018; Bastos, Costa-Lobo, & Pereira, 2017). The number of studies developed in educational contexts about creativity has been increasing since it has been perceived as a fundamental construct both for the intended advances in education and for student development (Costa-Lobo et al., 2017). The scientific literature reveals that the study of creativity encompasses various theoretical models that seek to reveal its origin, its performance and its subsistence. The objectives in terms of learning and teaching that the school suggests may or may not favor the development of creative potential, thus considering that several factors, interpersonal, individual or social, have significant consequences for the creative production of the individual and society (Costa-Lobo et al., 2017). It is assumed by Costa-Lobo et al. (2017) that early stimulation and experiencing creative thinking in the educational context are conditions that promote the development of capabilities for solving future problems and challenges.

Almeida et al. (2017) report the need to pay attention to the cognitive and learning processes of gifted children through the identification of measures that allow effective support for their psychological development and school learning; these authors characterize the cognitive abilities of gifted children and their particular forms of learning, evidencing how the current emphasis is no longer placed on quantity but on the functionality of cognitive abilities. The search for creative professionals, that is, innovative individuals who stand out for the strategies used to confront the new and solve problems, has been emphasized in the educational context, in different social and cultural settings. There seems to be a need for creative education, capable of covering all levels of education, stimulating students' desire to learn.

Pierre Bourdieu's Understanding about Resistance to Creativity

Pierre Bourdieu, a philosopher who made a significant contribution to anthropological studies with a decisive theorization in the field of contemporary sociology and an influence on educational research, does not specifically address gifted students, but careful reading of his work contributes to the education of these students, especially with regard to the theory of action. Lahire (2002, p. 45) points out that:

> It is evident from the work of Pierre Bourdieu that the greatest effort is made to explain the theory of action. In it we find specifically the notions of internalization or incorporation of objective structures, disposition systems, generating formulae or generating principles

and unifying practices, transposability or transferability of dispositions (Lahire, 2002, p. 45).

Bourdieu's theorization is structured in the concepts of field, habitus and capital, the latter being composed of subconcepts referred to as social capital, cultural capital, economic capital and symbolic capital.

The concept of habitus is central to Bourdieu's work, and it has roots in the Aristotelian thought and medieval scholasticism. In Bourdieu's philosophical studies, as Wacquant (2004, p. 65-66) highlights:

> We find the most complete sociological renewal of the concept [habitus] outlined to transcend the opposition between objectivism and subjectivism: habitus is a mediating notion that helps to break with the duality of common sense between individual and society by capturing the internalization of exteriority and exteriorization of interiority, that is, how society becomes deposited in people in the form of durable arrangements or trained capacities and structured propensities to think, feel and act in certain ways, which then guide them in their creative responses to the constraints and requests from their existing social environment.

For Bourdieu (1983) "habitus" can be understood as:

> A system of lasting, transposable dispositions which, integrating past experiences, functions at every moment as a matrix of perceptions, appreciations, and actions and makes possible the achievement of infinitely diversified tasks, thanks to analogical transfers of schemes

permitting the solution of similarly shaped problems. (Bourdieu, 1983, p. 65).

According to Bourdieu (1989, 1990, 1996a), Bourdieu & Wacquant (1992), "habitus" can be designated as a system of individual representations, socially constituted of structured dispositions and mental structuring, that emerges in practical experiences through the specific social conditions of existence, permanently configured for social functions and actions. Misconceptions occur in the understanding of habitus from Bourdieu's perspective, among them, habitus:

> It is never the replica of a single social structure [...] it is not necessarily coherent and unified [...] it is no less prepared to analyze the crisis and the change from what it is to analyze the cohesion and perpetuation [...] it is not a self-sufficient mechanism for action generation: it operates as a spring requiring an external trigger; it cannot, therefore, be considered in isolation from particular social worlds, or 'fields', within which it evolves (Wacquant 2004, pp. 68-69).

The concept of "field" is also essential in Bourdieu's work. For Bourdieu (2003, 2005), "field" refers to contexts with their own rules, principles and hierarchies, where conflicts and tensions, oppositions and concordances occur between social actors that interact daily. These actors may be education professionals themselves who follow established rules in the educational setting and a standardized form of teaching that ends up victimizing students by limiting their creative potential.

This situation often explains the resistance to creativity at school, because those people who are considered "non-standard" can break the rules that are pre-established in the field, that is, a student who does not accept learning in the same way as others can be excluded from the social group in which he/she lives. Bourdieu (1990) explains that every field, as a historical product, generates interest, which is the condition of its functioning.

Matos (2011) observes that creative resistance is based on a set of symbolic values that are reactive to the pre-established system, that is, a habitus that reacts to the conditions imposed by the field, re-signifying products and uses and avoiding the imposition of the field.

For Pontes (2002), each person through his/her habitus presents dispositions that put him/her in a certain social field, often without specific conditions for action. However, these dispositions called habitus, when practiced in a real action, may acquire differentiated forms as well as distinct responses, "since there may be a mismatch between the position an individual occupies at a given moment and his/her acquired habitus throughout his/her existence" (Pontes, 2002, p. 79).

In spite of the resistance to creativity impregnated in the school context, this context being considered the "Bourdieu field" where there are rules and disputes of power, it is possible to use the dispositions named "habitus" seized over time, to reverse the educational situation, where teaching staff repeat the same content to teach without reflecting on what they are teaching, much less generating possibilities for creative and innovative educational practices for learning.

Resistance to creativity can be defined precisely by the way the school offers teaching. Teaching with an emphasis on innovative and creative practices can generate significant changes for the school as a whole.However, teaching that focuses on a standardized and repetitive method establishes learning limitations and inhibits the possibility of generating something new (Gross, 2016; Kane, 2016; Piske & Stoltz, 2020; Guérios, 2019a; 2019b).

It is important to draw attention to a recurring fact in the didactic practice of teachers, since Guérios (2002) has identified that if teachers do not develop a didactic principle, which in the context of this text we can call didactic awareness, they can apply an innovative method in the classroom, but in a didactic directional way, without room for the development of the students' creativity.

Under the lens of Bourdieu, teachers will have incorporated a certain way of making socially dictated teaching into a historical perspective (habitus), whose reflection of accumulated cultural capital is manifested by the directivity in teaching action and reproduction in learning. In his research, he identified that "The innovative perspective of pedagogical practice did not lie in the pure and simple application of a new teaching technique, but in the differentiated posture that the teacher and students present in relation to knowledge" (Guérios, 2002, p. 198). In fact, as Wacquant (2004, p. 69) pointed out in a study of Bourdieu, as follows:

> Habitus is not a self-sufficient mechanism for action generation: it operates as a spring requiring an external trigger; it cannot therefore be considered in isolation from the particular social worlds, or "fields", within which it evolves. A complete analysis of the practice requires a triple elucidation of the social genesis and structure of the habitus and field and of the dynamics of its "dialectical confrontation".

Bourdieu (1998) points out that direct action, in the form of artistic teaching or the different types of initiation to practice (organized visits, etc.), remains weak [...] (Bourdieu, 1998,

p. 61). Medeiros (2007) explains that, according to the Bourdieu theory, the desire for ascension through the school cannot exist as long as the objective chances of success become cumulative, and as long as there is a rigidity of the social order that allows the monopoly of the use of the school institution. In this sense, a monopoly on the manipulation of cultural goods may also occur. The lack of freedom of expression and the reprimand of acting and thinking can generate aversion on the part of students to attend school (Piske et al. 2016a, 2016b). The monopoly of the use of the school institution discards all possibilities of educational measures that promote creation, invention and creativity.

Piske (2016) points out that the educational practices that take place in the school context can be determinant for gifted students to develop their high abilities and their creative potential. In this sense, it is up to the administrators of institutions, pedagogues and teaching staff to create possibilities for the achievement of creative and innovative work at school.

Contribution of Bourdieu to the Development of Creativity

Being creative can depend on how each person is instigated to think of a particular culture or social context. The dispositions that each person presents throughout their historical and cultural path can transform the field where he/she is inserted.

Bourdieu and Darbel (2003), in the work that explicits the love for art, emphasize its importance for the development of creativity and school performance. "The work of art considered as symbolic does not exist as such except for those who possess the means of appropriating it, that is, of deciphering it" (Bourdieu & Darbel, 2003, p. 71).

Pelaes (2009), by focusing on the works of Bourdieu, and making a relation on the teaching of art with the Bourdieu theory, identifies how much the universe of art can contribute to the development of creativity, as well as the recognition of the potential creator and self-knowledge enhanced by artistic activities. This idea is also found in Stoltz and Weger (2012, 2015), Veiga and Stoltz (2014), Machado, Stoltz (2016) and Stoltz, Weger and Veiga (2017) who, based on Rudolf Steiner, integrated between art and science in the sense of promoting knowledge and self-knowledge in the educational process.

Motivation is fundamental for the individual to be encouraged to create and be creative in order to enable the structuring of a knowledge that potentiates the student in the recognition of art and its aesthetic properties, and to carry out his/her own artistic representation, in the most varied languages, within the context of educational, aesthetic and everyday relations. Knowing the universe of art makes it possible to recognize the creative potential through its development. Education that occurs through artistic practices can be an important means for the development of creativity and the cultivation of aesthetic knowledge, "through the knowledge of consecrated artistic production and the elaboration of a personal aesthetic expression" (Pelaes, 2009, p. 30).

Artistic competence is important for the apprehension and appreciation of a work of art. The more accurate the artistic knowledge, the more the spectator allows himself to contemplate the appreciated work. For Bourdieu (2001, p. 271), the apprehension and appreciation of the work depend so much on the intention of the spectator that, in turn, is a function of the conventional norms that reacts to the relation with the work of art in a given historical and social situation, as an aptitude of the spectator to conform to these norms, that is, of their artistic competence.

Thus, it is possible to understand that the development of creativity depends on how the school works with the competence of each student. With regard to artistic competence, there must be educational means that will enable the student to improve his/her artistic potential and his/her talents through in-depth teaching in his/her area of interest.

Pontes (2002) makes us reflect, through Bourdieu's theory, that creativity is designated by the capacity for change that an action is capable of performing, as well as that action that could not be predicted and anticipated by social individuals.

This very important attribute for the development of potentialities can be present in each action, in its latent form, and emerges by means of injunctions of various opportunities and by the individual need to respond to the social demands presented to individuals everyday.

Creativity is an attribute that occurs from a mismatch between a specific habitus, in a specific field and from a dominated or dominant position, and the position of the actors in a field, as a result of transformations that are not only structural – for example, "A new status acquired from a particular type of training – as well as due to physical changes occurring everyday [...]" (Pontes, 2002, p. 81).

Thinking creatively goes beyond structural changes; physical and psychological changes lead us to create possibilities of invention and creation, making it possible to reinvent teaching practices in the educational setting.

For Bourdieu to be creative goes beyond creating new actions from a historical vacuum; the creative person possesses specific abilities developed in a habitus, in his/her mental and practical form, with the purpose of working with the elements available in his/her habitus in order to reinvent spaces for actions in different social fields. In this context, creativity is perceived as a situated action, established in a historical environment, susceptible to transformations because of its irregular character; this attribute requires changes of individual habitus and collective actions (Bourdieu, 1993, 1996b, 1998).

What is necessary to carry out a creative work?

For Sternberg (2006), Sternberg & Williams (1996), it is important to have the balance between the analytical, synthetic, and practical skills for creative work to occur.

In relation to analytical ability, Sternberg & Williams (1996) explain that it is considered as the capacity for critical thinking. A person with this ability analyzes and evaluates ideas. Everyone, even the most creative person, has better and worse ideas. The best ideas can also depend on a moment of inspiration. These authors explain that without a well-developed analytical capacity, the creative thinker is as likely to pursue bad ideas as to pursue good ones. The creative individual uses the analytical ability to discover the implications of a creative idea and to test it in the various areas.

As for the synthetic ability, it is what we usually consider creativity, that is, the ability to generate new and interesting ideas. Often, the person we call the creative individual is a particularly good synthetic thinker, capable of making connections between things that other people do not recognize spontaneously. This individual may develop innovative ideas easily.

The authors point out that practical skill is the ability to translate theory into practice and abstract ideas into practical realizations. One implication of the investment theory of creativity is that good ideas do not sell. The creative person uses the practical ability to convince other people that an idea is worthy. For example, each organization has a set of ideas that dictate how things, or at least some things, should be done. To propose a new procedure you must sell it by convincing others that it is better than the old one (Sternberg & Williams, 1996; Sternberg, 2006).

Thus, it can be said that to carry out a creative work according to Sternberg, there is also the need to consider what Bourdieu points out as changes in individual habitus and collective actions.

Important Attitudes for the Development of Creativity

According to Costa-Lobo et al (2016) the implementation of specific strategies and the promotion of an appropriate educational environment for the development of creativity signals the importance of the construct to be increased in psychoeducational practices, challenging and multifaceted environments.

For some specialists on the domain of Giftedness (Almeida et al, 2017; Piechowski, 2014; Pfeiffer, 2016; Gross, 2016; Kane, 2016; Fleith, 2000; Alencar, Braga and Marinho, 2016; Stoltz et al. 2015; Piske, 2013, 2016; 2018; among others) there are significant attitudes of teaching staff during the class that can favor working with creativity. Among them, it is possible to list:

- Provide a classroom environment in which the learning experience is enjoyable;
- Do not allow the limitations of the context in which it is found to inhibit creative potential;
- Value creative products and ideas;

- Allow the student time to think and develop his/her ideas;
- Consider error as a stage of the learning process;
- Encourage the student to imagine other points of view;
- Enable the student to make choices, taking into account his/her interests and abilities;
- Provide opportunities for the student to become aware of their creative potential, thus favoring the development of positive self-concept;
- Cultivate sense of humor in the classroom;
- Have positive expectations regarding the student performance;
- Demonstrate enthusiasm for the teaching activity and content of classes.

These attitudes could be seen as fundamental in the sense of the liberating action of the school, observed by Bourdieu.

Conclusion

As shown above, children entering the school system, which is a reality comprised of a large number of new rules, face a barrier that blocks their abilities. In this way, it is possible to confirm that the development and expression of creativity depends not only on the individual's own efforts, but also on the social context in which he/she is immersed. Reflection on the possibilities of developing the creativity of gifted students, avoiding resistance to this important attribute in the education of these students, leads us to think that artistic practices can give a new meaning to the teaching of these children (Machado &Stoltz, 2016). Coli (1998) points out that the artistic object has in itself the means to instill in us, in our emotions and reason, culturally rich reactions, "which sharpen the instruments of which we serve to apprehend the world around us" (Coli 1998, p. 109).

Costa-Lobo et al. (2016) and Costa-Lobo et al. (2017) signaled harmony promotion practices between educational research and psychological intervention, with regard to the development of skills and attitudes that encourage thinking and creative potential.

It is up to the school to enable freedom of expression and encourage the development of the gifts, talents and potential of its students to promote creative and innovative teaching. According to Bourdieu (1990, 2005) the school has a liberating role, whose success would depend on the individual gifts of each one.

The preparation of the teaching staff is essential to provide opportunities for gifted students to become aware of their creative potential, creating a classroom atmosphere in which the learning experience is enjoyable.

It is important that teachers do not allow the limitations of the school context to inhibit creative potential. These limitations include lack of investment in human and material resources. As such, teaching staff would have to present actions that generate transformations beyond structural changes, counting on physical and psychological changes to create possibilities of invention and creation at school.

References

Alencar, E. M. L. S., Braga, N. P. & Marinho, C. D. (2016). *Como desenvolver o potencial criador: Um guia para a liberação da criatividade em sala de aula.[How to develop creative potential: A guide to releasing creativity in the classroom].*Petrópolis, RJ: Vozes.

Almeida, L. S., Costa-Lobo, C., Almeida, A. I. S, Rocha, R. S., & Piske, F. H. R. (2017). Processos cognitivos e de aprendizagem em crianças sobredotadas: atenção dos pais e professores. In F. H. R. Piske, C. L. B. Vestena, T. Stoltz, S., J. M. Machado, A. A. O. M. Barby, S. Bahia & S. P. Freitas (Eds.). *Processos afetivos e cognitivos de superdotados e talentosos*: Curitiba: Editora Prismas, 15-39.

Bastos, F., Costa-Lobo, C., & Pereira, C. S. (2017). Práticas pedagógicas num Território Educativo de Intervenção Prioritária. *Educação e Pesquisa*. doi:10.1590/s1678-4634201706158555.

Bourdieu, P. (1989). *Poder Simbólico.[Symbolic power]*. Lisboa: Difel.

Bourdieu, P. (1990). Coisas Ditas. [In other words]. São Paulo: Editora Brasiliense.

Bourdieu, P. (1993). *The Field of Cultural Production*. New York: Columbia University Press.

Bourdieu, P. (1996a). *Razões Práticas: sobre a teoria da ação. [Practical Reasons: on the theory of action]*. Campinas: Papirus.

Bourdieu, P. (1996b). *As regras da arte. [The rules of art]*. São Paulo: Companhia das Letras.

Bourdieu, P. (1998). A escola conservadora: as desigualdades frente à escola e à cultura. [The conservative school: the inequalities regarding the school and the culture]. In M. A. Nogueira & A. Catani (Orgs). *Escritos de Educação [Education Writing]*. Petrópolis, RJ: Vozes.

Bourdieu, P. (2001). *A economia das trocas simbólicas. [The economic of symbolic exchanges]* (5th ed.) São Paulo: Perspectiva.

Bourdieu, P. (2003). Participant objectivation. *Journal of the Royal Anthropological Institute, 9*, 281-294. doi:10.1111/1467-9655.00150

Bourdieu, P. (2005). Secouez un peu vos structures! In J. Dubois, P. Durand, & Y. Winkin (orgs.). *Le symbolique et le social. La réception internationale de la pensée de Pierre Bourdieu* (pp. 325-341) Actes du Colloque de Cerisy-la-Salle. Liège: Éditions de l'Université de Liège.

Bourdieu, P. & Darbel, A. (2003). *O amor pela arte: os museus de arte na Europa e seu público. [Love of Art: European Art Museums and Their Public].* São Paulo: Editora da Universidade de São Paulo: Zouk.

Bourdieu, P. & Wacquant, Loïc J. D. (1992). *An Invitation to Reflexive Sociology.* Chicago: University of Chicago Press.

Coli, J. (1998). *O que é arte? [What is art?]*(15th ed.). São Paulo: Brasiliense.

Costa- Lobo, C., Pérez- Nieto, M. A., Castillo-Parra, G.; Carvalho, T., Sousa, M., Medeiros, A. M., & Vázquez-Justo, E. (2017). Creatividad en los centros educativos: ¿cómo promover? *Edupsyké, 15* (1), 109-139.

Costa-Lobo, C., Sousa, M., Campina, A., Vestena, C., & Cabrera- Cuevas, J. (2016). Potencial criativo e processos cognitivos em crianças: da identificação precoce às intervenções futuras. *Diálogos Possíveis, 15* (2), 65-93.

Cross, T. L. (2002). Competing With Myths About the Social and Emotional Development of Gifted Students. *Gifted Child Today,* 25(3), 44-65. Retrieved from http://sengifted.org/competing-with-myths-about-the-social-and-emotional-development-of-gifted-students/

Csikszentmihalyi, M. (1996). *Creativity.* New York: Harper Collins.

Fleith, D. S. (2000). Teacher and student perceptions of creativity in the classroom environment. In: Roeper Rewiew. Retrieved from http://www.tandfonline.com/doi/abs/10.1080/02783190009554022

Gross, M. U. M. (2016). Developing Programs for Gifted and Talented Students. In F. H. R. Piske, T. Stoltz, J. M. Machado & S. Bahia (Orgs.), *Altas habilidades/Superdotação (AH/SD) e Criatividade: Identificação e Atendimento [Giftedness and Creativity: identification and specialized service]* (pp. 61-75). Curitiba: Juruá.

Guérios, E. (2002). *Espaços oficiais e intersticiais da formação docente: histórias de um grupo de professores na área de ciências e matemática.* (Tese de Doutorado). UNIICAMP, Campinas. Retrieved from http://repositorio.unicamp.br/jspui/handle/REPOSIP/253667

Guérios, E. (2015) Influências e decorrências de diferentes concepções de supervisão na prática do estágio supervisionado em matemática. In

O estágio na formação inicial do professor que ensina matemática (pp. 147-172).Campinas: Mercado das letras.

Guérios, E. (2019a) *Contribuições do pensamento complexo para a formação de professores em uma perspectiva transdisciplinar.* [Contributions of complex thinking to teacher training in a transdisciplinary perspective] In R. Sá & M. Behrens (Eds.). Teoria da Complexidade: contribuições epistemológicas e metodológicas para uma pedagogia complexa. Curitiba: Appris. pp. 223-236.

Guérios, E. (2019b). *Principios didácticos para una práctica matemática transdisciplinar* [Didactic principles for a transdisciplinary mathematical practice]. Cuadernos de Investigación y Formación en Educación Matemática. N 18. 199-209 Retrieved from <https://revistas.ucr.ac.cr/index.php/cifem/article/view/39913>.

Kane, M. (2016). Gifted Learning Communities: Effective Teachers at Work. In F. H. R. Piske, T. Stoltz, J. M. Machado & S. Bahia (Orgs.), *Altas habilidades/ Superdotação (AH/SD) e Criatividade: Identificação e Atendimento [Giftedness and Creativity: identification and specialized service]* (pp. 77-94). Curitiba: Juruá.

Lahire, B. (2002). Reprodução ou prolongamentos críticos? *Educação e Sociedade, XXIII,* 78, 37-55.Campinas: CEDES.

Machado, C.L. & Stoltz, T. (2016). Art at school. Is there any perspective? *Creative Education,* 7(18), 2733-2747. doi: 10.4236/ce.2016.718255

Matos, E. B. (2011). Gênese da resistência criativa nas ideias de agência de Certeau e de habitus de Bourdieu. [Genesis of the creative resistance in the ideas of agency of Certeau and habitus of Bourdieu].*XXXV Encontro da ANPAD.* Retrieved from www.anpad.org.br/admin/pdf/MKT2526.pdf

Medeiros, C. C. C. (2007). *A teoria sociológica de Pierre Bourdieu na produção discente dos programas de pós-graduação em educação no Brasil [The sociological theory of Pierre Bourdieu in the student production of postgraduate programs in education in Brazil]* (Tese de Doutorado em Educação). Universidade Federal do Paraná, Curitiba.

Morin, E. (2000). Les sept savoirs nécessaires à l'éducation du futur. Paris: Seuil.

Pelaes, M. L. W. (2009). A Contribuição de Pierre Bourdieu para a Metodologia do Ensino da Arte. [Pierre Bourdieu's Contribution to the Methodology of Teaching Art]. *Revista Educação*, 4(1). Retrieved from revistas.ung.br/index.php/educacao/article/download/456/564

Pfeiffer, S. (2016). Leading Edge Perspectives on Gifted Assessment. In F. H. R. Piske, T. Stoltz, J. M. Machado & S. Bahia (Orgs), *Altas Habilidades /Superdotação (AH/SD) e Criatividade: Identificação e Atendimento [Giftedness and Creativity: identification and Specialized service]*. Curitiba: Juruá.

Piechowski, M. M. (2014). Identity. In F. H. R. Piske, J. M. Machado, S. Bahia & T. Stoltz (orgs.). *Altas habilidades/Superdotação (AH/SD): Criatividade e emoção [Giftedness: Creativity and emotion]*. Curitiba, Juruá.

Piske, F. H. R. (2013). *O desenvolvimento socioemocional de alunos com altas habilidades/superdotação (AH/SD) no contexto escolar: Contribuições a partir de Vygotsky. [The socio-emotional development of students with giftedness in the school context: Contributions from Vygotsky].*(Dissertação de Mestrado em Educação). Universidade Federal do Paraná, Curitiba, PR.

Piske, F. H. R. (2016). Alunos com Altas Habilidades/Superdotação (AH/SD): como identificá-los? In F. H. R. Piske, T. Stoltz, J. M. Machado & S. Bahia (Orgs), *Altas Habilidades /Superdotação (AH/SD) e Criatividade: Identificação e Atendimento [Giftedness and Creativity: identification and Specialized service]* (pp. 249-260). Curitiba: Juruá.

Piske, F. H. R. (2018). Altas habilidades/superdotação (AH/SD) e criatividade na escola: o olhar de Vygotsky e de Steiner. (Tese de Doutorado em Educação) Universidade Federal do Paraná, Curitiba, PR.

Piske, F. H. R. & Stoltz, T. (2020). *Altas Habilidades/Superdotação (AH/SD) e Criatividade: Contribuições do Sociointeracionismo de Vygotsky e da Pedagogia Waldorf de Rudolf Steiner.* Curitiba, Juruá.

Piske, F. H. R.; Stoltz, T.; Guérios, E. & Freitas, S. P. (2016a). Creativity and Complex Thoughts of Gifted Students from Contributions of Edgar Morin and Rudolf Steiner. *Creative Education, 7*, 2268-2278. Retrieved from http://file.scirp.org/pdf/CE_2016092716142766.pdf

Piske, F. H. R., Stoltz, T., Vestena, C. L. B., Freitas, S. P., Valentim, B. F. B., Oliveira, C. S., Barby, A. A. O. M. & Lopes, C. L. (2016b). Barriers to Creativity, Identification and Inclusion of Gifted Student. *Creative Education, 1899-* -1905. Retrieved from http://file.scirp.org/pdf/CE_2016082517133903.pdf

Pontes, N. L. M. T. (2002). *É possível uma ação criativa? Elementos para uma teoria da ação na obra de Pierre Bourdieu. [Is creative action possible? Elements for a theory of action in the work of Pierre Bourdieu].* (Dissertação de Mestrado em Sociologia). Universidade Federal de Pernambuco, Recife, PE.

Steiner, R. (2003). *A Arte da Educação I: O Estudo Geral do Homem – uma base para a Pedagogia. [The Art of Education I: The General Study of Man – a basis for Pedagogy].* São Paulo: Antroposófica.

Steiner, R. (2015). *Educação na puberdade: o ensino criativo.*[Education at puberty: creative teaching] (4th ed.). São Paulo: Antroposófica.

Sternberg, R. J. (2006). The nature of creativity. *Creativity Research Journal, 18,* 87-98. doi: 10.1207/s15326934crj1801_10

Sternberg, R. J. & Williams, W. M. (1996). *How to develop student creativity.* Alexandria, VA: Association for Supervision and Curriculum Development. Retrieved from http://www.ascd.org/publications/books/196073.aspx

Stoltz, T., Piske, F. H. R., Freitas, M. F. Q., D'Aroz, M. S., & Machado, J. M. (2015). Creativity in Gifted Education: Contributions from Vygotsky and Piaget. *Creative Education, 6,* 64-70. doi:10.4236/ce.2015.61005

Stoltz, T., & Weger, U. (2012). Piaget and Steiner: Science and Art in the Process of Formation. *Research on Steiner Education (RoSE), 3,* 134-145. Oslo: Rudolf Steiner University College; Alfter: Alanus University of Arts and SocialSciences. Retrieved from http://www.rosejourn.com/index.php/rose/article/viewFile/106/131

Stoltz, T., & Weger, U. (2015). O pensar vivenciado na formação de professores. *Educar em Revista, (56),* 67-83. Retrieved from http://www.scielo.br/scielo.php?script=sci_arttext&pid=S0104-406020150002000 67&lng=pt&tlng=pt. 10.1590/0104-4060.41444.

Stoltz, T., Weger, U. & Veiga, M. (2017). Higher Education as Self-Transformation. *Psychology Research,* 7(2), 104-111. doi:10.17265/2159-5542/2017.02. 004

Wacquant L. (2004). Esclarecer o habitus. *Sociologia Revista da Faculdade de Letras da Universidade do Porto,* 14, 35-41.Retrieved from http://ojs.letras.up.pt/index.php/Sociologia/article/view/2459/2249

Veiga, M., & Stoltz, T. (Orgs.). (2014). *O pensamento de Rudolf Steiner no debate científico.*Campinas, SP: Editora Alínea.

ABOUT THE AUTHORS

Alberto Rocha

Psychology graduate. Phd student in Education Sciences, specialized in Educational Psychology. Effective member of the Order of Portuguese Psychologists. Specialist in Educational Psychology, Special Educational Needs and Early Intervention from the Order of Portuguese Psychologists. Alberto Rocha is the President of the Board of the National Association for the Study and Intervention of Giftedness (A.N.E.I.S), while also being Coordinator of the Enrichment Program in the Areas of Aptitude, Interest, and Socialization (P.E.D.A.I.S), for which the Delegation of Porto and Gondomar is responsible, and finally, he is the director of the scientific journal "Sobredotação". Dr. Alberto Rocha led the Project of Identification of Giftedness and Talent in 1st Cycle Students (PISTA|1). He is the representative of "Red Internacional de Investigación, Intervención y Evaluación en Altas Capacidades Intelectuales" (REINEVA) in Portugal. Rocha is a member of the Editorial board of the scientific digital magazine in the disciplines of Psychology and Education, "Talíncrea": talent, intelligence, and creativity. He is also a member of the Research Group on Cognition, Learning, and Performance (GICAD), as well as a member of the European Council for High Ability (ECHA) and World Council for Gifted and Talented Children (WCGTC). Alberto Rocha is part of the research group of CIEd – Center for Research on Education of the University of Minho. He is the author and co-author of several papers presented at national and international conferences, in addition to papers published in the areas of giftedness and talent.

Carmen Ferrándiz

Dr. Doña Carmen Ferrándiz García. Professor of Evolutionary Psychology and Education (University of Murcia). Principal Investigator of different research projects. She has taught on High Skills, and participated in different specialization and Master's courses at several Spanish universities. She has spent time at prestigious research centers (Yale University, USA, University of Coimbra, Portugal, Institute of Education, IOE, UK). She is the author and co-author of books published by national and international publishers on high skills and intelligence (cognitive functioning, educational enrichment programs, emotional intelligence, multiple intelligences and scientific-creative thinking). She has published different articles on JCR impact in national and international journals (Gifted Child Quarterly, Psicothema, Anales de Psicología, Psicodidactica), among others. She obtained the First National Prize for Educational Research (doctoral thesis, CIDE) and was also awarded an extraordinary doctoral prize.

Charlina Gozali

PhD candidate in education at Claremont Graduate University. Her research interests include teaching, learning, and child development, particularly that of children in developing countries. Recently awarded the Claremont Graduate University Dissertation Grant, her research focuses on the individual, school, and environmental factors that contribute to talent and leader development in Indonesia. She also recently presented a professional workshop to teacher leaders in Indonesia on productive giftedness and creativity. Gozali has presented her research at national conferences such as the American Educational Research Association (AERA), Comparative and International

Education Society (CIES), and the Wallace Research Symposium. She has published in international and other journals, including in FIRE: Forum for International Research in Education.

Cristina Costa-Lobo

Degree, Master and Doctorate in Psychology. Post Doctorate in Education. Coordinating Professor, Integrated researcher and Director of Educational Innovation at the Fafe Institute of Higher Studies. Coordinating Professor at the Institute of Higher Studies in Fafe (IESF-Portugal). Editor in Chief of International Journal of Innovation and Research in Educational Sciences. Director of Strategy, Development and Internationalization Department at Optimus Creative and Technology School (Brasil & Portugal). Member of the Board of Directors at the Research, Development and Innovation Center (CIDI-IESF). Integrated researcher at the Center for Organizational and Social Studies at the Polytechnic of Porto (IPP, Portugal). Associate Member of the International Network for Research, Intervention and Evaluation in High Intellectual Capacities (Spain, http:// reineva.gtisd.net/ en/apresentacao/), Brain and Behavior Institute at Universidade Fernando Pessoa (Portugal), INPP-UPT (Portugal), REMIT-UPT (Portugal, Research Group on Economics, Management and Information Technologies), Research Group of the Autonomous University of Madrid (Spain), UNIFACS (Brazil) and UNICENTRO (Brazil). Founder and Vice-President of the Portuguese Association for Career Development (APDC, Portugal, http://www.apdc.eu/ corpos.html). Founder and Director of the Center for Research and Intervention in Sport, Education and Welfare (CIIDEBE, Brazil and Portugal).President of the Portuguese Observatory of UNESCO Chair in Youth, Education and Society. Researcher of the Interactive Ecosystem for Portuguese Business Internationalization (IEcPBI) project approved and funded at the 2017 Call for SR&TD Project Grants FCT. https://orcid.org/0000-0003-4459-8676

Daiana Yamila Rigo

PhD in Psychology from the University of San Luis. Master in Educational Psychology, University of Murcia, Spain. Degree in Psychopedagogy from the University of Río Cuarto. Professor of University of Río Cuarto degree and postgraduate courses. Researcher of the National Council of Scientific and Technical Research -CONICET-. Director, co-director and collaborator of various research projects and postgraduate theses. Her research works refer to the field of multiple intelligences, education, instructional design, engagement and evaluation. Author of articles for books and magazines on topics of her specialty nationally and internationally.

Ettiène Guérios

Doctor of Mathematical Education from Campinas State University (Unicamp). Master of Education, Bachelor of Science in Mathematics and Bachelor of Arts in Pedagogy from the Federal University of Paraná (UFPR). At UFPR she teaches at the Department of Teaching Theory and Practice, in two different Programmes: the Postgraduate Education Programme (Academic); and the Postgraduate Education Programme – Teaching Theory and Practice (Professional). She is a member of the following CNPq certified Research Groups: "Cognition, Learning and Human Development"; "Science and Mathematics Teaching and Learning Research Group"; "Pedagogy, Complexity and Education Studies and Research Group". She coordinates the Studies and Research Group on Mathematics Teachers. The main subjects she works with are: complex thinking, teacher training (initial and continuing), education in mathematics, learning didactics and methodology at all teaching levels.

Eva Gyarmathy

Senior researcher at the Institute for Cognitive Neuroscience and Psychology of the Hungarian Academy. Her research interests focus on multiple exceptional gifted individuals such as talent associated with specific learning difficulties, ADHD, autism and/or social, cultural differences. She is university lecturer at several universities. As a psychotherapist her activity directs toward the care of the profoundly gifted and multiple exceptional talent. She is a consultant to private schools that serve gifted children and adolescents who could not be integrated in main stream school. She founded the Adolescent and Adult Dyslexia Centre and the Special Needs Talent Support Council.

Fernanda Bachini de Oliveira

Graduated in Pedagogy from the Federal University of Paraná. Post-Graduate in Special and Inclusive Education from ITECNE. She is a teacher at the Curitiba Municipal Education Department. She has experience in Education and in studies related to Giftedness.

Fernanda Hellen Ribeiro Piske

Doctor of Education from the Federal University of Paraná (UFPR), on the theme of Cognition, Learning and Human Development. She took a Ph.D. sandwich course at Purdue University, West Lafayette, United States, focusing on the area of Creativity in teaching high ability/gifted students. Master of Education from the Federal University of Paraná. Postgraduate Specialist in Special Education and Inclusive Education from the UNINTER International University Centre. Bachelor of Arts in Pedagogy from the Federal University of Paraná. She also holds a Higher Technology Education Degree in Foreign Trade from the Curitiba International Technology Faculty. Member of the UFPR Creativity and High Ability/Giftedness Research Group. She works as a school teacher for the Curitiba Municipal Education Department. She is a researcher, author and organizer of books on themes relating to Creativity, Affectivity, Socio-emotional Development, Teacher Training, Human Rights, Special Education, principally in relation to the area of High Abilities/Giftedness. ORCID: https://orcid.org/0000-0002-1516-6455. E-mail: ferhellenrp@gmail.com.

Letícia Fleig Dal Forno

Professor at the Master's program in knowledge management in organizations at Unicesumar. Graduated in special education and Master in Education from Universidade Federal de Santa Maria, and PhD in education (specialty of Education psychology) from the University of Lisbon. Researcher in knowledge management, community of practice, collaborative learning, inclusive education and teaching processes. Scholarship productivity of the ICETI program.

Lola Prieto

University Professor in the area of Educational Psychology (UM). 6 years of research. Primary Teacher, Lic. Philosophy and Letters, Pedagogy and Psychology. Collaboration and pre-doctoral fellow from MEC. Extraordinary doctorate award Training stays: Hadassah-Wizo-Canada Research Institute (Israel); Lancaster University (UK), Yale University (USA), University of Newcastle Upon Tyne (UK), Harvard University (USA), Warwick University (UK), Minho University (Portugal), Canterbury Christ Church University (UK), Roehampton University (UK). IOE (Institute of Education, London (UK) Research lines: Intelligence, Creative-Scientific Thinking, Creativity, Emotional Intelligence, Triarchic Intelligence. She has taught High Skill training to education professionals in the following communities: Canary Islands, Andalusia, Madrid, Region of Murcia, Balearic Islands and Castilla la Mancha. She has held different research management positions (ANEP, Ramón y Cajal, ANECA: Academia Program, president of the Andalusian Evaluation Agency, member of CNEAI, member from the Valencia Agency for the Evaluation of Research Activity.) Reviewer of different Journals (Thinking Skills and Creativity, Learning and Individual Differences, Annals of Psychology, Thinking Skills and Problem Solving, Spanish Journal of Psychology, International Journal of Creativity and Problem Solving, among others) Member of the scientific committee of journals such as: Annals of Psychology, International Journal of Creativity and Problem Solving. Member of the organizing and scientific commission of different International Congresses.

María Laura de la Barrera

PhD in Psychology from the Faculty of Psychology of the University of San Luis. Master in Neurosciences and Behavioral Biology, Pablo de Olavide University, Seville, Spain, Master in Neuropsychology, University of Córdoba, Graduate in Psychopedagogy, University of Río Cuarto. Associate Professor (graduation and postgraduation). She has carried out and carries out research and teaching tasks in relation to CONICET, FONCyT, SECyt-UNRC. Director and collaborator of several research projects, national and international, aimed at educational improvement and quality. Director and co-director of Degree, Master's and Doctorate theses. Evaluation member of Master and Doctorate projects, as well as publications, articles and projects. Her research refers to the field of neuroscience, neuroeducation, learning patterns. Author of numerous national and international articles, books and book chapters.

Marta Sainz

Professor at the Department of Evolutionary Psychology and Education, University of Murcia. Her thesis won an extraordinary prize. Master in Hearing and Language. She has been hired for research on different topics, highlighting the field of High Abilities: giftedness and talent; sponsored by public entities. As a researcher she has done different stays at foreign universities, both predoctoral and postdoctoral, specifically, at the University of Minho, Portugal (with Professor Leandro Almeida). She has published several chapters of national and international books of prestige on high skills, and articles in indexed journals of impact and great projection such as Psicothema, International Journal of Creativity and Problem Solving, Psychodidactic, Gifted Child Quarterly, among others. Plus the development of various teaching materials aimed at the exceptionality of students. Likewise, as a member of the Research Group of High Skills of the University of Murcia led by Dr. Prieto, and in collaboration with the Specific Team of High Capabilities of the Ministry of Education of the Community of Murcia she has contributed to the identification process of highly skilled students of the Region of Murcia; as a collaborating Professor in the first and second edition of the "Enrichment Workshops for Students with High Intellectual Capacities"; in the design and writing of the report-memory of these workshops and in the writing of evaluations and psycho-pedagogical reports of high-skill students from various centers of the Community of Murcia. She participates in different University Master's degrees, in particular the Master's Degree in Neuropsychology of the High Intellectual Capabilities (on-line) of the University of La Rioja. Finally, she participates in the organization of international congresses on High Skill, as a member of the organizing and scientific committee.

Mercedes Ferrando

She is a member of the High Skills Research Group, a Contracted Professor of Educational Psychology at the University of Murcia. She has been a predoctoral research fellow, studying at different universities (Universidad do Minho, Portugal, Warwick-University, UK, Canterbury-University, UK). Her Bachelor Thesis was on Multiple Intelligences and Creativity and her Doctoral Thesis on Creativity and Emotional Intelligence in High Skills students. Later, she was granted a Seneca postdoctoral fellowship (Murcia Region) working with Professor Robert Sternberg (PACE Center-Tufts-University, USA) and Professor Elena Grigorenko (Yale University, USA). She has enjoyed a Seneca research contract and a Juan de la Cierva contract. She has been coordinator of the CREANET project in Spain and has collaborated in a teaching innovation project to encourage creativity from the ordinary curriculum in Primary Education. She has also participated in the design of workshops to improve the Scientific-Creative Thinking of Secondary Education students with High Skills. Her research focuses on the study of creativity, intelligence, giftedness and talent. Currently, she is coordinating the works for the adaptation and scaling of the C-SAT (Creative-Scientific Ability Test, Sak & Ayas, 2011).

Natanael Matos

He is a graduate in Clinical Psychology from Fernando Pessoa University. He holds a post-graduate degree in Clinical Psychology and Health, also from Fernando Pessoa University. Natanael is a psychologist in the Enrichment Program for the Gifted, in the Areas of Aptitude, Interest, and Socialization (PEDAIS), and in the Little Explorers Program, both at the National Association for the Study and Intervention of Giftedness (ANEIS), at the Porto and Gondomar branch. He graduated as a psychotherapist in Emotion-Focused Therapy, at the University of Strathclyde (Glasgow, Scotland), and has complementary training and supervision in mindfulness-basedapproaches (Acceptance and Commitment Therapy, Compassion Focused Therapy). He is a member of the Portuguese Society of Constructivist Psychotherapies (SPPC) and of the Portuguese Association of Mindfulness (APM).

Otto Schmidt

Education consultant who specializes in giftedness and other areas of special education. He has over 40 years of experience in gifted education. Otto is an author (Accent on Essential Life Skills and Accent on Educating the Highly Intelligent). His Masters degree is in curriculum design. He does speaking engagements and presents at workshops and conferences. He works mainly with educators, parents and their gifted children, and also with corporate/business leaders and employees. His unique personal competency skills training courses are recognized nationally and internationally. The inventing courses that he has designed challenge people to use the skills he teaches. He holds professional teacher status through the Ontario College of Teachers, has been president of the Educators of the Gifted Organization, was Education Director of the Inventors Circle co-operative inventors association, is the former Founder/ Director of a Canadian inventions show, and is a member of the Advanced Technology Think Tank. He resides and works in Toronto, Canada.

Romina Elisondo

PhD in Psychology from the University of San Luis (Argentina) and the University of Murcia (Spain). Master in Education and Bachelor of Psychopedagogy from the University of Río Cuarto.

Researcher of the National Council of Scientific and Technical Research (Argentina). Associate Professor at the Department of Education Sciences in University of Río Cuarto. Coordinator of the Master of Social Sciences (UNRC). Director of Research Projects and Postgraduate Theses. Author of books, chapters and articles related to creativity and education. Speaker at national and international scientific events.

Rosario Bermejo

Professor of Evolutionary Psychology and Education (University of Murcia). Principal investigator of different research projects related to high abilities, emotional intelligence and creativity. She has taught at various universities, different specialization and Master's courses. Her works have been published in prestigious national and international journals (Psicothema, Anales de Psicología, Psicodidactica, Revista de Investigación Educativa, Thinking Skills and Creativity, Learning and individual Differences). She has supervised different doctoral theses. Currently, her research focuses on the line of High Skills and the cognitive-emotional configuration of this type of students, the effectiveness of the intervention in the development of high skills, executive functioning, management of intellectual resources, improvement and stability to the extent of the skills and intellectual profiles. In addition, for a few years she has included among her research lines the study of scientific-creative thinking. She is participating in the specialized Master's course in Neuropsychology of the High Intellectual Capabilities (on-line) of the University of La Rioja.

Sara Bahia

Professor of Developmental and Educational Psychology at the Faculty of Psychology of the University of Lisbon and researcher in the areas of creativity, artistic education and inclusion, with over 300 national and international publications and has supervised over 100 master's and doctorate theses. Collaborates regularly with master's degrees in theater, dance and art education. Coordinates the Lisbon Creative Enrichment Program ANEIS for Gifted, is part of committees in the Order of Portuguese Psychologists and a Member of the European Awarding Committee of EFPA (European Federation of Psychologists Associations).

Susan J. Paik

Associate Professor at the School of Education at Claremont Graduate University. Her research interests include educational productivity, productive giftedness, talent and leader development, and research methods and evaluation. Dr. Paik has participated in education projects in Africa, Asia, Central America, Europe, and the U.S. She has presented her work nationally and internationally in over 150 venues. Dr. Paik has also received several fellowships, grants, and awards including the Early Outreach Award for her commitment to underserved populations. She has published a number of articles and books, including related topics such as Nurturing Talent, Creativity, and Productive Giftedness (2013) and Educational Productivity in the International Encyclopedia of the Social and Behavioral Sciences (Elsevier Ltd, 2015).

Susen Smith

Senior Lecturer in Gifted and Special Education and GERRIC Senior Research Fellow at the School of Education, University of New South Wales, Australia. She has held many leadership, consultancy, and educator roles from early childhood through to tertiary. Susen's research interests include differentiating curriculum and pedagogy for underachieving gifted students and their social and emotional learning, and she developed the Model of Dynamic Differentiation (MoDD). She has been a visiting scholar at Columbia University and CUNY, USA, the National Taipei University of Education, Taiwan, and the Hong Kong Institute of Education, China, guest editor of the Australasian Journal of Gifted Education (AJGE), is published in top international journals in the field, is a popular invited speaker on teaching strategies for diverse student learning needs, and has keynoted internationally. Susen is co-recipient of the UNE Vice-Chancellor's Award for Outstanding Achievements in Interdisciplinary Research Innovation and recipient of the UNSW Excellence in Postgraduate Research Award. Contact: susen.smith@unsw.edu.au

Tania Stoltz

Bachelor of Arts in Pedagogy from Tuiuti University, Paraná (1987). Bachelor of Arts in Artistic Education from the Paraná Faculty of Musical Education (1984). Master of Education from the Federal University of Paraná (1992). Doctor of Education (Educational Psychology) from the Pontifical Catholic University of São Paulo (2001). Postdoc from the Jean Piaget Archives, Geneva, Switzerland (2007) and Postdoc from Alanus Hochschule, Germany (2011-2012). She coordinated the scientific cooperation agreement between the Brazilian Federal University of Paraná and the Jean Piaget Archives, Geneva, Switzerland (2003-2008). Since 2008 she has been the Coordinator of the scientific cooperation agreement between Alanus University in Alfter, Bonn (Germany) and the Federal University of Paraná. She has taught full-time at the Federal University of Paraná since 1996 and is currently Full Professor. She is also a CNPq Productivity Research Fellow. ORCID: 0000-0002-9132-0514. E-mail: tania.stoltz795@gmail.com.